NEIL OLIVER

Not Forgotten

The Great War and Our Modern Memory

HODDER

In memory of
Robert Miller Oliver and James Cameron Neill

First published in Great Britain in 2005 by Hodder & Stoughton
An Hachette UK company

This paperback edition published in 2018

1

A CIP catalogue record for this title is available from the British Library

B format ISBN 9781473676923
eBook ISBN 9781473695481

Printed and bound by CPI Group (UK) Ltd, Croydon, CR0 4YY

Hodder & Stoughton policy is to use papers that are natural, renewable
and recyclable products and made from wood grown in sustainable
forests. The logging and manufacturing processes are expected to
conform to the environmental regulations of the country of origin.

Hodder & Stoughton Ltd
Carmelite House
50 Victoria Embankment
London EC4Y 0DZ

www.hodder.co.uk

Contents

Women

Contents

Class

Survivors

'It is the function of the brain to enable us not to remember but to forget.'

Henri Bergson

'Objects contain absent people.'

Julian Barnes

Preface to the 2018 Paperback Edition

At 11am on Remembrance Sunday this year I was boarding a plane at Heathrow Terminal 5. There had been announcements over the public address system inviting all passengers to observe the two minute silence, but those of us booked on the 1130 to Edinburgh were ushered through the gate as normal. As I waved my e-ticket under the scanner, I glanced at the nearest television screen and saw the princes in their places in Whitehall. It felt wrong to be going about everyday business while elsewhere other people were standing still and silent, remembering.

I was on my way home after attending the funeral of a friend, another act of remembrance. The service was held in Christ Church in Spitalfields, one of six London churches designed by Nicholas Hawksmoor and built of the same bone-white Portland stone as the Cenotaph. Inside it's huge – half the volume of St Paul's Cathedral – and yet there were enough mourners to fill it. Hundreds of people, all connected by just one other.

After the service, we were all invited to the wake. It was to be held in our friend's home just around the corner. Determined not to miss one last party, she was coming too and her coffin led the way down Fournier Street. Hundreds of people flowed slowly along behind. It took the best part of an hour to get everyone inside and I was struck again by how many folk's lives had been affected, altered forever, by the loss of her.

While I was boarding my flight in London, my wife and children were at the war memorial near our home, in Stirling, for the wreath laying. We go most years. For a while our daughter was in a local company of Girl Guides and on one occasion she laid a wreath herself. When our eldest boy was in the Boy's Brigade, he was part of the parade. And so it goes.

The memorial is just a few minutes walk from our house. It's on the way to the primary school all our children have attended, so we've been walking past it, five days out of seven, for the best part of the last 10 years. It's fairly grand, built of blond sandstone and complete with lions bearing Saltires. In shape it resembles the Cenotaph, but smaller. It's surrounded by a stone balustrade and sits up high, overlooking one of the main roads into the city. Nearby is a statue of Robert Burns and one of Rob Roy MacGregor. A few years back, given the run up to the centenary and all, it had a bit of a makeover. Stonemasons came and re-pointed all the stonework and now it's good for another hundred years.

In order to check the details for what I wanted to write here, I took a walk to the memorial. I knew it well enough, but it's always worth another look. An object like a war memorial is so much part of the street furniture, it sometimes takes an effort to see it properly for what it is – a gravestone, an empty tomb for those buried elsewhere.

On a panel on one side are words in raised letters that read, 'This memorial was unveiled by Field Marshall Earl Haig on 14th October 1922.' Below are more words, advising that a book of remembrance containing the names of 692 'Fallen Men' is kept on view at the public library. In all the years of knowing this, I had never been to see it. I did this year, though. The names of those fallen men are also listed on bronze plaques around the memorial of course, and early on I'd noticed three Olivers – Charles, David and William. I always look for our family name on war memorials and it's a strange, disconcerting feeling to find it fossilised among the lists of the dead.

The library is within sight of the memorial, built with funds donated by Scottish industrialist and philanthropist Andrew Carnegie, and inside I found the book in question, under glass in a finely carved oak display case. I had to ask a member of staff to open it for me, with an old-fashioned key, and he stood by while I turned the pages in search of the Olivers.

The information about them was as sparse as could be. Charles was a private in the Black Watch and had lived in a house on Abbey Road Place. David was a private in the Highland Light Infantry. His address was given as Baker Street – near where my children attended nursery school. William's details were the briefest of all. No rank or address listed – just that his regiment had been the 1st Cameron Highlanders. Carved into the oak above the glass were the words:

'They have left a name behind them and their glory shall not be blotted out. Their bodies are buried in peace but their name liveth for evermore.'

We have three children – three more Olivers, a daughter and two sons. I think about how much love and nurturing we have invested in them, my wife and I. I thought about my friend, whose funeral had been attended by hundreds of people, and wondered how many were affected by the loss of Charles and David and William. Then I remembered that 692 Fallen Men were listed in just that one book in front of me and I wondered how many hundreds, maybe thousands of folk had been hurt beyond healing, hearts broken by all the dying.

I was about to take out my notebook to record the details when the young librarian said, 'Why not just take a photo?'

He was right, of course, and I reached for my phone instead and took a snap of the page. I wondered what the Oliver men would have made of that – a mobile phone in every pocket now, connected to the entire world and complete with camera and just about everything else besides. What a world.

'What have they done with the lives we laid aside?' asks The Soldier in Humbert Wolfe's 1916 poem of the same name. 'Are they young with our youth, gold with our gold, my brother? Do they smile in the face of death, because we died?'

What have we done with the lives they laid aside?

Old habits die hard, and I took out my notebook after all. Jotted down the words I had photographed, just to be sure.

On my way back home I walked past the memorial once more and the strangest thing happened. As I approached it, I noticed a man carefully re-positioning the wreaths of poppies laid the Sunday before, propping each in turn against the stone steps. He was just finishing the job as I passed and he turned and we made eye contact.

'Blown by the wind,' he said.

I nodded and we started talking. He told me how he'd been born in the Wirral, but moved to Stirling as an adult. Turns out we know some of the same people. He pointed at the statue of Robert Burns and said he was a Burns as well. In just a few minutes we found out quite a bit about each other. His mother was a MacWilliam, from the Isle of Whithorn, he said. Last of all we talked about the memorial, how it was important to keep it tidy.

I've walked past that memorial countless times, stopped and looked at it often. But never before have I had a conversation about it with a stranger. It was surely just my overactive imagination but for a moment it seemed to me that by seeking out the book of remembrance, the book of names, I had somehow activated it, brought it back to life like a computer screen coaxed from its slumber. Whatever it was, I felt better – as though together Mr Burns and I had paid some proper attention to the memory of the fallen men.

As I say, overactive imagination. But the truth is my mind often drifts towards the events of the First World War, and always has. Ever since I learned, as a child, that both my grandfathers had taken part in it – been injured but survived – it has felt like part of my family's story. For many people now, Gallipoli and the Somme are just words from the ancient past, no more relevant than Troy, or Carthage. On account of my two men who came back from the war and then made the man and woman who made me, the places and events of those four years feel like my personal belongings.

I wrote this book in 2005. Our daughter was just a toddler then. She's 14 now. My wife was pregnant with our eldest son. He's 11. They are both at High School. Our youngest son was born here in Stirling. He's nine now and still at the primary school up the hill from the memorial. It's all enough to make a person think about time – and about how it stopped for so many millions of men and boys between 1914 and 1918. When *Not Forgotten* was first published, a handful of the veterans were still alive. They are all gone now.

It's finally a hundred years since the end of the war. Even I find it hard to believe that my parent's parents lived through it. How can I be alive in a world of Internet and driverless cars and plans for missions to Mars, and yet be so closely connected to men from a horse-drawn Edwardian world of crinoline and cavalry charges?

But I am. I shake my head in wonder. All I can do is remember.

Stirling, November 2017

Foreword

There are so many First World War memorials in this country that it is easy to stop seeing them. They have become so much a part of the landscape of our towns and villages that you can walk past them without registering what they are, or stopping to think why they were originally put up. It is only when you are looking out for them that you realise the scale of this act of commemoration. There are roughly 36,000 memorials to the dead of the Great War in Britain and they represent a massive and unprecedented outpouring of national grief. Nearly a million men from Britain died in this conflict and were buried where they fell, in Rupert Brooke's 'some corner of a foreign field'. But this was never going to satisfy their mourning relatives and they needed a way of remembering all those sons, brothers, fathers, uncles, cousins and friends that made up the endless casualty lists from the front. The process began during the war itself with small street shrines and rolls of honour which then developed into larger and more permanent monuments, culminating after the war in Edwin Lutyen's great Cenotaph in Whitehall. The design of these memorials varies in terms of size and ambition but what they nearly all have in common are the inscriptions of the names of the dead. It is no coincidence that Rudyard Kipling, whose son Jack was killed in action, chose as the wording on some of the official monuments the biblical quotation 'their name liveth for evermore'. The name is what people considered essential to the act of remembrance, and that recognition is what the relatives wanted, and it is what the returning troops wanted for their comrades who had not survived. That is why it seemed natural for both the television documentary and this accompanying book to take the names of individuals as their starting point.

As a child I remember looking at rolls of honour in school chapels or beneath stone crosses in villages, trying to imagine who these young men were who had gone to the front and never come back. If I came across two surnames that were the same I felt doubly sad, thinking that these boys were probably brothers who left grieving parents behind. As an adult making this series I stood in front of the memorial in the church at Great Rissington where the names of *five* brothers are carved in stone. Five boys from the same family were killed between the years 1916 and 1918 and almost unbelievably their name was Souls. As an emblem of the sacrifice made by the entire country 'the lost Souls' could hardly be more poignant. Can we begin to imagine what this meant? For those smiling farm boys who were so keen to join up? For their mother left behind? For the village that put up the memorial?

This is just one of the stories behind the names on the stones, and they are fascinating stories. Of grief and suffering certainly, but of courage and resolution too. And the individual stories tell the wider story of this cataclysmic war and the great changes that it made to Britain. Neil Oliver's book compiles a wealth of this rich material with sections on the role of class, of women, of the survivors of the war and of the memorials themselves. But he also makes it into a personal story. Oliver's grandfather fought in a Scottish regiment during the war and survived. So did mine. Yet their generation did not talk much about it and it is their grandsons who have ended up trying to tell their stories a hundred years later. Perhaps that is our act of memory.

When I was making a programme about my grandfather for the TV series *Who Do You Think You Are?* I went to the battlefields of France to see where he had fought. I visited a cemetery filled with rows and rows of headstones of men from the Highland Light Infantry. There was of course no Hislop there, nor is there a D.M. Hislop on the memorial in Ayr Academy where he went to school, nor on the monument in the town where he lived. Yet as I read the names of his fellow soldiers, fellow pupils and fellow townspeople I realised how easily it could have been him, not them, and how easily I could not have been here at all. And I wondered again about all those lives cut short while his and mine continued on through the century.

That, then, is the motivation for *Not Forgotten*. I recently went to see R.C. Sherriff's brilliant first world war play *Journey's End* which is running in the West End. It ends with a blackout and the sound of a bombardment by the guns. Then the lights come up on a tableau with the actors standing completely still like statues on a monument. The entire backcloth is then filled with lists of names of the fallen. Their lives have turned to stone. It is an extraordinary effect and as my vision began to blur it struck me that the point of this series and this book is to try and achieve the opposite. To turn the names in stone back , however briefly and incompletely, into remembered lives.

Ian Hislop, 2005

1

War is Over

It's a long way from the Great War to Scotland's Western Isles. The men waiting at the Kyle of Lochalsh for the crossing to their homes on Lewis had travelled a distance best measured in time.

It was the last night of 1918, seven weeks after the fighting stopped, and they were on the last leg of a journey back from another world. These Scots had taken longer to make it home than many British servicemen. Their English comrades, in particular the navy men, had wanted leave at Christmas, as was their tradition, and many Scottish seamen had manned English bases to let them get away. Now it was New Year's Eve and nothing stood between the island men and their homes and families but a few tens of miles of cold, black sea.

They had come a long way, all the way from a great war that had taken them from their families and crofts and fishing boats. They'd been gone, give or take, for four years – four years that had changed everything. The population of Lewis in 1914 was around 30,000 – and 6,200 had joined up. Almost a thousand of them were dead now – one in six. It seemed every home had lost a father or a son, a brother or an uncle. As a proportion of their population, the Western Isles had given up twice as many men to the Great War as any other part of Britain.

The soldiers waiting to board a ship home had survived bullets, shells, poison gas, barbed wire and disease. The sailors had experienced miracles too, among them Kenneth Macphail, from the village of Arnol, sole survivor of a merchant ship torpedoed in the Mediterranean in October 1917. He'd spent a day and a half in the water before glimpsing land beyond the swell. He'd struck out for shore – Algeria, as it turned out, where he was found and cared for by English missionaries: a lucky man.

Now there were thoughts of home and family. The mood on the quayside was cheerful and loud with talk in Gaelic, the language of the islands, too light a sound for machine guns, tanks and war.

Soldier and civilian alike piled aboard the SS *Sheila*, the MacBrayne steam ferry scheduled for the crossing. Soon she was full, leaving scores of men still waiting to board. The thought of another night away from homes so close they could almost be sensed out there beyond the dark was too much to ask. Signals had been sent across the Minch to summon a second ship.

She'd sailed out from her berth in the harbour town of Stornoway. Originally she'd been called the *Amalthea*, but on arrival in Lewis nearly two months previously she'd been renamed in honour of the naval base that was now her home. It was the Gaelic word for sea-eagle – 'Iolaire'.

As she came alongside the quay, she hit the wall. Men who saw it happen put it down to the nature of the tides at Kyle, puzzling to sailors unfamiliar with the place. She'd been there only once before, and then with a different crew. There was a conversation between her master, Commander Mason, and the man in charge at Kyle, Commander Walsh. Mason knew – or would soon learn – that he was to carry nearly three hundred men back to Stornoway. A train from Inverness had arrived at the railhead carrying hundreds more sailors, bound for Lewis, Harris and Skye. Mason and his crew had never sailed the *Iolaire* into Stornoway at night, a tricky enough manoeuvre in daylight. All this was talked through before Mason and Walsh agreed the crossing would go ahead.

The Harris men were told they'd make the crossing the following morning and cursed their luck. Hogmanay parties in full swing from one end of the island to the other, and here they were, stuck at Kyle. Room for sixty more Lewis men was found on the *Sheila* and the sailors fresh from the train boarded the *Iolaire*. It was around half past nine.

Given the occasion and the crush, no final list of passengers was tallied, but something like 284 sailors boarded the yacht. Leading Seaman Angus Nicolson went aboard. He had a few friendly words with Commander Mason and noticed that in spite of the occasion there was no hint of alcohol on the man's breath. The same could be said for all the crew. The wind was right astern and rising, but it was a fair enough night for a homecoming.

All passengers aboard, the *Iolaire* cast off. The *Sheila* would be half an hour behind.

James Macdonald was on the deck of the fishing boat *The Spider* later that night, making for Stornoway and Hogmanay. He spotted the lights of a vessel on a similar line to his own, but some way behind. Still a dozen miles out from Stornoway, the weather turned grim. A gale tore at the night, ripped away the tattered remnants of 1918 and left a new year in its place, wailing and raw. Midnight had come and gone.

Macdonald knew the safe course into Stornoway well enough. Lying in wait, close by the harbour's narrow mouth, were rocks they called Biastan Thuilm, 'The Beasts of Holm'. Nine miles before the mouth, and the Beasts, was the Arnish light showing the line of safe passage. As always, *The Spider* turned now towards port, directly in front of the following vessel. When Macdonald saw the other fail to change course likewise, he knew.

All of Stornoway stood around the harbour, peering out into the dark, oblivious to wind and sleety rain. It was a new year and the war was ended and the men were coming back to the island. They had watched Macdonald's fishing boat come in safe enough and now they waited for another's approach.

And then what happened . . . happened. In the charthouse of the *Iolaire* Nicolson was sitting quietly. There had been music and singing and laughing earlier, but not now. Now there was anticipation. A group of his friends had been out on deck, had seen the passing of the Arnish light. They came in to make ready for arrival. These were men who'd been away too long, faced the worst. They were going home.

'Well, boys,' said one, 'she's near in.'

In the charthouse Nicolson looked at his watch. The time, the moment, registered clear in his mind and stayed with him. It was ten minutes to two on the morning of the first day of 1919. War was over.

And then the *Iolaire* struck Biastan Thuilm. Immediately she started to roll, pitching men headlong. All was noise, the screeching of a ship dying. Seaman that he was, and well drilled, Nicolson shouted towards the bridge, telling whoever might hear him over the din to blow the whistle and sound the alarm. Three or four long blasts. Rockets were fired from the bridge and by their light Nicolson saw, no more than 25 feet away, the blatant red of the warning beacon on the Beasts. He knew then where he was. There were no shouted orders to make for the lifeboats – and not enough of those in any case. She had lifeboats for just 100 souls and life jackets for only 80 more. Provision of life-saving kit for government ships was based on strength of crew. There was nothing for passengers on the *Iolaire* because she was not a passenger ship.

Both lifeboats were launched anyway but soon swamped and sunk as too many jostled for too few spaces. The ship was right down on her side, separated from safety by too many yards of freezing, angry sea. Dozens made a jump for it and drowned, weighed down by winter clothes and stunned by cold. Still no orders from the bridge – Nicolson had no idea why not, and others would later say the same.

Then the *Iolaire* broke her back and slipped away, farther out and farther away from any hope of safety. There was little for most to do now but drown. There was to be no happy landfall for Kenneth Macphail, survivor of the Mediterranean. When his body was found later, his hands were still in the pockets of his greatcoat. No swimming this time.

John Finlay Macleod, a boat-builder from Ness, took to the water and made it to land with a line tied to a hawser still aboard. A handful of others followed, desperate and grateful. Once on dry land they pulled the hawser home. At least thirty more saved themselves by hauling their way along its length through the breaking waves.

Two brothers still aboard, the Morrison boys, climbed the masts to get clear of the water. Only one, Donald, nicknamed 'The Patch', was plucked alive from his perch – at around 10 a.m. on that New Year's morning. Around and below him, his elder brother Angus among them, 205 men who had lived out the worst war yet known were dead on the doorstep of home.

Dawn came to Lewis and with it the news of something unbearable. Parents expecting sons, wives expecting husbands, children expecting fathers – they put to sea in their boats to look for bodies.

Some on the island had feared the worst that New Year's Eve. Throughout the night red deer – messengers of deaths to come – had walked black eyed and silent down the empty streets of village after village.

COMMEMORATION

2

A Story I Feel I Should Know

This isn't a military history of the Great War. I don't know enough to try and explain why it happened. It doesn't have lists of regiments, battalions and companies. I haven't tried to understand the strategies of the generals, so it's beyond me why the events of August 1914 to November 1918 unfolded as they did. There are a lot of books that tackle those themes, but this isn't one of them.

This is a *story* of the Great War. It's also about remembrance and memory. It comes from cities, towns and villages, and every word that matters is someone's name. Some places come up with page after page, others just a line. It's about people who lived and died between 1914 and 1918, and it's written in stone. It's scattered like instalments between thousands of stones in thousands of different places.

War memorials are everywhere, urging remembrance. Beside main roads, at the corners of town squares, by village churchyards, blanketed in hedgerows by the sides of country lanes. Stone soldiers with bowed heads look down from plinths in public parks, from niches on grand buildings. Sculpted plaques punctuate the brickwork of railway stations, department stores, hospitals, factories, libraries, schools. Sad-faced angels keep watch over columns of names in town after town. As the years ticked by their voices quietened to a whisper and the story they had to tell became harder to hear, muffled.

One Sunday each year, the closest to 11 November, men and

women in dark clothes deck the nearest memorial with wreaths of poppies. Later in the day, and for a few days thereafter, little crosses appear, made from what look like outsize lollipop sticks. On other days (birthdays, death-days, wedding anniversaries – who knows?) there are single offerings. A bunch of flowers, or a card wrapped in cellophane to keep out the rain – left for some-one who has not been forgotten. For the rest of the year the memorials are mostly overlooked.

These are the dead. Reduced to name and rank, they have found an immortality of sorts. Their stories are noted in the briefest shorthand, simply their names. Often there's a line or two about not forgetting them, but nothing by way of per-sonal detail. They're difficult stories to read at first, hard to decipher.

The house I'm writing in is part of a scheme on top of a hill on the outskirts of Falkirk. A quarter of a mile down the road there's a quiet corner. The houses are all more or less the same – detached or semi-detached, rough-cast exteriors, knee-high breeze-block walls round well-kept gardens. Modern. There's no sense of history. But at the quiet corner there's a gap. The plot is big enough for at least one more house and garden. But there's nothing but grass and a scattering of trees – each one looking at least a hundred years older than the homes on either side. One tree has nailed to it a white sign with black writing. 'No Ball Games', it says – which seems a bit of overkill given that no one plays football in a stand of trees.

People hereabouts, those in the know at least, will tell you the plot is empty because it's a mass grave of dead soldiers. They say no one's allowed to build on it. A mile from this spot, away on the other side of the house my family lives in, there's a memorial. For a while it was a sorry sight, the facing stones cracked and falling off to reveal rough bricks. It wasn't that it had been vandalised or anything. For a long time no one had been interested enough even to damage it. The weather and the years had begun the job of demolition all on their own. It had just been forgotten.

Over a few weeks in the early spring of 2005 a mason restored it. Someone must have found some money in some or other budget, and now it looks good again – a 23-foot column of blond sandstone pointed with white mortar. While it was being done up, and often since, my family talked about the memorial, thinking about what happened, remembering wars. Six bunches of artificial white roses have been placed round the base of the column. The plaque on it says:

THE BATTLE OF FALKIRK
WAS FOUGHT AROUND HERE 17TH JANY 1746

(Soldiers died on this hillside by the hundred; 'around here' seems a casual reference somehow.)

In among a modern scheme the remains of dead soldiers are close by, whether anyone remembers them or not. Living and dead are neighbours here. This has always amazed me – a housing scheme complete with a mass grave. Other developments might have a swing park, or a row of handy shops. This one's got dead soldiers all in a heap: ball games prohibited. Who would have thought it?

Falkirk's no stranger to fighting. Long before Bonnie Prince Charlie's men turned round for a set-to with the soldiers who'd hounded them, off and on, since Derby, the locals had a reputation. It's carved on the gable end of at least one building in the town centre. 'Better meddle with the de'il than wi' the bairns o' Falkirk' it says. Hard folk. Fighters. William Wallace had his army crushed here in 1298 and the dead in that grave might even be his. No one remembers anymore.

Upper Newmarket Street, parallel to the High Street, is one of the main drags. It's the home of buses jostling for position by a row of metal shelters. Off-centre on one broad pavement is a memorial to yet another war. A stone plinth topped by two bronze figures. A kilted soldier wielding a rifle, bayonet fixed, protects a fallen comrade. The dedication says it's for the men of the eastern district of Stirlingshire who died in 'the South African War' of 1899–1902: the Boer War. Captain Dudley Henry Forbes of the 3rd Battalion, The Royal Scots, heads a list of thirty-five corporals, lance corporals, bombardiers and privates. There are Argyll and Sutherland Highlanders, Dragoon Guards, Royal Field Artillery, The Black Watch, others. On and on it goes, the list of the usual suspects. William Graham Bastarde, of the South African Constabulary, sounding like a bit-part character from an episode of *Blackadder*, has found his way into the company too.

I don't know how often I walk past the thing without looking at it. Sometimes I notice the figures, think about how I've seen the same figures posed much the same way on other memorials in other places, but mostly it's just part of the furniture like the red post boxes and the litter bins.

But when I stood in front of it to write the names into a notebook – PRIVATE JAMES COULTER, PRIVATE THOMAS SPROUL, PRIVATE ARCHIBALD LYON, PRIVATE GEORGE RALSTON PEDDIE-WADDELL – an old man stopped by my side.

'What are you doing, then? Writing down the names?'

We chatted for a while and it felt good to be paying the memorial some proper attention. Reading the men's names, checking I'd spelled them right. Is that remembrance?

The point is that neither of us gave a thought to the memorial until one of us found the need to look at it properly. And then it was . . . activated? My standing in front of it with notebook and pen made someone else stop and look at it too. It gave us something to talk about, and we discussed the war and the names and what it must have been like for these men. It's almost as if the memorial was dormant, on stand-by like a television set or a computer monitor. Read a name off it, though – look at it or touch it when you walk past – and it's as if it comes back on. Is that remembrance?

I don't think you're supposed to say this kind of thing, or even think it. Writing about war is a specialised and serious business. There are libraries dedicated to nothing else, and whole intimidating, overwhelming sections in bookshops.

Apart from what's in all the hundreds, thousands of books that have been written about the Great War, it's another story which gets to me the most. To work, to be read and understood, it needs people to play their part, I think.

Memorials to the dead are everywhere, and still being built. At the time of writing, a memorial to the dead of the Holocaust has been newly unveiled in Berlin. Two thousand seven hundred concrete blocks arranged in undulating waves across a space the size of two football pitches near the city's Brandenberg Gate. Like many memorials, it's controversial – not least because the company that won the contract to vandal-proof the blocks once made poison gas for the Nazis' death camps. Is that remembrance? I don't know.

In the middle of a housing estate in Falkirk there's a plot left empty because it's supposedly full of dead soldiers from an eighteenth-century civil war. The living surround those dead, and still they're all but forgotten. The only sign is the one banning ball games, and the only memorial is a mile away, tucked into the corner of a winding country road.

I don't know why the Great War affects me as strongly as it does, but it always has. I know it gets to people of all ages the same way. I was aware of its memorials before I'd read a single word about the war they commemorated. They are my continuing connection to it. Whenever I see one, I check the names for my own and I'm relieved every time 'Oliver' is missing. I can't explain that feeling either.

Some of it comes from knowing that my grandfathers fought in the Great War and survived. How did they manage that when those litanies of names mouthed by memorial after memorial can make it seem as if every young man in the world died between 1914 and 1918?

. Some of it is the mystery posed by the names themselves. Who were they, these men who came from the same Edwardian world as my grandfathers, went to the same foreign places, followed the same routines, ate the same food and wore the same clothes, but never returned?

My grandfathers came home, went to work, met my grandmothers and found enough time to set about the business of making the people who made me. The men on the memorials were reduced to nothing more than name and rank. Deprived of any detail, they became mysterious characters, fascinating to me.

Julian Barnes says the historian is 'a sort of novelist' who has to discover and understand the characters given to him, rather than inventing his own: 'This may well be the harder sort of work, especially when the sought plot proves nugatory, fragmented, trampled into indetectability by previous searchers . . .'

Every name I read on a memorial to the Great War seems to remind me of part of a story I've half forgotten, a story I feel I should know. As long as the memorials stand and the names remain legible, it might be possible to rediscover the story, even a part of it, to read it and understand it.

3

Death-or-glory Work

Before I started writing this book Trudi and I took our daughter Evie to Edinburgh for a family day out. It was one of those afternoons, warm sunny spells mixed with showers of hailstones, that make springtime in Scotland such an adventure if you have to make clothing choices for a two-year-old.

We were walking at Evie's pace through Princes Street Gardens, so it was easy to read the little brass plaques on the backs of the park benches. Most of them are for mothers and fathers missed by grown-up children. They often say something about how much the loved one enjoyed the gardens.

About halfway along the path there are benches in the shadow of a soldier on horseback. The towering mounted figure complete with bearskin is a memorial on Princes Street itself, dedicated to the officers and men of the Royal Scots Greys. Below it in the gardens, one plaque on one bench stood out from the others:

IN MEMORY OF

CORPORAL JAMES McPHIE V.C.

AND HIS COMRADES OF

THE 416TH (EDINBURGH) COY [company],

ROYAL ENGINEERS

WHO FELL IN ACTION DURING

THE 1914–1918 WAR

PLACED HERE BY SURVIVING MEMBERS

OF THE COY

JULY 1961.

Corporal James McPhie, VC.

Trudi wandered on, holding Evie's hand. I leant on the empty pushchair to copy the words on Corporal McPhie's plaque on to the back of an envelope I had in my jacket pocket.

Back in Falkirk, away from the hailstones, he was easy to track down. A website maintained by the Commonwealth War Graves Commission lets you type in the names of dead soldiers. One click and up come all the likely suspects. Corporal McPhie's VC made him stand out.

Son of Allan and Elizabeth McPhie, of 112 Rose Street, Edinburgh – just a few minutes' walk away from the bench that now bears his name, in fact – he was twenty-four when he was killed on 14 October 1918. He is buried in Plot II, Row E, Grave 4 at the Naves Communal Cemetery Extension, in Nord, France. There's a photograph showing rows and rows of those familiar white gravestones. The cemetery is just outside Naves itself, a little village three or so miles north-east of Cambrai. I remember the name 'Cambrai' from a history lesson at school – it's where tanks were used in force for the very first time, after a more tentative debut at Flers, on the Somme.

Dig a little further and there's a photograph of Corporal McPhie in uniform. He's handsome, as a young hero should be, with a shock of wavy dark hair. His standard-issue khaki looks as if it was made in a hurry. The rumpled flaps of the breast pockets obviously resisted any and all attempts at ironing them flat. Photos like these seem familiar, there are so many of them.

Knowing that all the men in those photographs are dead – that so many died so soon after posing for them – makes it feel as if they were taken *because* they were about to die. Not for remembrance, but for reference: 'Yes, he's dead as well, of course, but don't worry, I can show you what he looked like.'

Beside the photo of James there's a snap of his gravestone at Naves. It has on it an engraving of the Victoria Cross he didn't live to see. The medal itself is held now in the collections of the Imperial War Museum, in London. Everything about being Corporal James McPhie is about being dead.

On a page headed 'Casualty Details' is the citation they gave to his parents along with his medal. Printed in The *London Gazette*, no. 31155, of 28 January 1919, it records his 'conspicuous bravery' in trying to repair a floating bridge across the Canal de la Sensée near Aubencheul-au-Bac. British soldiers were trying to cross the thing under heavy German machine-gun fire when it started to come apart. In broad daylight and in full view of the enemy, Corporal McPhie led a party of men to try to carry out repairs. 'It's death or glory work which must be done,' he said before heading off.

Back on the bridge he was shot and severely wounded, 'falling partly into the water, and died after receiving further several wounds'.

(Did he really say that stuff about death or glory? I hope so.)

All this comes from one name on one bench, in one park, in one city.

4

The Sound of Scarp

It was a long way from the Western Isles of Scotland to the Great War. The tiny island of Scarp hides behind the western coast of Harris, where the scratchy Tweed comes from. It's separated from its bigger brother by half a mile of Atlantic Ocean – half a mile that has always made its presence felt in the strongest terms. The only way across, in this century or any other, is by a little open boat that seats about six. There's nothing quite like a trip in a little open boat across part of the Atlantic – even just a half-mile strip of it – to remind a person what the Atlantic Ocean really is. There's no official crossing either – you have to make your own arrangements with someone who actually owns a little open boat. And there's not as many of them as a person might think. Mine was owned by a quiet man called Murdo who could steer a course with one hand and keep a hand-rolled cigarette lit in the other, despite the wind and the rain and the spray.

The Scarp school register, long since filled in for the last time and kept now at the library in Tarbert, Harris, is full of references to the island being cut off for weeks at a time by storms. Any more than a Force 5 through that narrow channel, what they call the Sound of Scarp, and half a mile might as well be twenty. A Force 5 comes through quite often.

No one lives on Scarp now, not full time. The last family to leave were evacuated to Harris in 1971. Life had got that hard. Their old home looks as if it might have been abandoned two hundred years ago. The roof is gone, along with the internal walls and doors. A single pair of chimney pots stands defiant. The rectangle of space seems too small ever to have contained the family of seven that lived there. It's nothing more now than a shelter for animals.

Lying in front of the space left by the missing front door is a brass tap on the end of a black plastic pipe. This, the remains of a standpipe, was the only water supply to the house – cold water at that. There was no indoor toilet – flushing or otherwise – and no electricity either, in this house or anywhere else on the island. Gas mantles provided the only indoor lighting (and this in 1971).

The whole island is just 3 miles or so across and very little of it was ever suitable for growing crops. There's just one patch of arable-looking green, where the houses are. It's no more than a few acres, and every square foot of it was put to use by the crofters. The rest of it, lovely though it looks, is nothing but heather and bare rock.

A handful of the old houses have been taken over as holiday homes by occasional visitors with a taste for isolation, and during spring and summer there's smoke to be seen coming from a few chimney pots (the local word has it that it was in one of the houses here that the pop group the Moody Blues composed 'Nights in White Satin'!). The rest of the buildings are being slowly taken apart by the weather, and the only permanent inhabitants are sheep.

It's easy to imagine that the life lived on Scarp, right up to the beginning of the 1970s, was much like that being lived there when news of the war arrived in 1914.

Donald MacLennan was forty years old then, son of Finlay MacLennan.

Nicknames were often used to differentiate between men of the same Christian name. This Donald of Scarp was known as Domhnall Ban, 'Fair Donald,' because of his blond hair. He lived the life of a bachelor on the family croft.

Donald John MacLennan, twenty-nine-year-old son of Alexander MacLennan and apparently no direct relation to Fair Donald, had a croft on the other side of the channel, at Husinish. His family hailed from Scarp originally, but in 1885 the place was deemed overcrowded and the landlord moved twelve families back to Harris. They were allocated crofts in six different villages, but after a while the landlord became convinced that the newcomers were poaching his herds of deer. In 1900 some of the MacLennans, Donald John among them, were moved a second time, away from the deer, to Husinish, within easy sight of Scarp. They were glad to be back, close to where they had started, and found the land there much more to their liking. By the time war broke out, Donald John was a fisherman, based at Diorsgail and chasing the great shoals of herring.

The Great War reached even here. Fair Donald would serve as a Royal Engineer, Donald John as a deckhand with the Royal Naval Reserve.

5

The Reach of Memory

What is remembrance anyway? *The Chambers Dictionary* says it's: 'That which serves to bring to or keep in mind . . . to bear in mind as someone or something deserving of honour or gratitude . . . the reach of memory.'

'The reach of memory': that's good.

But how does remembrance work? When does it start?

I have a handful of images of my dad as a younger man. They are fixed, and when someone mentions him my mind selects one at random and presents it like an upturned playing card. Once the image comes it starts to move, playing in my head like a short clip of film.

In one he is on the highest diving board in the swimming baths in Dumfries (we called it the top dale for reasons that escape me). He must be around forty years old, nearly the age I am now. Dad always wore the same pair of trunks when he took me swimming – vertical stripes in shades of dark green and black, gold-coloured buckle. He is right on the edge, toes flexing and curling over, dripping water, readying himself for the plunge. I only remember him performing the feat on a handful of occasions. It was terrifyingly high to me (and to him, I suspect: it meant a near 20-foot drop into just 12 feet of water and the possibility of going in too straight and driving yourself into the tiled floor of the pool like a carpet tack) and I would watch from the side, holding on to the scum channel in the deep end beneath the board. In the memory he never actually dives. He just stands straight, handsome, slim and focused, looking outwards not down, dark hair and sideburns slicked to his head with water. He reaches up with his right hand and straightens his side-parted hair across his forehead with a movement so much a part of him he wouldn't realise he had done it.

Robert Miller Oliver, my dad's dad, died in Erskine Hospital, a home for ex-servicemen, near Glasgow, in 1986. He was ninety-two years old.

He was already ancient, at least to my eyes, by the time I was old enough to understand who he was, his relationship to me. Because he was so removed from my life and world, I never got to know him while he was alive. In the family photo album there are several of Grandpa holding me as a baby, and I've got a clear enough picture in my head of what he looked like from about the age of seventy-five onwards – medium height, slightly plump, thinning white hair, thick black-framed glasses, large nose – but he's just a vague memory.

Mum and Dad and my two big sisters and I used to drive up from our home at 50 Alder Bank, Masonhill, Ayr, maybe once every couple of months, to the flat Grandma and Grandpa shared with Aunt Margaret, at 5 Albert Road on the south side of Glasgow. The grown-ups would talk over cups of tea (it was always proper china cups and saucers, the tea poured from a teapot that had a little sponge tied round its spout to collect stray drops. One tea set had the delicate profile of a woman's face moulded into the bottoms of the cups. When you finished your drink and held the base up to the light, she would appear in ghostly silhouette) and I would wander, bored and restless, from room to room.

As you're supposed to, I remember the flat being huge. But it seemed elderly as well, frail like Grandma and Grandpa. Every floorboard creaked, every door groaned, dust motes hung in the air too weary to move. There were ghosts everywhere, not just in the teacups, but I couldn't recognise them. In the good room, the front room where nobody seemed to go, was a glass-fronted cabinet containing fragile treasure – glass figurines, china ornaments of all kinds, musical boxes. The cabinet was kept locked, and I wasn't allowed to handle any of the choice items on my own (from time to time I would be granted supervised access to the musical boxes, one of which played 'Lara's Theme', from the film *Doctor Zhivago*). In much the same way that I was separated from those trinkets, I was cut off from my grandparents as well. They were too breakable for my childish grasp and, in any case, too far away from me in time. Out of reach.

My memories of Grandma are uselessly faded, of someone fragile as a bird, with white hair, back rounded by a dowager's hump. I would watch as Aunt Margaret handed her a cup of tea, expecting the weight of the fine bone china and its cargo of Twinings' finest to snap her wrist like a dry twig. She died in the Victoria Infirmary, in Glasgow, before I was in my teens, after a fall in the flat which broke one of her hips.

There are, however, a couple of things about Grandpa that I remember clearly: the first is that if I ran a finger behind his left ear, I could feel a serrated metal edge just beneath the papery skin. It felt like a fragment from a dull bread knife. Grandpa never said what it was but Dad told me it was a piece of 'shrapnel' that had hit Grandpa's head while he was fighting in 'the Great War'. I was probably about six or seven years old at the time and had no idea what 'the Great War' might have been. But I could tell from Dad's tone that it was significant.

He said that that piece of shrapnel – what he described as a jagged sliver of steel – had come from a bomb that had exploded near my grandpa. It had hit him in the head, stuck there, and made him deaf in that ear. He said the doctors had been either unwilling or unable to get it out and so there it had stayed.

The second thing I remember about Grandpa is his right hand. The pinkie and ring fingers were permanently clenched against his palm – as though he were holding a one-pence piece there.

Dad said Grandpa had hurt his arm and hand during this war – maybe at the same time as he hurt his ear, no one seemed to know for sure. Those two fingers had been so badly hurt they had stopped working and curled against his palm for ever.

Those two oddities made Grandpa fascinating – not only did he have a bomb fragment in his head, actually *stuck* in his *head* but the fingers of his right hand had the same configuration as that of my Action Man!

As I grew older and progressed through history classes at school, I learned more about the Great War (they called it the First World War there) and shells and bombs and shrapnel. For one thing I learned that 'shrapnel' was the correct name not for jagged bits of metal from shell casings – as most people think – but the pile of lead balls inside the shell that turned into a deadly hail when it exploded. It was named after the imaginative General Shrapnel who invented it.

But at home I learned that there was precious little detail anyone in the family seemed able to provide about Grandpa's role in any of it. Barring a few anecdotes, all I knew was this:

He volunteered for, or was conscripted into, the Ayrshire Yeomanry in 1916. He smoked untipped Navy Cut or Capstan Full Strength cigarettes (having smoked many a day from the age of eleven he quit, without telling anyone, in his late eighties. His health took a turn for the worse until his GP asked him some questions and discovered that nicotine and tar were no longer on the menu. The good doctor told him not to be ridiculous and to start smoking again at once before he caused any more problems for his ancient system.) The Ayrshire Yeomanry became part of the Royal Scots Fusiliers, who saw action at various locations in the Ypres Salient and at the Second Battle of the Somme. He also fought near the town of Albert and on the Menin Road. Family legend had it that he could have been killed on the Menin Road when a 'whizz-bang' (a smallish German shell) landed beside him – but it was a dud and didn't explode.

Somewhere else he got himself wounded in the head and hand and invalided out of the army. He recuperated at a temporary hospital in Beeswing, near Dumfries.

So – I knew he'd joined up, been sent to France, got hurt and been sent back home. I realise too that whenever I picture him in action – going over the top of a trench, advancing towards massed ranks of machine guns or whatever – it's old Grandpa that I see. Grandpa was so old and round shouldered and white haired it seemed to me he could never have been a young man. So the image I have when I think about him in the thick of things is more or less that of Private Godfrey in *Dad's Army* – for me, that's Grandpa, fighting in the Great War.

He returned to Glasgow, picked up his old job in a now long since defunct supermarket chain called Cooper & Company's Stores, and worked there till he retired.

After he died, I inherited the gold wristwatch he was presented with as his retirement gift. The inscription on the back reads:

Presented to
R. M. OLIVER
In appreciation of
41 years
loyal service with
Cooper & Co's Stores Ltd
1913–1954.

I like the way his war years are swallowed up, without a mention, within his record of service at the supermarket. It's as though Coopers thought he was working for them all the time he was in France. 'Where is that man Oliver? Haven't seen 'im in days. Must be out in the storeroom.'

What else can I tell you? He met and married my grandma and they had their honeymoon on the Isle of Wight. There's a photograph of them, arms round each other's waist, smiling. They look as if they might be in their twenties but it's hard to say; young then doesn't look like young now. Grandpa has his sweater draped round his shoulders, like a tennis player. He reminds me of someone. No one remembers when the photo was taken.

They had four children – eldest son Robert junior, Mona, then my dad and finally Margaret. Grandpa was a volunteer fire-watcher in the Second World War. My dad remembers looking out at the bombing of Glasgow's Clydebank from the back door of the family home in Orchard Park. Instead of an Anderson shelter they had a steel-framed bed supplied by the authorities. They were supposed to lie under it during air raids.

Grandpa supported 3rd Lanark Football Club and also turned out every Saturday afternoon to watch my dad play in his Boys Brigade side. His favourite film star was Myrna Loy, he voted Conservative and he never learned to drive. When he was old – old as I remember him being, after Grandma died – he started wearing a woolly hat while indoors, to keep his head warm. He wore outdoor shoes around the flat all the time as well, because he figured it was good exercise. Maybe he was right.

But as for his war years, he wrote no poetry, made no sketches, drew no maps and kept no journal. Most inconveniently of all from my point of view, when he came home and until he died it seemed he breathed hardly a word about any of it to a living soul. Why should he have, anyway? I can imagine it was a bad time and nothing he wanted to talk about. But it meant that when he died his real, personal memories of that war were lost as completely – as irretrievably – as those of any medieval soldier who fought at Agincourt, or any Jacobite at Falkirk.

That information about a family member can vanish so completely and so easily – and vanish to all intents and purposes while that family member is still alive – fascinates me.

6

Rod and His Time Machine

Dansom Lane in Hull has had a bit of a tidy-up in recent years, landscaping and the like. The name 'Dansom Lane' seems like a misnomer, though, a genuine anachronism, since there's no longer any lane to speak of. In 1914 there were homes here – rows and rows of terraced houses looking on to the then Reckitt and Sons factory on Dansom Lane itself. The houses are long gone, swept away along with much of the original factory. To be honest, it's a bit of a neatly manicured wasteland. There's still a factory, making over-the-counter medicines, and its buildings occupy some of the footprint of the old place. On one neatly pointed new wall, beside a car park, there's something that looks vaguely out of place, or at least out of time: a large carved wooden plaque bearing a list of men's names. At the top it says:

GOD BLESS OUR BOYS.

This is the Dansom Lane roll of honour.

Between September 1914 and January 1915, Hull raised four whole battalions, Pals' battalions, from among its menfolk. Its teachers and clerks joined the 1st Hull Commercials. Its blue-collar men – shipyard workers, joiners, plumbers and so on – made up the 2nd Hull Tradesmen. The athletes, amateur and professional, joined the 3rd Hull Sportsmen and the rest joined the 4th Battalion, known simply as 'T'others'.

By 1916 there were loud calls for ways to mark and remember

all this effort, and the creation of honour rolls was one of the earliest responses.

Scores of men working at Reckitt's had joined up and marched away and the factory owners took it upon themselves to put up a roll of honour on the wall outside. Reckitt and Sons were a big deal at the outbreak of the war. They made starch and cleaning products and had grown from their founding in 1840 to become one of the most successful businesses in Hull. The Reckitt family were Quakers and, in that way of members of the Society of Friends, looked on their employees as though they were members of the family. They had their own 'garden village' built, with 600 homes for the workers. The first stone was laid in 1908 and Sir James Reckitt put £150,000 of his own money into the project.

As Quakers they officially opposed the war, but they still managed to enter into the spirit of things. They raised their own company of men, mostly serving with 1st/4th Battalion, East Yorkshire Regiment. They had their social hall converted into a military hospital as well. By the end of it all 153 of the company's men would be dead.

There was a company magazine and it kept the staff up to date with what was happening to the local servicemen. It carried the news of the death of Lance Corporal Thomas Borrill of the 2nd/8th Sherwood Foresters. He was the son of Edwin and Sarah, of 50 Bright Street, off Holderness Road. He was fourteen when he joined Reckitt's in September 1911. He joined Reckitt's boys' club as well and had a flair for woodwork.

Thomas's great nephew Dave Borrill has spent hundreds of hours studying his uncle's military career. Among other documents he has a letter Thomas sent to his family three weeks before he died: '. . . I don't think old jerry has made anything to put me out yet, well at least I hope not as I want to see a bit more life before I throw up the sponge.'

Dave has one photograph of his uncle in his Sherwood

Foresters uniform – and another that he bought on eBay, showing Thomas with his platoon in Ireland during the Easter Rising in 1916.

He was killed on 26 September 1917, aged twenty. He has no known grave and his name is among the thousands on the Tyne Cot memorial in Belgium.

On 21 October 1916, Mr W. H. Slack from the Reckitt's board of directors unveiled the roll of honour. As well as Reckitt's employees it listed the servicemen from homes in seven surrounding streets. It was a snapshot of the day in 1916 when it went up – names of men already dead were grouped together in a separate box surrounded by a black border.

One of those listed as still being on active duty in 1916 was Lance Corporal Herbert Farrow. He was a farrier before the war, good with horses. During one leave back home there was a Zeppelin raid on the city and an incendiary bomb started a blaze in part of the factory. It was where the company's horses were stabled, and Herbert risked his own neck going in to lead them out to safety.

Herbert's granddaughter Norah Wilburn is seventy-five now. She grew up hearing stories about her grandfather, and for years she's been piecing together what she can about his war years. There's a photograph of him wearing a kilt – after swapping uniforms with a Jock, for a laugh – and a postcard he sent the family from St-Omer. There doesn't seem to be any definite record of exactly when or even where Herbert joined, up but he definitely started out in the 12th Battalion, East Yorkshire Regiment. Norah thinks it might have been in the October of 1915. Later on, with many men dead and a need to fill the gaps, he was switched to the 11th.

He was married to Rosa, and the couple had eleven children together, although only three survived into adulthood. One of them was Louisa, Norah's mother. They lived on Dansom Lane, but Norah's not sure at what number. Herbert was injured twice during the war and made it back to Hull on leave a few times. Louisa remembered the last time he was home, walking with him to the station when he had to go back. He took her on an unfamiliar route that day, through the town's backstreets, and she asked him why. 'I've overstayed my welcome,' he said. 'And I'm keeping out the way of the Red Caps.' Herbert had extended his leave by a day without telling anyone, and on his return to the front he was demoted to private.

Norah's mum, Louisa, was twelve years old when word reached the family that Herbert had been injured, for a third time, in a fierce battle at a place called La Becque Farm, near Aval Wood, on 28 June 1918. Around 350 men of the East Yorkshires were killed or injured that day, and Norah has visited the cemetery where most of them lie. She's been told the Allies used a 'creeping barrage' at La Becque – supporting the infantry attack with artillery – and that it crept a bit too close to the East Yorkshires. She thinks Herbert, and many of his comrades, may have been victims of what nowadays they would call friendly fire.

Half an hour after the first letter arrived saying Herbert was hurt, there was a second knock at the front door. This time it was a letter saying he had died of his injuries, in a field hospital, on 11 July. Bad news travels fast. He was thirty-four. Rosa was pregnant when she got the news but lost the baby soon afterwards. Norah believes it was the shock of grief. As well as her husband, Rosa lost two brothers and a brother-in-law in the Great War. Left with three children to raise – Louisa and two sons – she was almost made destitute by the ten shillings a week poor-relief money she was paid as a widow.

Norah was five years old when her grandmother Rosa died, but she remembers her. Now Norah keeps her grandfather's dead man's penny on proud display in the hallway of her home. She's been out to see his grave, at Longuenesse (St-Omer) Souvenir Cemetery, Plot 5, Row C, Grave 65.

As well as on the Dansom Lane honour roll, Herbert's name

appears on the East Yorkshire's memorial in Beverley Minster. He's listed on the local cenotaph in Goole as well – where Rosa lived after Herbert's death, to get away from the risk of air raids – and on the memorial at St John's parish church in the town.

Private Wilfred Farmery of the 12th Battalion, East Yorkshire Regiment, is another among the names at Beverley. His wife was called Alice and his mum and dad were Thomas and Sarah. His granddaughter Shirley Waite has followed his story all the way back to the copse in Oppy Wood in France where he was killed, on 13 November 1916.

He was a seaman before the war, but after one fateful night out in Hull with his pals he came home with something rather more worrying than a new tattoo. He stood unsteadily in front of Alice and delivered the news that he and his pals had joined up. They were off to the war. Apparently she hit him all round his sorry, drunken head.

Wilfred was a family man. Shirley has a photograph taken not long after he enlisted. It shows Wilfred's children – Muriel (Shirley's mum) together with Hilda, Jessie, Frank and Wilfred junior. Muriel is wearing Wilfred's watch. He had given it to her as a keepsake, to ensure its safety while he was away.

But Wilfred would not be coming back. Not to collect his watch or anything else. On 13 November 1916, during the closing stages of the battle of the Somme, he was killed. He has no known grave and his name is listed among the missing, on the memorial at Thiepval. Alice was left alone to provide for her family, and like all war widows she struggled to get by. She found herself a job, and Muriel, as the eldest, had to look after her brothers and sisters while her mum was out at work. Life took its toll on Alice, and finally she became ill with pneumonia. Muriel and the rest of the children did their best to nurse her, but she died. Family history has it that young Frank was trying to feed her at the time.

The children joined the thousands of others made orphans by

the Great War. The eldest of them were put into an orphanage in Hull, while Wilfred junior was taken in by a friend of their father. Their family home was broken up, the furniture and everything else sold off by their relatives. Now the children had nothing with which to remind themselves of the life they had had before.

Shirley was just three when her mum died. Her dad remarried and insisted that his new wife be called Mum now. From that day on there was to be no mention of Muriel. It was best she be forgotten, he said. It was only after he died that Shirley felt able to track down her missing family history, find out more about her birth mother. In a local library she found records of the Seaman's and General Orphanage, where Muriel and the other children had lived out their childhoods. Muriel had been awarded prizes for her handicraft skills, and for good behaviour. Shirley also made contact for the first time with her Aunt Jessie, Muriel's youngest sister. It was Jessie who told her about her grandfather, Wilfred, and how he had been all but forgotten. She had photographs of Muriel, as well as the ones of her grandfather, which Shirley had never seen before.

Now Shirley has tracked down as much information as she can about Private Wilfred Waldamar Farmery, service number 1258. She says the process of carrying out the research has helped her as well. In addition to bringing back the memory and the name of her grandfather, she has filled in gaps and missing pieces in her own life.

Shirley is sixty-seven now and has been out to France several times to see the places where Wilfred fought and died. Because he has no known resting place, she has adopted the grave of an unknown soldier of the East Yorkshire Regiment, and she tends that now instead. Who knows, perhaps it's Wilfred's.

The Dansom Lane honour roll eventually fell victim to decades of Hull weather. What's there now is a carefully executed replica based on surviving photographs of the original. It's back in the right place, though, on a wall specially built to mark the old line of the factory.

When I was little, I loved the film *The Time Machine*, the version with Rod Taylor. I was particularly taken with the bit near the start when he throws the crystal-topped control switch forward for the first time, taking him into the future. The room, the house, the garden, his street – all of it decayed and crumbled away in moments, leaving behind nothing of the old world; only Rod and his time machine.

There's something of that sensation to be had on Dansom Lane today. In 1916 this was the wall of a factory. Over the road were the houses where the workers lived, the soldiers' families. The whole point of the honour roll was that it was in the heart of the community that had given up its men to fight a war. Every moment of the day those left behind were forcibly reminded of the names. Now, in the manner of the time machine, everything that once surrounded it has gone. The only enduring constant from that day to this has been a list of names.

Nothing but the names of the men who were not to be forgotten. But if no one lives here any more, no one who knows who those men were, what they looked like, the things they used to say – no relative, no descendant – is that remembrance?

7

Gold Flake Cigarettes

My mum's father is even more lost to me than my dad's.

James Cameron Neill died aged fifty-one in 1949 – eighteen years before I was born, thirteen years older than I am now. There aren't many photographs of James in the family album (I realise now that I think of him not as 'Grandpa' or 'Grandad' or 'Papa' – nor any other of the familiar names reserved for grandfathers – but as 'James'. This is because I never knew him and so think of him mostly with the kind of curiosity I reserve for interesting-sounding strangers). In my favourite snap of him – which is also my favourite of my mum – he's dressed in casual clothes and holding a bag of golf clubs. My mum, who looks about six, is trying to pull the golf bag away from him. It's a black-and-white snap, obviously, but you can see he's got sandy-coloured hair (mine is dark brown) and that he's either frowning or, more likely, protecting his eyes from the sun. And I don't recognise a single thing about him. If I hadn't been told he was my maternal grandfather, I wouldn't be able to work out that he's connected to me at all (if anything, he reminds me more of the actor Edward Fox at about the time he starred in *The Day of the Jackal*). But he's my mum's dad. He accounts for one whole quarter of my DNA.

Here's what I know about him:

He was born on 26 October 1897 in Surrey Street, Gorbals, Glasgow. He smoked Gold Flake cigarettes (I don't know why I know the brands of cigarettes favoured by both my grandfathers).

When he was sixteen, he gave a false age in order to join the Royal Marines. His battalion went to Turkey and took part in the Gallipoli campaign. One night James and some other men were trying to get back into their encampment when they were challenged, and then shot at, by their own sentry, who was drunk. James was badly wounded, the bullet entering high up on one arm, passing down through his body in a diagonal line and finishing up embedded in his other forearm. He was invalided out of the Army and shipped home, probably aged about eighteen or nineteen. He never fully recovered and when he died, prematurely, his death was attributed in part to those old wounds.

Just recently I asked Mum whether she could tell me any more, but there's not much to be had. He played bowls and golf. He voted Tory like my grandpa. He tried to enlist for service in the Second World War, on more than one occasion apparently, but without success on account of his old war wounds, and became a sergeant in the Home Guard instead. The family, James and my grandmother Peggy, my mum and her big sister (my Aunt Elma), lived in Renfrew, and soldiers were regularly billeted in a nearby school. James went to each commanding officer in turn and said the soldiers would be welcome at his house any time. My mum's mum cooked them scones and pancakes while they played table tennis on a makeshift table in the living room.

It's not much – but then how much *do* you remember? You love someone and you remember them but how much of the detail comes out in words when someone asks you?

My grandfathers are two men who survived the Great War, who came home again more or less intact, and yet their experiences of the war are all but lost.

Is that remembrance?

8

The Birkenhead Drill

It is a dreary unexpected little town . . . The people are thoughtful
and solid, great readers and churchgoers. They have a capital
library. Like all natives of such forlorn, out-of-the-world places,
they cannot understand how any one can be happy anywhere
else; and when one of them leaves the wild, unlovely place,
they accompany him with wondering pity to the outskirts
of their paradise, and never cease to implore and expect
his return for good.

Dr John Brown, writing about Leadhills, in 1865

The village of Leadhills sits in the Lowther Hills on the border
between Lanarkshire and Dumfries and Galloway. On the
map it looks as if it might be just out of sight of the M74
motorway, but on the ground it feels as remote any Hebridean
island. At 1,295 feet up in the Southern Uplands, it's almost
the highest inhabited place in Scotland, second only to nearby
Wanlockhead. It feels like it too. The road up through the
hills west of the motorway is a steady climb. It has those unnerv-
ing red markers by the side of it – the ones designed to give
motorists some clue to direction when the area is blanketed by
snow.

I can't say I found Leadhills dreary myself – or unattractive in
any way – but it was certainly unexpected. Just before I arrived
at the boundary, I had all but persuaded myself I was lost on a

road leading nowhere but up. When I finally reached my destination it seemed more like Brigadoon.

Miners made a village here from at least the seventeenth century and turned the place into one of Britain's biggest producers of lead right up into the twentieth. There's always been gold here too, and people still come with pans and sieves in search of riches. Once upon a time they called it 'God's Treasure House in Scotland'. It's quiet now, though, home to a few hundred people and Britain's oldest subscription library, opened in 1741.

The Cook brothers, William and James, grew up in the village, sons of John and Mary. There were two sisters as well, Marion and Jenny, and a younger brother, Dick. They all lived together at Ramsay Place. As had been the case for as long as anyone could remember, work in the lead mines was the principal occupation for Leadhills men. At the start of the twentieth century there were around a thousand people living there and the mines were still going full tilt. John was a smelter, and had it not been for the war maybe all his boys would have joined him there. As it was, William, born in 1884, and James, born in 1888, were just the right age for the great adventure promised by the international events of August 1914. They joined up for service with the Highland Light Infantry.

This had been the first regiment raised from the clans to fight in the king's service and it cut its teeth in India. Its first battle, at a place called Perambucam, was a famous disaster. Two companies, under Captain David Baird and Captain John Lindsay, suffered a surprise attack by an overwhelming force of the enemy. Fighting in their squares to the last, they were finally offered quarter and surrendered. They'd been promised honourable treatment but the survivors were chained together in pairs and locked in the dungeons of the victor, Hyder Ali. Told of the fate of her son, Captain Baird's mother apparently replied: 'Lord pity the man that's chained to oor Davie!'

Legends like this, in which fortitude and grim refusal to buckle are shown even by the soldiers' mothers, formed part of the allure of the regiments which was irresistible to so many young men.

The HLI were famous too for the events aboard the troopship HMS *Birkenhead*, which foundered on rocks near Cape Town, South Africa, on 25 February 1852. Of the 693 aboard, there were thirty-one children and twenty-five women, families of the soldiers. The officers, most of them young and inexperienced like the majority of the enlisted men, nonetheless saw to it that the safety of the women and children was made paramount. Their cry was 'Women and children first!'

Such an order had never been given before, never been thought necessary. But all of them were swiftly assembled and put into the three lifeboats that could be launched. The men were brought to attention on what remained of the deck. Before the boats were rowed away, the few remaining spaces were filled subject to what the armed services have always called 'funeral order' – youngest first. Even when the ship sank, into shark-infested waters, not one of the remaining soldiers struck out for the lifeboats – which would have been quickly overwhelmed and swamped had they done so. Faithful to their orders, they trod water while their families made for safety. Only 116 men, women and children were saved. In all, 438 men lost their lives.

What happened on that ship that day – the saving of women and children first – is remembered now as the 'Birkenhead Drill' and it set the rules for emergencies aboard ship from then until the present day.

Rudyard Kipling was moved to commemorate their valour in a poem: '. . . To stand and be still, to the Birken'ead Drill, is a damned tough bullet to chew . . .' And the King of Prussia, later the first Emperor of Germany, ordered an account of the incident to be posted in every barracks of his army.

William and James Cook were joining a force that had taken honourable part in just about every campaign of the British army to date. The Highland Light Infantry had garrisoned Gibraltar, fought throughout the Penisular War, taken part in the immortal retreat across Spain and Portugal to Corunna with Sir John Moore. Many of them had been killed at Waterloo.

During the course of the Great War, the regiment would expand to twenty-six battalions and nearly ten thousand of its men would die in places as far apart as Ypres and Mesopotamia, Gallipoli and Archangel.

It's not recorded whether the Cook boys' neighbours accompanied them to the village boundary to see them off. It seems fair to imagine that John and Mary, and Marion, Jenny and Dick at least, implored and expected their return.

9

Waterloo Teeth

Lance Corporal Herbert Farrow from Hull was remembered, is remembered, as a man who mattered and was missed. His name is cut into three separate memorials and his granddaughter visits his grave at St-Omer. He is not forgotten.

It hasn't always been like that for a dead British soldier. For a long time he was of no consequence, valued less than the often ill-fitting uniform he wore, the weapon he bore. He was called scum, used until broken, and thrown away without a thought.

Legend has it that, walking the field after another battle, Napoleon Bonaparte heard someone make a comment about how many had died. 'One night in Paris will replace these men,' he said.

It's a hackneyed anecdote now, every military historian knows it, but it makes a point about the dead of any army in the early nineteenth century. Individually, they didn't exist, didn't matter. They were bought in bulk and used in bulk – and so long as none had an identity in death, they could be replaced again and again without a thought. Without a name, a dead soldier didn't count as a man in his own right. In death as in life they existed only in the plural: not man, just men.

By the time Kitchener's new soldiers were dying in Flanders, uncounted thousands of Wellington's and Napoleon's men had found a home in its soil, if only briefly. By ten o'clock on the evening of 18 June 1815, the battle of Waterloo was over. Blucher had arrived in the nick of time with his Prussians. The French

42

were defeated, Napoleon was finished and more than fifty thousand men were dead. It was a huge heap of slain by any standards, but one man's dead meat is another man's business opportunity. Among the first on to the darkening ground were entrepreneurs known as tooth robbers.

The sunken cheeks of toothlessness have never been a good look, it seems. The spluttering talk and bad breath caused by decaying, missing teeth were a social handicap as well. They say the fashion for carrying a fan and holding it in front of the face was developed to hide blackening teeth and waft away the smell of their rot.

At the beginning of the nineteenth century, the best replacement teeth money could buy were someone else's. Unwanted healthy teeth were usually thin on the ground, though, and cost a fortune. A poor man might sell his for a few pounds – what point in having teeth if you can't afford the food to chew with them? But even that source was limited.

Healthy, unwanted teeth were not thin on the ground of Waterloo. Out into the gathering darkness came teams of specialist scavengers. In addition to clothes, coins, weapons and the rest of the detritus, they were after the newly dead corpses' teeth. Consider the desirability of white incisors and eye-teeth pulled squealing and squeaking from the strong jaw-line of a young man who, up until his final moment, had been a fine and healthy specimen. British, Prussian, French – no matter. At a time when other sources of the raw material might be corpses exhumed from civilian graveyards after God alone knew how long, corpses riddled with who knew what – or thieves and murderers fresh from the gallows – the smile harvested from the mouth of a dead hero was a prize.

The Napoleonic Wars took a toll on the fighting classes, but their carnage meant a boom time for the denture industry. So many sets of false teeth were manufactured out of the skulls from that one climactic battle that they were shortly known, on both sides of the Channel, throughout Europe and even in North America, as Waterloo Teeth.

Without their teeth, or much else of their dignity, the fifty thousand-odd naked, nameless dead were buried. Unmarked, they were left in peace just long enough for nature to do her artful work of decomposition. Months or years later, skin, muscles, vitals gone, the remains were dug up on to the field of Waterloo one last time. The bones were ground into fertiliser and this used on the fields on and around the former battlefield and shipped elsewhere – including to the arable farms of England. The barrels arrived at Hull and companies in York carried out some of the grinding work and the distribution.

These were the dead of war in the nineteenth century and this was their fate. Fathers, sons, brothers, husbands – each as missed and mourned by his family as any who would fall on the same ground a century later, but condemned by society as a whole to nameless, forgotten death.

If Royal Naval Division volunteer and poet Rupert Brooke had been among the dead of Waterloo in 1815 – instead of dying a sordid death of poisoned blood aboard the hospital ship that carried him away from the Dardanelles and the Gallipoli campaign – his corner of a foreign field would just as likely have been repatriated.

The 'dust whom England bore, shaped, made aware' might well have come back to that England in a lucky-dip of a barrel, mixed with the dust of nameless others, and been scattered across some ungrateful waiting acre. 'Under an English heaven', maybe, but hardly a hero's rest.

Before the turn of the twentieth century Britain cared for her war dead as she did her living poor, from among whose ranks they were mostly drawn. Which is to say not at all.

This national disdain, lack of interest at best, was to do with the way the common soldiery were seen by civilians. In the nineteenth century and before, a career as a foot soldier was hardly desirable. Poor men joined up to escape unemployment, poverty, even jail. Working-class families felt no pride in a son 'gone for a soldier', and society looked down its nose at the rank and file taken abroad to do God knew what, God knew where. They were professional soldiers – they had chosen their path through life and so hell mend them. Victories and conquests reported in the newspapers might be cause for short-lived celebration, bolsters for national pride, but when the soldiers themselves came home they were usually unwelcome. When they died in foreign fields they were easily forgotten by the country that had borne them.

Not that the Empire, or the wider world, had always been so dismissive of its dead warriors.

Thermopylae is as good a place to start as any. There in the middle of a sweltering July in 480 BC, King Leonidas, a few hundred of his Spartans and seven hundred Thespians fought to the last man to hold at bay the innumerable army of Xerxes of Persia.

Spartan mothers used to send their sons to war, their ears ringing with the words: 'Come back carrying your shield, or on it.' What they meant was: 'Come back victorious or come back dead'. It was a tough old life for a Spartan, right enough. Cheers, Mum.

The fighting at Thermopylae was so ferocious that towards the end, in lulls in the combat, the Spartans were seen combing the blood and entrails of their victims out of their long hair. When it was over, every one of the defenders was dead. In the way of the best heroic stories, though, their sacrifice was avenged. By the time the greater war was ended, Xerxes and his Persians had been crushed and driven out. Some time later the Greeks put up a stone to mark the place, bearing words by their poet Simonides. Roughly translated they read: 'Stranger, tell the Spartans that those who died here obeyed their orders.'

That sentiment has been echoed on a thousand war memorials since – but not one Spartan foot soldier was named on any stone at Thermopylae. They died anonymously. Unlike the dead of the Great War – and of every war thereafter – their names do not live evermore.

I've had a hand in the examination of a few supposed 'mass graves' on some of the battlefields littering British history. From Bannockburn to Culloden – the last pitched battle ever fought on British soil – most have stories of mass graves associated with them, and I've had a good go at trying to find many of them. Using documentary research, geophysical survey, ground-penetrating radar and excavation, I've done my best, along with my fellow archaeologists, and haven't seen so much as a single human tooth.

The remains of forty individuals killed at the battle of Towton on 29 March 1461 were found by chance during building work on a hotel in recent times. Tossed into a pit in a grim jumble, they were indeed occupants of a mass grave. But the spot had gone unmarked. Here are the dead as rubbish, dumped out of sight and forgotten. The contemporary accounts of Towton put the death toll on the day at 28,000. That's a lot of bodies. Where are the rest of them?

Maybe mass graves demanded more work than most victorious armies of the past were prepared to offer.

In the days before the musket, or the precision rifle, machine gun and explosive shell, the greater part of killing in battle was often done not face to face, but in the rout. Once one or other army broke and ran, it was pursued. Fatigue, injury, grim resignation – whatever – would string the runners out. Rather than a disciplined body of men, a rout probably looked more like the later stages of a London Marathon, stragglers trailing for miles.

In ones and twos and threes they would be overtaken and cut down. By the time the victors lost their appetite for the chase, the dead might be strewn over miles. Rather than go to the trouble of collecting them into one place, they likely left them where they lay.

What had briefly been a battlefield was farmland before and farmland again immediately after. Workers reclaiming the land and finding bodies might do no more than heap enough soil over them to put them out of sight, mask the smell of decay. Once the ploughing season came round again, the shares would soon accelerate the work of worms. Hardly a mass grave and nothing at all by way of a memorial.

A medieval soldier, pressed into service by a landlord and marched far from home, would fall dead a long way from anyone who knew him or cared that his remains were accorded rightful burial. Anonymous death was all that awaited him. So it was for most of them as far as the available evidence suggests. Henry IV dispatched Hotspur and his rebel army at Shrewsbury on 21 July 1403, the eve of the day dedicated to St Mary Magdalene. As penance he built a church near by and paid monks to pray for the dead. It was commemoration of a sort – but without a mention of a single common soldier's name.

They'd come from all over, some pressed and some driven by their own zeal. Once dead on the field and stripped of everything of value by scavenging locals, who was there to remember their names anyway? The Church of St Mary Magdalene was at best a sop to a king's guilty conscience and no proper memorial – none that mattered – to those killed in his name.

It was sometimes different for sons of grand families with proud traditions of military leadership. The rank and file they commanded were neither here nor there when it came to commemoration. But rich families would sometimes go to the lengths of bringing home a dead husband or son. If he could be identified on the field, by his relatives or attendants, he could be got home for burial under his rightful name. He might also be buried on the field of battle, or in the nearest available churchyard. Captain Henry Kingsmill, Cavalier and Royalist, was a commander at Edgehill, the first battle of the English Civil War in 1642. He was killed by a cannonball and buried in Old Radway churchyard, close by the scene of the fight. Twenty-eight years later his mother, still grieving, had a statue of a reclining Captain Kingsmill built over the grave, that he might be remembered.

It's a poor-looking thing nowadays. The church was knocked down and replaced by a new one a quarter of a mile away. Someone must have seen fit to move Captain Kingsmill's statue to the new building – but he didn't travel well. Lodged now in a niche at the foot of the bell tower he is missing his left hand as well as his floppy Cavalier hat. Both legs have been chopped off at the knee and one forlorn, severed foot sits by the statue like an afterthought.

A year after Edgehill, at the battle of Lansdown Hill, near Bath, another Royalist gentleman was killed. Sir Bevil Grenville led his regiment of Cornish foot soldiers up a steep slope to stand stubbornly in the face of Parliamentarian musket and cannonballs.

Near the spot where he fell dying from his wounds there's a memorial. It says Sir Bevil and his men stood 'as unmoveable as a rock', as good soldiers do.

Clarendon's *History of the Great Rebellion* says:

In this battle on the King's part were more Officers and Gentlemen of Quality slain than Private Men; but that which would have clouded any victory and made the loss of others less spoken of was the death of Sir Bevil Grenville. He was indeed an excellent person . . . and his temper and affection so publik that no accident which happened could make any impression in him . . . In a word, a brighter Courage and a Gentler Disposition were never marryed together to make the most cheerful and innocent Conversation.

More officers and gentlemen of quality than common soldiers, then – and their collective death remembered in stone on the spot, even if only one of them lies together with his name.

Lansdown Hill is one of those places where it's easy to imagine things. At the end of a winter's afternoon when the light is going out of the sky, the past edges forwards with the shadows. The memorial to Sir Bevil is carved from the same yellow stone that gives Bath its light. It's part of the strangeness. Knowing the name of one man who died there, reading about how much he mattered to whomever paid for the stone, is part of the strangeness too. It gives the place an identity. A name in stone makes things different.

10

A Good Soldier

Charles Henry Kirman was a regular family man when the Great War broke out. Married with a couple of kids – a son to carry on the family name and a daughter to take care of him in his dotage – he and his wife had made their home in Immingham, in Lincolnshire. They lived in the last house on Battery Street.

Charles had had his thirtieth birthday in the July of 1914 and under normal circumstances he might have been able to relax and look forward to many more years with the Great Central Railway, the company that had taken him on as a plate-layer the year before. But things were different for Charles: he was a reserve soldier.

Born in the nearby village of Fulstow, he'd joined the 1st Battalion, Lincolnshire Regiment, as a twenty-year-old. For the next nine years he'd followed the colours, as they say, serving for more than seven in India. There's a photograph of him there, standing on the left of the back row of his troop. You can see that whatever other qualities he may have had as a soldier, regulation hair wasn't one of them. A cow's lick of blondish brown kicks up on the right-hand side of his head, giving him some of the look of the scruffy boy in the average school photograph. Also visible in the snap are a set of 'good conduct' stripes on his uniform. Cow's lick or not, Charles was a good soldier.

With all that behind him, he transferred to the Reserve in 1913 and came back to England. He'd married a girl from Southsea and brought her home with him to Lincolnshire with their two kids.

And then a war broke out and Charles, in that way of men of the Reserve, found himself recalled to his regiment.

11

The Well of the Dead

Nearly a century after the English Civil War ended, the last pitched battle ever to take place on British soil was fought at Culloden. Three months after the battle at Falkirk, the one commemorated by the newly restored memorial near where we live, Charles Edward Stuart's ambitions for the throne were wiped out in less than an hour.

According to the contemporary accounts of the aftermath, the dead Jacobites and government soldiers were buried separately from one another.

In the middle of the nineteenth century, landowner Duncan Forbes set about making more of a tourist attraction of the battlefield. Building on the folklore of the place, he used rough boulders as markers for the 'Clan Graves'. Each has a clan name engraved on it: 'Clan Stewart of Appin', 'Camerons', and so on. It's not clear what if anything was still visible of the graves before Duncan Forbes 'commemorated' them in this way, but the effect he achieved has made the place one of the most popular tourist attractions in Scotland. People come from all over the world, notably expat Scots from North America, Canada and the like, to mourn at the place where a line was drawn under a way of life.

The site of the government graves is more mysterious, and Duncan Forbes's memorial to it near by makes his sympathies easy to read. There's just a single boulder, bearing the inscription 'Field of the English – they were buried here'. In more recent times the field supposedly containing the mass grave of government soldiers was fenced off and visitors were invited to use the area to exercise their dogs.

Is that remembrance? Soon the battlefield will get a makeover for the twenty-first century, but the overall impact of the place will remain the same. What Duncan Forbes started – and what the National Trust for Scotland has continued – is the preservation of the battlefield. The clan graves have always been the focus, and whenever you visit you see wreaths, bouquets and cards left beside one stone or another in memory of someone's ancestor, real or imagined. The centrepiece, also built in the mid-nineteenth century, is a huge cairn. The plaque on it says:

> THE BATTLE OF CULLODEN
> WAS FOUGHT ON THIS MOOR
> 16TH APRIL 1746.
> THE GRAVES OF THE
> GALLANT HIGHLANDERS
> WHO FOUGHT FOR
> SCOTLAND & PRINCE CHARLIE,
> ARE MARKED BY THE NAMES
> OF THEIR CLANS.

Even here, at one of Scotland's holy of holies, the names of individuals are missing from all the memorials: all but one. Only Alexander MacGillivray is mentioned by name on one of Duncan Forbes's stones. Chief of the MacGillivrays at Culloden, he was found afterwards face down in a natural spring that's remembered now as 'The Well of the Dead'. Perhaps he drowned, weakened by wounds. Maybe he died trying to slake his thirst. In any case it is his name alone which is commemorated in stone there.

As time wore on, there were occasional exceptions to the lot of the common soldier. By the later years of the nineteenth century, the names of ordinary men were appearing on memorials in other countries of Europe and on the battlefields of North America as well. Scattered across the acres of Gettysburg are something like 1,300 memorials to the dead thousands.

In the gardens of the Royal Hospital in Chelsea, home to the familiar crimson-coated pensioners, is an obelisk put up in 1853. It has on it the names of every one of the 255 officers and men of the 24th Foot (later the South Wales Borderers) who fell at the battle of Chillianwalla, during the Sikh Wars, on 13 January 1849. Near by are two cannon captured from the enemy.

Such an exception was a whim on the part of individuals caught in the moment, not a change of national mood.

12

Known Unto God

Of the 5.7 million British men who took part in the Great War, fewer than twenty are still alive at the time of writing. That's the kind of fact I struggle to make sense of, like a list of a million dead men's names. In any case those survivors are a hopelessly endangered species. Some day not too far off, they will all be gone.

Their dates of birth have years beginning with an '18'. These people, some of them still alive today, were born not in the last century but in the one before.

Peter Stoddart died in 1988 following a stroke. He was born in 1896, one of eight children, in Leith, Edinburgh. One of the thousands caught up by Kitchener's recruitment campaign, he joined the 1st Battalion of the Royal Scots, the local Lothian regiment. He was just below the official enlistment age of eighteen but no one was asking questions. 'And I was a real tough young Scotsman,' he said. 'I was a born soldier.'

The Royal Scots, Peter's chosen brotherhood, was the oldest of the Scottish regiments and had seen action everywhere from Tangier to Niagara, Culloden to Sedgemoor, Blenheim to Havana, Corunna to Egypt, Waterloo to Burma, and more besides. Their history and the history of the British Empire are entwined.

In 1915, when their reputation was still based purely on the achievements of regulars, not volunteers such as Peter, Lord Rosebery could write:

The Royal Scots have stamped their name on almost every battlefield in which our army has engaged. They have been commanded and trusted by such consummate commanders as Turenne, Marlborough and Wellington. It has indeed been their habit to fight all over the world: there is scarcely a region where they have not left their mark. That is the way with all our regiments, but the Royal Scots have been longer at it.

I've never given a day's military service in my life. If I'm honest, I'd have to say the thought of it frightens me. I've wondered how I'd cope if conscription ever came looking for me, marched me into a war. But I can't read about regiments of the British army without feeling an involuntary pricking of the hairs on the back of my neck. Part of me understands what possessed boys like Peter Stoddart, who didn't know then what I know now.

Born soldier or not, the first weeks of training for new recruits were tough. Richard Holmes says that in the army a man 'survived easiest if he set out to conform'.

To meet regulations in August 1914 he had to be over 5 feet 8 inches tall and passed physically fit by a medical examiner. By October, the need being greater and the pool that bit more depleted, the height restriction had dropped to 5 feet 5 inches. By the end of the year it was, in general, 5 feet 3 inches.

(At High Wood on the Somme battlefield is a recently constructed memorial cairn to the 9th Battalion, Highland Light Infantry. It's built from 192 stones and stands exactly 5 feet 2 inches tall. On 15 July 1916, 192 men of the 9th were killed at High Wood. A man wanting to join the regiment had had to be at least 5 feet 2 inches tall.)

Every soldier was given a number (Peter's was 1463) and then kitted out with a uniform of rough khaki serge. Khaki was an adaptation of the old white dress uniform thought up by troops in India. Colours like white and red had made soldiers highly visible to the enemy, and so the men started dying the white fabric with substances like mud, curry powder, coffee, tea and tobacco. The effective, camouflaging earth colour that resulted was named 'khaki', after 'khak', a Hindustani word for dust.

A canvas webbing worn like a waistcoat enabled him to carry most of his regulation gear, which in total added up to about a third of an average man's weight. It consisted of a haversack, pack, ammunition, water bottle and sundry other items. Later on, and with the death toll mounting, he would have received a metal helmet and a gas mask to improve his chances.

He was also given an identification disc, what my generation of American war-movie viewers would call a 'dog-tag', giving his name, army number and religion. Here at a stroke was the fighting man's best hope of being identified – and remembered – in death. Before the dog-tags a man killed in battle might never be identified, even with the best will in the world. There are lots of stories of soldiers in the American Civil War carrying notes in their pockets bearing the handwritten details of their identities: if you find me when I'm dead, this is who I am.

At the start of the Great War, soldiers wore a single red circular disc made of vulcanised fibre. During the carnage of the Somme, these were collected from the dead – for the combined purpose of having the relevant details to send a letter home to the family and to ensure his pay was promptly stopped. The army didn't pay wages to dead soldiers. This practice, logical enough at the time and in the desperately confusing circumstances, caused problems later on. By the time there was a sufficient break in the fighting to allow for collection and burial of the dead, the decomposing and therefore unrecognisable bodies were no longer identifiable. This is part of the explanation for the legend 'The Missing of the Somme' that appears on the memorial at Thiepval. Having earlier collected the red identity discs, they knew *who* was dead; the problem was they could no longer connect the names they had to the bodies. It was for this reason that so many graves had to be marked:

A SOLDIER
OF THE GREAT WAR
KNOWN UNTO GOD.

It was also behind the decision to create the haunting memorials such as Thiepval, the Menin Gate and Tyne Cot, bearing lists of names of men known to have died but whose actual resting place could not be identified.

From September 1916 the men wore a second identity tag as well – an octagonal green one carrying the same information as the red. Now when a body was found, the red disc was taken so that pay could be stopped and relatives informed. The green was left behind to ensure that if and when burial took place, the man could be laid to rest with his name.

Peter would also have worn puttees, strips of cotton wound round each leg from ankle to just below the knee. He carried a short-magazine Lee Enfield rifle – the SMLE, but known affectionately by one and all as the 'smelly' – a weapon that would remain the mainstay of the British army infantryman's kit right up into the 1960s. Finally he had a 'frog', a metal clip on his belt to hold his bayonet and a trenching tool. The trenching tool, a modified shovel, would become the item of kit most likely to save his life.

As a private, he was entitled to 35 pence a week in pay. His food, board and clothing were free.

He would have lived in a communal barrack room, part of a troop of recruits between twenty and forty strong. Privacy was non-existent, the discipline unwavering and the routine relentless. His day would start at five o'clock in the morning in summer time and at six o'clock in winter, an endlessly repetitive round of drilling, weapons training, cleaning and preparing equipment.

To begin with, Peter's battalion stayed close to home, on routine coastal defence work. Because he had joined right at the start, in 1914, he had almost certainly been able to pick what regiment he wanted to join. Later on this element of choice was often taken away, and volunteers were assigned to whatever regiment was most sorely depleted at the time.

In April 1915 they moved to the town of Larbert, in Stirlingshire, for further training. Among the men, the assumption was they would soon be heading for France. Though they didn't know it yet, they were in fact destined for Gallipoli and the Dardanelles campaign.

In the early hours of Saturday, 22 May, Peter was among almost five hundred officers and men of A and D companies loaded into twenty-one wooden-framed troop train carriages, bound for the docks at Liverpool. The atmosphere was tense, excited. Another train, similarly loaded, had left half an hour before.

At first, there was chatter as the men discussed where they might be headed, what might happen when they got there. As the train wound its way south through the night, most of them fell asleep.

13

How Soon I'll be Forgotten

Before Evie was born – before Trudi was pregnant with her – it bothered me how little I knew about my family history. It wasn't just my grandfathers' missing war years – it was everything. I come from what most people, including me, would consider a close family. There's my mum and dad, Norma and Pat (both seventy-two in 2005) and my two big sisters (Lyndsay, forty-seven, and Jane-Ann, forty-two). Lyndsay is married to John Guttridge, and they have two grown-up children, my niece Emily and my nephew Jack. We love each other and we get along pretty well. We are all up to date with what we are all doing, most of what we've done in the past and what we have planned for the immediate future.

But move the questions just one generation away from the nuclear family, to the subject of our grandparents, and the certainties slip significantly. I've been thinking about the subject for a while now (and I've asked Mum and Dad a few pertinent questions so I could fill in some gaping holes) but I'd bet you good money my sisters would struggle to come up with all four Christian names of our grandparents. Given a while to think about it, they'd probably manage it (Robert and Margaret on my dad's side, James and Peggy on my mum's) – but I'd be surprised if those names tripped off their tongues at the first time of asking. As for where those people were born or what they did for a living . . . not a chance.

I don't think this lack of knowledge on the part of my family about our recent forebears is remarkable. Both Mum's parents were dead before Jane-Ann was born, so she and I never knew them at all. Lyndsay was no more than a baby and has nothing much to add in terms of real details. My dad's mum died when I was about twelve or thirteen, my dad's dad when I was nineteen. That's getting on for twenty years ago now – and memories fade. I know from talking to them that both my parents loved their own parents dearly – and were loved in return – but they've been gone a long time now.

This absence of knowledge bothered me for a long while. I was even embarrassed by how little I knew about the people I was made of. But now that we have Evie other implications have become unsettling. Dad's dad held me as a baby – I've seen the photographs that prove it, my old grandpa appearing to almost buckle under my mighty weight (I was 11 pounds at birth) – and he once patted *my* baby head, smelled *my* baby smell. But I never properly knew him while he was alive and now he's long gone.

Will Evie's children know as little about me? Is that how soon I'll be forgotten?

14

Five and a Half Thousand a Day

Remembering war could scarcely have been less familiar for British
society than during the Victorian period, when martial experience
was confined to the specialist recall of battles at the beginning of
the 19th Century such as Trafalgar and Waterloo, by professional
soldiers and statesmen . . . British society saw little of war other
than at a distance or in the peacetime activities of the voluntary
movement, whose memories were of military camps on Wimbledon
Common, musketry in city drill halls, or marching through the
streets of Britain's towns and cities to Sunday Church parades.

*Bob Bushaway, 'The obligation of remembrance or the
remembrance of obligation: society and the memory of world war'*

Nameless in death was a fate brought to an end by two wars
that changed everything for Britain – not least the way she
viewed her fighting men.

First in South Africa, 1899–1902: relations between the Boers
– descendants of the original Dutch settlers – and the British
colonists of the Cape and Natal had been tense at best for
sixty years or more. The special tension of bellicose neighbours
climaxed in the bloodshed of the Boer War. To win, Britain had
to throw 450,000 men at it.

The core of the British army that fought the Boers was the
product of reforms by Secretary of State for War Edward Cardwell. Understanding that recruitment in peacetime was a task

not unlike kicking a dead whale up a beach, he set about making the counties back home feel proud of the men fighting abroad in their name. The logic was simple enough: if a young man felt proud of his local regiment, he might feel motivated to enlist in it. Rather than an option to be avoided, a career as a professional soldier was to be recognised as an objective to be proud of. With this in mind, Cardwell sought to forge connections between the soldiers and the communities they came from.

From now on, regiments were made up of linked pairs of battalions: one serving overseas and one back home building links with likely recruiting grounds. Infantry regiments had always been identified by number; now they got names to tie them inextricably to parts of the country. Local teams, as it were. So the 28th and 61st came together as the Gloucestershire Regiment; the 14th Foot became the West Yorkshire Regiment, and so on.

Despite these reforms, by the time the Boer War broke out the army still didn't have enough 'regular' soldiers to fight it. It was still too small. It took a quarter of a million last-minute volunteers to deliver victory in South Africa, and nearly six thousand of them died along the way.

But thanks to Cardwell's reforms, the men who had died in South Africa were identified in the public mind with the towns they had left behind. As well as fighting 'for Queen and Country' as they always had, now they fought and died on behalf of their communities.

Dead soldiers had been missed before, if only by individual families quietly mourning the loss of a son, a husband. From the time of the Boer War, soldiers, whether regulars or volunteers, started to die in a different way. From now on they were valued members of society first and soldiers second. Their deaths could no longer go unnoticed. War memorials in the villages, towns and cities mourning men lost in South Africa bear the names of lowly private and commissioned officer alike. The lot of the dead had changed.

When the Great War broke out it was obvious that the available army wasn't going to be big enough to cope. The British Expeditionary Force that sailed for France in August 1914 numbered around 100,000 professional soldiers. It was a rapid-response army shaped by further reforms led by Secretary of State for War R. B. Haldane. But although it was designed to go into action in a hurry, it was tiny compared to the standing armies of Britain's principal allies France and Russia, and more worryingly that of her principal enemy, Germany.

This was the state of affairs that had been inherited by Kitchener in 1914. His response, his demand for whole new armies of volunteers, unleashed the flood that swept away Donald John MacLennan, Donald MacLennan, Herbert Farrow, the Cook brothers, Peter Stoddart, Charles Kirman, and the rest.

The fate that befell them would turn a softening of opinion inspired by the Boer War into a seismic shift. The Victorian world had been affected by an average daily death toll in South Africa of ten men per day. The Edwardian world that had succeeded it would learn to endure an average of five and a half thousand a day during the Great War. It would change their world, or at least the way they saw it.

15

Hundreds of Thousands of Names

Scattered across England, Ireland, Wales and Scotland there are more than 36,000 memorials dedicated to the Great War. A team at the National Inventory of War Memorials (NIWM) is at work tracking them all down and putting them on a computerised database – along with memorials to the war of 1939–45 and every conflict since that has claimed the lives of British servicemen and women. The number of memorials to *all* wars in this country is thought to be in excess of 53,000.

So many were raised over the years it's hard for everyone to settle on one final total. This is another of the numbers churned out by the Great War that defies precision.

The NIWM was originally the brainchild of Dr Alan Borg, at the Imperial War Museum, who was concerned by the dilapidated condition of many of the war memorials around London and across the country as a whole. In order to try to ensure that there was at least a central record of them, he set in place a project encouraging volunteers to record and photograph the memorials, setting down for posterity every architectural and social detail of the things. Members of the public were asked to send in descriptions of the memorials in their towns and villages as well.

Work began in 1988 and has resulted in the collection now housed in premises connected to the museum. Two full-time staff and a few volunteers look after rows of filing cabinets, each filled with countless plastic and manila envelopes containing the hard

65

copies of nearly seventeen years' worth of research. Some of it is on the specially printed forms composed and sent out for the purpose by the NIWM. Much is in the form of personal letters from members of the public, even scribbled notes on pages torn out of notebooks. There are photographs of thousands of the memorials as well, but not of all of them. In more recent times a great deal of effort has being going into collecting all the hundreds of thousands of names engraved upon them.

The database will form the basis of an online service, and people in search of the memorial or memorials carrying the names of their relatives will finally have a starting point.

The Commonwealth War Graves Commission website lets you track a man down to his grave, where one exists, or to his particular part of one of memorials to the missing, such as the Menin Gate, or Thiepval or Tyne Cot.

Georgina Binks, one of the two full-timers in charge of the inventory, said something about the aims of the NIWM: something that made me understand the way in which the new website will be crucially different from that of the CWGC. She said it was one thing, an important thing, to be able to find out where a relative lies. 'But what we're doing at the National Inventory is about finding out in how many places that person is *remembered*.'

I liked that. It's important for people to be able to find the last resting place of a loved one. But maybe there's just as much comfort, or even more, to be had from knowing that that person's name is simultaneously remembered in the village where he was born, at his old school, where he lived with his family, where he worked before he went off to war.

16

An Empty Tomb

If Britain has one mass grave for all her Great War dead, then it's a place of mind and memory. If that place has a single marker in the living world, a gravestone, then it's the Cenotaph in London's Whitehall.

Whatever each individual war memorial in England, Ireland, Wales and Scotland means to some of those who have not forgotten the Great War, only the Cenotaph commemorates every one of its victims, all in one place. There seems to be general agreement that the Cenotaph is the daddy of them all.

Its inception and creation owed more than a little to a strongly felt need to keep up with the Joneses. In this case, the Joneses were the people of France. In the run-up to the first anniversary of the Armistice, on 11 November 1919, plans were well under way for a victory parade involving surviving veterans and their commanders. Sensitive to the wider public mood, the government of Lloyd George was adamant that any such parade would involve commemoration of the dead. London was aware that Paris, as part of its own preparations for a similar parade, had commissioned a huge, sculpted catafalque (a temporary tomb-like structure for use in a funeral) to stand as a centrepiece and to provide something for passing generals to salute. Not to be outdone, Lloyd George's government asked sculptor Edwin Lutyens to design something similar.

The parade would pass through Whitehall, on a route chosen to ensure that those marking the anniversary would pass like blood through the still-beating heart of the victorious nation's capital city. Lutyens had his site and the object he created would have to signify all that had been sacrificed to make victory a reality. What he came up with, literally an 'empty tomb', was a catafalque of sorts as well.

Ironically, the French took one look at their own temporary tomb once it was finished, decided it owed too much to the German style of monumental architecture and took it down before their own parade took place.

A crucial point in all this was that to begin with, Lutyens's Cenotaph was meant to be *temporary* – something to focus hearts and minds on the day of the anniversary itself, to then be taken apart and put away. What Lutyens created, out of timber and board, seemed to lay an unbreakable claim on the conscious-ness of everyone who marched past it or looked up it that day.

Some of the impact of the thing came from what Lutyens left out of his design, rather than what he put in. Most conspicuous of all is the absence of any religious symbolism on the Cenotaph: no crosses, no weeping angels, no Christ (when I look at it I'm always reminded, more or less, of the shape created from the simplest stacking of toy bricks).

In the aftermath of the war many people had turned, in their desperation to find their lost loved ones, to spiritualism. Self-styled mediums were kept busy by bereaved families needing some word or reassurance from the dead or missing. Elsewhere, explanations for all that had happened were being sought in theosophy. Lutyens was on the fringes of the theosophy move-ment, through his wife, and some say there's more than a nod to spiritualism in his work as well.

Even as people looked at the Cenotaph for the first time, they seemed to decide as one that it should be made permanent. At first the authorities allowed it to remain for a few days after the march, to give more people a chance to make their pilgrimage to it. Such was the clamour for it to remain for ever that a permanent replica of the original, in Portland stone, was duly commissioned. It would be ready for the Armistice Day ceremony of 1920.

17

Cities of the Dead

Bellamy Street Roll of Honour

Shrine was dedicated on Saturday by the Rev A. Berry
(St Andrews). It was an impressive service. The drum and fife
band attended. The Rev R. Robinson assisted and the
unveiling ceremony was performed by Mr J. Moore. East Hull
Prize Silver Band played immediately before the dedication.

A collection was made for disabled soldiers. Dr Lilley
proposed a vote of thanks to all who assisted. Alderman G. L.
Scott was the chairman. The 10th Company B. B. Scouts and
St Peters Boy Scouts were also present. A collection is being
made daily by a dog in this street, clothed in flags . . .

Bellamy Street Roll of Honour

TO THE EDITOR OF THE 'DAILY MAIL'
SIR, – We, the residents of Bellamy-street, beg to record our
grateful appreciation to all the workers in connection with
the above 'Roll of Honour', those responsible for the
unveiling ceremony, the decorators, and those who so kindly
loaned bunting, etc., and to Mr Green, the secretary of the
street patrol, to whose untiring efforts a good deal of the
success is due.
– Signed, on behalf of the residents,
J. H. SILBY,

4, Bellamy-street.
October 5th, 1916.

Bellamy Street Roll of Honour

TO THE EDITOR OF THE 'DAILY MAIL'
SIR, – We have 51 houses in the above street; 38 men are
serving their country, three have fallen in the war, and we have
given to the wounded soldiers and sailors the sum of £4 4s,
the surplus of our collection in behalf of the roll of honours.
I am SIR, etc.,
H. Green (Patrol Secretary).
Bellamy-street, October 16th, 1916.

The willingness of thousands of young men to join the fight
generated a wave of pride among the families they left behind.
It wasn't only acknowledged by the nation as a whole, but by
countless pockets of people throughout the land. Desperation to
escape unemployment and poverty may have motivated some
volunteers, but there can be no denying how many were called
by duty and determination to do their bit. The folks back home
wanted to show how much they thought of their men.

As early as 1915 this pride showed itself at the local level in
the creation of 'street shrines', like the one in Bellamy Street, in
Hull, mentioned above. They sprang up in countless villages,
towns and cities, and though their form varied, they shared
certain features. Often based around a simple cross and a photograph of the king, every shrine included a steadily growing list
of those on active service, together with snapshots and other
souvenirs such as letters and cards from the front.

There was opposition to the shrines in some quarters, owing
to their allegedly Roman Catholic overtones, but by late 1916

some shops were selling them ready made – a frame, a flagpole and some flower holders for six shillings and sixpence.

These commemorations were, first and foremost, about the living, and were an expression of raw emotion, of pride. One of the first – or at least among the first documented – appeared in a cul-de-sac in London's East End, its precise location lost to memory now. From just forty houses, sixty-five men had volunteered and those left behind were determined to acknowledge the sacrifice their men were making.

Present even before the shrines were the 'honour rolls', such as that in Hull's Dansom Lane – straightforward lists of those who had enlisted. This form of remembrance was instantaneous and not a response to death – men taken away from home by the war were being remembered even as they marched away.

As 1914 wore on the realisation of something darker, less blindly optimistic, entered the mix. On 23 August 1914, Irish Dragoons and German cavalry met in the first clash of the war. In among the pit-heads and slag heaps on the outskirts of the industrial town of Mons, just a handful of miles from the battlefield of Waterloo, they fought one another to a standstill.

Private Charles Henry Kirman, service number 7423, 7th Battalion Lincolnshire Regiment, old India hand and erstwhile platelayer for the Great Central Railway, was right in among it. The soldier with the 'good conduct' stripes and the cow's lick in that photograph with the lads was doing his duty all over again. He played his part in the legend of the great retreat from Mons and was active in the capture of the first half-dozen guns captured from the enemy.

Farther south the French were in retreat, and while Mons was a victory of sorts, stubborn resistance in the face of what had looked liked an unstoppable German force, those same British soldiers were soon in danger of being outflanked.

At school I remember being told it was the Kaiser, Wilhelm II, who had dismissed the British Expeditionary Force as a 'contemptible little army'. While reading the books in preparation for writing this, I learned that the infamous slur is part of the mist of folklore surrounding the subject. It turns out it was originated by Sir Frederick Maurice, at the War Office in London. He thought something was needed to get the Tommys' backs up – and what could be more effective than telling them that Kaiser Bill was calling them names? And so the circulation of black propaganda began.

The BEF eventually pulled back as far as the River Marne. John Terraine described the latter stages of the retreat as 'men stumbling more like ghosts than living soldiers, unconscious of everything about them, but still moving under the magic impulse of discipline and regimental pride'.

At the river, together with the hastily regrouped French, they managed to halt the German advance. Germany turned its attentions then to the French-held, strategically important Channel ports of Dunkirk, Calais and Boulogne. To hold the enemy at bay, there in the borderlands between northern France and Belgium, called Flanders, the Allies dug in their heels. The battle that followed – called the First Battle of Ypres – was the first real clash on what was soon known as the Western Front.

After a month of fighting, British and French casualties numbered 60,000. A stalemate had emerged that would last, by and large, for the rest of the war. In order to stay alive, both sides had begun to dig trenches in which to shelter. Soon the network stretched like 500 miles of hurried stitching all the way from the English Channel to the Swiss border.

Some time in October, Private Kirman was hurt badly enough to be invalided home to Lincolnshire. Back in Britain he may have noticed that some of the energy once focused on remembrance of the living had been diverted into mourning the dead.

Those willing to join the fight had been celebrated for their actions while they lived, their names added to lengthy lists of relations, workmates, neighbours – people everyone knew. By the time they began to die in ever increasing numbers it was already unthinkable to let them be forgotten: impossible, even.

On village greens and town squares wooden crosses began to appear, bearing the names of dead soldiers. It was soon the custom to leave flowers – bouquets or single blooms – at the foot of them. Such places commanded instant respect. Objects left there, flowers and what have you, were never disturbed, never stolen.

That sons, fathers and husbands were being killed was devastating to families and communities. It was made even harder to bear by the absence of the loved one's body. Logistical problems alone made it impossible to bring the dead home for burial by their families; repatriation of the war dead was officially banned.

During the 1920s the awe-inspiring war cemeteries of France and Belgium were designed and built. When you pass through the gates of any of those that contain the bodies of British servicemen, you walk on to British soil gifted for ever by the nations in whose clay our dead are enfolded.

The scale of some, such as Tyne Cot, is too much to comprehend – whole silent towns and cities of the dead. The burying has not stopped either: every year more of the missing dead are unearthed by farmers, construction workers, road builders. The fields of France and Belgium are still giving up their Great War dead and each one is accorded a proper burial.

The cemeteries were originally the work of the Imperial (later Commonwealth) War Graves Commission, and it's hard to imagine how they knew where to start, so great was the task. To some extent each cemetery is shaped by the form of the land on which it was placed: some hug the contours of gentle slopes, others stretch away across level plains or cluster in hollows. But while there is something individual about every one of them, there is a basic, almost numbing, uniformity as well.

Central to all are a few carefully designed and chosen keystones. Most prominent are the 'Cross of Sacrifice' designed by

Sir Reginald Blomfield and the 'Stone of Remembrance', by Sir Edwin Lutyens (Lutyens was apparently unhappy with the blatantly religious message of the cross). These two items are in every Commonwealth War Graves Commission cemetery and they were mass produced. Every Stone of Remembrance was the same: a 12-ton block priced at £500. There were four different sizes of cross starting with Type A1, deemed suitable for cemeteries containing between forty and 250 burials. At the top end of the scale was Type B, to be used whenever there were more than two thousand. Where the details were known, the stone carried the appropriate regimental crest, the man's name, rank and regiment and date of death. The bereaved family could also pay to have a personal inscription added. Where the dead man could not be identified, his grave was marked as that of an unknown British soldier, known unto God.

It is the rows upon rows of these gravestones which are most affecting, hardest to accept. Each one represents a man, and yet there are often too many to count or even to take in with one glance. The regimented rows and columns are a deliberate aspect of the overall design of these places. Sir Frederick Kenyon reported to the IWGC that such a layout would '. . . carry on the military idea, giving the appearance as of a battalion on parade'.

In this way two objectives were met: there was a uniformity that suggested the much-vaunted 'equality in death' – officers and enlisted men lie together, row on row; at the same time, families and next of kin had the opportunity to personalise the individual graves.

Every cemetery is immaculate, grass as neatly clipped as a regulation short back and sides, every grave tended: the ongoing efforts of the CWGC. Walk between the rows and there are cards and flowers here and there, left by recent visitors. Not forgotten.

For those with no known grave, the memorials to the missing

were created. Greatest and most terrible of all is Thiepval. Located near the main Bapaume-to-Albert road it commemorates the fight for the village of Thiepval itself. It had been strongly fortified by the Germans and was a key objective of 1 July 1916. Despite savage fighting it was not taken until September. The loss of men involved was obscene, both before and after the fall of the place into Allied hands. More than 72,000 officers and men of the British and South African forces who died fighting around here up until 20 March 1918 have no known grave.

There is a small cemetery too, in which British and French soldiers lie together, in memory of the combined force that fought here from the start. But it's the Thiepval memorial itself which delivers the greatest impact. Standing around 150 feet tall, it was designed by Lutyens and built between 1928 and 1932. A series of interconnecting arches is supported on sixteen massive square columns (when we visited the place together, my dad described it as looking 'like a cathedral without walls'). It's built mostly of red brick, but the flat surfaces are faced in white stones. It's these that are engraved with the seemingly endless list of names.

Tens of thousands of soldiers were marched out of the Belgian town of Ypres on their way to the battles of the Ypres Salient, and it was here that the Menin Gate memorial was built to remember more of those with no known grave. There were too many to list in one place and so there are four such memorials, spread across the whole of the Ypres Salient. The Menin Gate was designed by Blomfield and opened in 1927. It has on it more than 54,300 names.

On the Tyne Cot memorial, 5 miles or so north-east of Ypres, there are nearly 35,000 more.

Back home in Britain, in the world left behind, the absence of mortal remains, to tend and to visit, must often have felt unbearable. Worse even than dying, the men were disappearing. Even where a family could be notified that a burial had taken place, a grave site in France or Belgium was cut off from the bereaved in a way that is hard to imagine from the point of view of the twenty-first century.

It was this void that memorials – temporary at first but increasingly permanent – filled. For want of anything better to visit, such as a graveside, a wooden cross on a town green bearing a man's name at least gave his family somewhere specific to take their grief. If his name survived – there among those of other local men who'd been killed alongside him, who shared his sacrifice – then maybe he hadn't quite ceased to exist.

Those wooden crosses and later the stones that replaced them could in some way personify the dead. The weight of the stones could anchor them and keep them in place; weigh them down.

18

Here was a Royal Fellowship

Age may not weary them but the years have condemned.
Sun-dozed and snow-dazed, they sweat in greatcoats in the
summer or freeze in shirtsleeves through the long winter
months. Sprayed by feminists – 'Dead Men Don't Rape' – and
damaged by vandals, all are rotted by pollution. Powerless to
protect themselves, their only defence, like that of the blind,
is our respect.

Geoff Dyer, The Missing of the Somme

Long before the building of the permanent Cenotaph in 1920,
the work of raising memorials to the dead was under way in
cities, towns and villages. Such was the scale and the variety of
the nationwide effort it has been called the greatest public art
project ever undertaken in Britain.

They are so commonplace now, so familiar, they can be hard
to spot. In truth it's hard to walk through any town or village
without passing a few, whether you notice them or not. If and
when you do start to notice them, to see them for what they are,
it's impossible to imagine the landscape without them.

The Boer War had changed the nation's perception of its fighting men – particularly those who had died as volunteers – and
inspired a wave of memorials naming ordinary soldiers. But it
was the death toll of the Great War which seemed to leave almost
every community in the land clamouring for a permanent marker

to commemorate its dead. The question became not *if* the dead were to be memorialised, but *how*?

It is easy to imagine that some government body must have taken on the job of ensuring that the dead of each community were properly remembered on a suitable memorial. This was not the case. In fact each community had to go through the entire process alone – compiling the list of the dead; identifying and purchasing a suitable site; interviewing artists and sculptors; supervising the drawing up of plans; overseeing the construction and preparing for the unveiling.

As early as 1915 the newly formed Civic Arts Association was circulating advice on how best to reconstruct the country after the war – and central to its aims was finding the right ways to remember the dead. In the same year the Church Crafts League was talking about the need to properly channel the 'pious intentions' of grieving families.

There was general concern in high places that the public need for sites at which to grieve and to remember lost loved ones might be exploited by individuals or organisations seeking to use memorials to make a point or advance their own causes. There were worries too that some groups acting alone and without guidance might commission artworks that would be memorials to bad taste rather than commemorations of the honoured dead. In 1918 the Royal Academy published 'Suggestions for the Treatment of War Memorials' and the Royal Society of British Sculptors circulated advice. The Royal Academy of Arts put on a War Memorials Exhibition at the Victoria and Albert Museum in 1919, with a view to pointing groups and committees in the right artistic and architectural directions.

In 1916 the then Imperial War Graves Commission made a fundamental decision about the rules governing the commemoration of the dead in the cemeteries overseas. There was to be 'no distinction . . . between officers and men lying in the same cemeteries in the form or nature of the memorials'.

This caused some upset – by 1916 there were already private memorials in some French and Belgian cemeteries that the commission was powerless to do anything about. This led to disparity and caused ill feeling for those families that lost a son after 1916 but were barred from putting up their own memorial. The commissioners felt that the only fitting place for personal memorials was at home. Although they would press for uniformity here too, they were powerless to prevent private individuals and families from creating what they felt were fitting symbols.

The commission did allow the bereaved to include their own inscriptions on the regulation gravestones – and next of kin were entitled to the wooden crosses that had marked the graves before the stones were set in place. The collection of these most poignant of symbols became the object of pilgrimages organised by the Church Army. More than two thousand crosses had been brought back to Britain by 1923. Those that went unclaimed became the focus of ceremonies where they were burned en masse, and the ashes buried on the battlefields.

The options for memorials at home seemed endless: a work of art in the form of a statue, or something useful such as a hospital, an art gallery, a village hall? Figurative forms such as soldiers, angels, grieving mothers, or architectural forms such as crosses, obelisks or catafalques? Some people wanted to dedicate areas of open space such as gardens or parks, bowling greens or recreation grounds; others preferred the idea of using the money to provide scholarships for war orphans, relief funds for wounded servicemen or even for the provision of district nurses.

(There were also so-called 'thankful villages', which had all their servicemen returned to them safe and well by the end of the war. With no dead to mourn, such communities usually found no need for a traditional war memorial, the roll of honour of those who had served being seen as record enough. It is generally accepted that the term 'thankful village' was first used in the

'King's England' series of books by the writer Arthur Mee, published in the 1930s. The exact number of places passed over in this way is the topic of ongoing debate – many chat rooms and message boards on the Internet continually amend and add to their running lists of contenders – but the consensus seems to be fewer than forty. Of these, the village of Arkholme in Lancashire is regarded as the 'most thankful', at least in terms of the number of servicemen. It sent fifty-nine men to the Great War and got them all back again. Arthur Mee singled out Somerset as the most thankful county in England, with a total of eight 'thankful villages': Aisholt, Chantry, Chelwood, Rodney Stoke, Stocklinch, Stanton Prior, Tellisford and Wooley.)

Returning servicemen also tended to have strong opinions on the matter of memorials. Having experienced the day-to-day realities of life in the services, many of them were vocal about what they wanted to see on the memorials dedicated to those who had died. In the main they spoke out against attempts to render the experience of the trenches, of fighting and dying, too realistic or dramatic or lurid. This call from the survivors for literal, straightforward, even plain memorials had its impact in the form of most of those we see around us.

And then, of course, there was the question of money. Never mind what it was going to look like, who was going to pay for it? A general consensus emerged that there would be no centralised memorials project paid for from the public purse. Instead each community would take responsibility for organising payment by public subscription, voluntary donations. Committees were duly formed and cash collected. Controversy could arise at every step of the project, even the fund-raising. In Workington it was proposed to keep a permanent list of subscribers in the town hall; in Pudsey it was decided that only 'large' donations would be publicised.

Memorials themselves, meanwhile, were springing up across the country. Monumental sculptors began to offer a range of 'off the shelf' designs to speed the process along. Other committees appointed designers and artists and took votes on their proposals. In *Sites of Memory, Sites of Mourning*, Jay Winter says: '. . . commemoration was and remained a business, in which sculptors, artists, bureaucrats, churchmen and ordinary people had to strike an agreement and carry it out'.

There was a lot of money to be made – by the end of it there were over 36,000 memorials in Britain – and the endeavour made the artistic reputations of men like Charles Sergeant Jagger, who designed the Royal Artillery memorial at London's Hyde Park Corner.

(I'd heard about Jagger's RA memorial – even glimpsed it once or twice over the years through taxi windows – but I visited it on foot for the first time this year. I got off at the wrong stop on the London Underground and had to walk the length of Pall Mall and all the way along Constitution Hill in warm spring sunshine. The plot of ground it dominates feels almost like an elaborate traffic island. If you were to pass by on a bus you might hardly notice the memorial itself. From the ground it's truly monumental. On both towering sides of the central column, behind a massive sculpted howitzer, are engraved the words:

IN PROUD REMEMBRANCE OF
THE FORTYNINE THOUSAND AND SEVENTY SIX
OF ALL RANKS OF
THE ROYAL REGIMENT OF ARTILLERY
WHO GAVE THEIR LIVES FOR KING
AND COUNTRY IN THE GREAT WAR
1914–1919.

'Fortynine thousand and seventy six' – in words the death toll looks bigger, even worse, than in numbers. Giant bronze artillerymen, twice life-size, stand around the base in wet-weather gear. One wears on his right leg an arrangement like a

1. In all conscience: the iconic image of Field Marshall Lord Kitchener, Secretary of State for War, adorned countless recruitment posters.

2. Shame on you: women in London's East End raise the 'White Feather' flag as part of a campaign to humiliate men not in uniform.

3. Fulstow's men on active service in India before the Great War. Charles Kirman is on the extreme left of the photograph.

4. 'Death or glory': Corporal James McPhie, V.C.

5. 'I don't think there was ever anyone like him; he was absolutely glorious': Major William 'Billy' La Touche Congreve, V.C., D.S.O., M.C.

6. Our Boys God Bless Them: street shrines like this one in Hull began the process of immortalising men's names.

7. Sergeant Ernest Artus.

8. A day to remember: Ernest Artus and his comrades of the 10th Battalion, Gloucestershire Regiment, bid farewell to their families as they leave for the front from Cheltenham Railway Station, 3 August 1915.

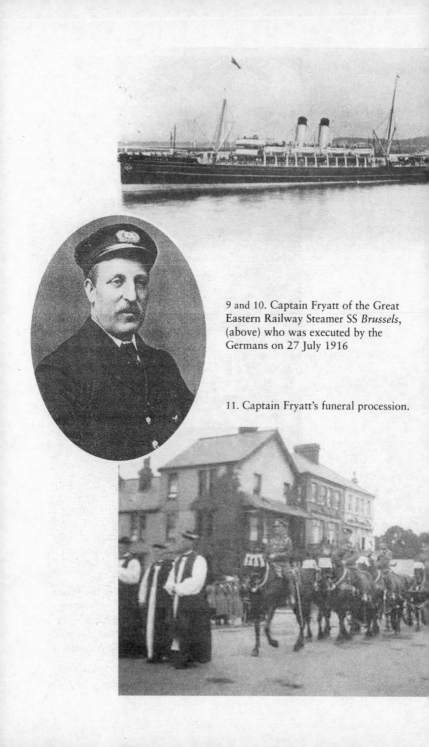

9 and 10. Captain Fryatt of the Great Eastern Railway Steamer SS *Brussels*, (above) who was executed by the Germans on 27 July 1916

11. Captain Fryatt's funeral procession.

12. Quintinshill, 22 May 1915. Firemen tackle the blaze hours after the troop train crashed.

13. Helpers wander among the dead and injured: of the 490 soldiers on the train, 225 men perished in the accident.

14. 'Munitionettes' – women at work in the Brunner, Mond and Company explosives factory at Crescent Wharf in east London's Silvertown area.

15. Acres of Silvertown were laid to waste when the munitions factory exploded.

16. Lost Souls: the five Souls brothers, pictured among the war dead of Great Rissington.

17. Their mother, Annie Souls, on the left of the photograph.

IN GRATEFUL MEMORY OF THE GALLANT MEN OF THIS PARISH
WHO SACRIFICED THEIR LIVES FOR KING AND COUNTRY IN THE
GREAT WAR 1914-1918.

ALBERT SOULS PRIVATE 2ND WORCESTERSHIRE REGT. FRANCE 1916
JOHN VELLENDER PRIVATE 8TH GLOUCESTERSHIRE REGT. FRANCE 1916
FRED G. SOULS PRIVATE 16TH CHESHIRE REGT. FRANCE 1916
WALTER D. SOULS PRIVATE 2ND WORCESTERSHIRE REGT. FRANCE 1916
OLIVER J. PORTER PRIVATE 8TH GLOUCESTERSHIRE REGT. FRANCE 1916
GARNET MORRIS LANCE CPL. ROYAL WARWICKSHIRE REGT. BELGIUM 1916
FRED J. VELLENDER PRIVATE 12TH HAMPSHIRE REGT. SALONICA 1917
THOMAS SPENCER GLOUCESTERSHIRE TERRITORIAL FRANCE 1917
WILFRID H. HENSLEY CAPTAIN 6TH SOMERSETSHIRE L.I. FRANCE 1918
ARTHUR W. SOULS LANCE CPL. 16TH CHESHIRE REGT. FRANCE 1918
ALFRED E. SOULS PRIVATE 11TH CHESHIRE REGT. FRANCE 1918
FRED MASTERS PRIVATE 10TH ARMY CYCLIST CORPS DIED AFTER DISCHARGE 1916
THOMAS W. BOLTER PRIVATE 11TH LEICESTERSHIRE REGT. DIED AFTER DISCHARGE 1919

"DEATH IS SWALLOWED UP IN VICTORY."

18. The memorial in Great Rissington church.

19. The redoubtable Elizabeth de T'Serclaes, née Elsie Shapter – nurse, baroness, adventurer.

modified cricket pad – used to protect his leg against crushing when he had to ride between a pair of the horses used to pull the heavy guns. Another figure lies in death – his body covered by his poncho, his face by his tin helmet. He is laid out upon a slab inscribed with:

HERE WAS A ROYAL FELLOWSHIP.

And beneath it, on a bronze plaque:

BENEATH THIS STONE IS BURIED
THE ROLL OF HONOUR OF THOSE WHOSE MEMORY
IS PERPETUATED BY THIS MEMORIAL.
THEY WILL RETURN NEVERMORE
BUT THEIR GLORY WILL
ABIDE FOREVER.

Near by is another memorial to other men of the Great War, much smaller than that of the Royal Artillery but as affecting in its way. It commemorates the men of the Machine Gun Corps and has on it:

SAUL HATH SLAIN HIS THOUSANDS
BUT DAVID HIS TENS OF THOUSANDS.

How can a person not be moved by all this? How could any of it ever be overlooked, far less forgotten? Or is it just me?)

If anything unites the mass of the memorials dotted across the landscape, it's the names of servicemen and women. Whatever else was incorporated into the designs, the highest priority was given to recording their identities, fixing them somewhere and making them permanent. Sometimes they are arranged in order of rank, officer class followed by enlisted men. Often even this distinction is omitted and lists are ordered by the alphabet alone.

There are similarities between many of the memorials around the country – testament to the 'off the shelf' service being provided by monumental sculptors at the time. There is also an undoubted element of variety as well, of communities finding their own unique ways of remembering their dead.

The memorials described below are chosen almost at random from the collection amassed by the National Inventory of War Memorials. They have been selected to give a sense of the range of works created both in the inter-war years and after, right up to the present day.

Memorial Bell, St Margaret's Church, Blackwood, Gwent

Dedicated to Sergeant James Spencer, 'H' Company, 1st Monmouthshire Regiment. Life above ground in the countryside around places like Ypres was impossible for men within range of the enemy. Tunnels were dug – both to provide cover for troop movements and to make it possible to undermine enemy positions and blow them up. The Royal Engineers, men with specialist skills, pioneered the tunnelling, but soon less experienced men were being drafted in to keep up with demand. Sergeant Spencer was a member of one of these first 'tunnelling companies', having sailed for France with his company on 14 February 1915. The work was foul as well as dangerous. Strafed on the surface by enemy machine-gun fire and artillery, they faced the prospect of encountering rotting corpses in the ground they were digging through. It wasn't for nothing that they were paid bonuses for the job. Sergeant Spencer was one of thirty-eight men of the 1st Monmouthshire Regiment called in to bulk out the 171st Tunnelling Company. He was killed near 'Hill 60', a man-made mound created by the cutting of the Ypres–Comines Railway, when the Germans set off explosives in one of their own tunnels close to where the British teams were digging. He was twenty-seven years old. In a letter to his mother, Sergeant Spencer's commanding officer wrote:

'Your son was in charge of a party working up at the trenches
... The Germans blew in one of our mines, burying one man
and partly burying another. There was a large amount of poison
gas in the mine at the time. Your son very gallantly went down
... to try and rescue one other man, but was overcome by the
fumes, and when he was brought out of the gallery he was dead.
He had been buried behind the trenches, and his grave marked
by a cross. He was always conspicuous in the trenches for his
zealousness and he met his end fearlessly and doing his duty as
a soldier should. I can only again express my sympathy with
you in your loss, yours sincerely – E. Wellesley, Capt. R. E.,
O. C. 171 Coy, R. E.'

Despite the initial burial, Sergeant Spencer's grave was lost in the
confusion of later fighting. His name appears among the missing
on the Menin Gate.

The Memorial Bell in St Margaret's Church at Blackwood, in
Gwent, was engraved in his honour. The inscription says:

TO THE GLORY OF GOD IN MEMORY OF
SERGT. J. H. SPENCER,
WHO WAS GASSED AT HILL 60, FRANCE,
JUNE 2ND 1915,
WHEN NOBLY ATTEMPTING
TO SAVE A COMRADE.

Chattri War Memorial, Brighton

Located on the downs at Patcham, just outside Brighton, the
Chattri War Memorial remembers a group of thirty Sikh and
Hindu soldiers who died of their injuries while being treated in
hospitals in the town. It is also dedicated to the rest of the twelve
thousand or so Sikhs who convalesced there during the war years.

A service honouring all the Sikhs and Hindus who fought on the Allied side is held every year. The inscription says:

TO THE MEMORY OF ALL INDIAN SOLDIERS
WHO GAVE THEIR LIVES FOR THEIR
KING-EMPEROR IN THE GREAT WAR,
THIS MONUMENT, ERECTED ON THE SITE OF
THE FUNERAL PYRE WHERE HINDUS AND SIKHS
WHO DIED IN HOSPITAL IN BRIGHTON
PASSED THROUGH THE FIRE,
IS IN GRATEFUL ADMIRATION AND
BROTHERLY AFFECTION DEDICATED.

Cleopatra's Needle, London

This unmistakable landmark on Victoria Embankment was given by the Egyptian government to Britain in 1878 to commemorate both Admiral Nelson's famous victory over the French at the battle of the Nile in 1798 and Abercromby's triumph at Alexandria in 1801. On 4 September 1917, during a German air raid on the capital, a bomb exploded close to Cleopatra's Needle, killing three people in a passing tram. The memorial itself was damaged in the same blast and, as tradition dictates, the scars made on the needle and on the sphinxes at its base were left as battle honours. Cleopatra's Needle, though not formally recognised as such, is also therefore a memorial to the Great War.

Saughall clock tower, Cheshire

The specially designed and built clock tower at Saughall in Cheshire commemorates twenty men killed in the Great War. It has on it the words:

THIS MEMORIAL WAS ERECTED
BY THE PARISHIONERS OF
GREAT AND LITTLE SAUGHALL
AND SHOTWICK PARK
TO THE MEMORY OF
THE MEN FROM THESE PARISHES
WHO MADE THE SUPREME SACRIFICE
IN THE GREAT WAR 1914–1918.

Great Gable Memorial, Lake District

Set into the summit of the Great Gable climb, this plaque commemorates those members of the Fell and Rock Climbing Club of Great Britain who died in the Great War. It has on it the words:

IN GLORIOUS AND HAPPY MEMORY
OF THOSE WHOSE NAMES ARE INSCRIBED
BELOW – MEMBERS OF THIS CLUB
WHO DIED FOR THEIR COUNTRY IN
THE EUROPEAN WAR 1914–1918.
THESE FELLS WERE ACQUIRED BY
THEIR FELLOW MEMBERS AND BY THEM
VESTED IN THE NATIONAL TRUST
FOR THE USE AND ENJOYMENT OF
THE PEOPLE OF OUR LAND FOR ALL TIME.

Canadian Memorial, London

Designed by French-Canadian artist Pierre Granche, the memorial to Canada's dead of both the Great War and the Second World War is a recent addition to the landscape of Green Park. It was unveiled on 3 June 1994 and is a break from the more conventional, traditional ways of remembering the dead.

If you come at it from the Mall it is first visible as two dark triangles rising up out of the grass. On a sunny day, the triangles shimmer with tiny movements. Closer examination reveals that the blackened surfaces of the stone triangles have impressions of maple leaves in them. A continuous flow of water cascades gently down, giving the leaves a lifelike quality, as though they had just fallen from the tree.

Between the triangles is a narrow path sloping upwards; the gradient is very slight, hardly noticeable. The central axis of the memorial, as defined by the pathway, is carefully aligned east to west, and there is also a plaque in the form of an old-fashioned compass rose. The whole thing is pointing towards Halifax, in Nova Scotia, the place back home where most of the Canadian servicemen had congregated at the start of their journey to the war.

Saighton Lane Memorial Pump, Cheshire

An ornamental pump in the village of Saighton lists the names of six of its men who died in the Great War:

Lieut Percy Lyulph WYNDHAM Coldstream Guards	Lieut George William MASON 3rd King's Liverpool Regt
Pte Frank STOKES 1st King's Liverpool Regt	Pte Harry GRACE 3rd Batt Cheshire Regt
Gnr William GRINDLEY Royal Field Artillery	Pte Wilfred SALISBURY East Kent Regt

Maybole Memorial Park, Ayrshire

The people of the town of Maybole bought a piece of farmland some time after the end of the Great War, and had it turned into a memorial park in honour of their dead. The specially commissioned ornamental gates of the entrance were opened for the first time in 1925 by a Mrs Clark. She was the mother of seven sons, four of whom were killed in the war. The original gates went missing some years ago, after being taken down for repairs and refurbishment, and have been replaced with new ones.

St Peter's Memorial Church, Blaina, Gwent

The brass plaque on the wall of the church is inscribed:

> DULCE ET DECORUM EST PRO PATRIA MORI.
> TO THE GLORY OF GOD AND IN HONOURED
> MEMORY OF THE MEN OF THIS
> CONGREGATION WHO FELL IN
> THE GREAT WAR 1914–1918.

It names twenty-seven men.

There is also a memorial in the form of wood panels behind the pulpit, bearing the names of the men of the parish who died. The dedication reads:

> TO THE GLORY OF GOD AND THE
> IMMORTAL MEMORY OF THE MEN
> OF THIS CHURCH WHO SERVED AND
> THOSE WHO GAVE THEIR LIVES IN
> THE GREAT WAR 1914–1918.
>
> THE MEN WERE VERY GOOD UNTO US,
> AND WE WERE NOT HURT,
> THEY WERE A WALL UNTO US BOTH
> BY NIGHT AND DAY.
>
> I SAMUEL 25 (15.16.)

All those who served are named, those who survived as well as those who fell. The dead are indicated by the letters 'RIP' and the year in which they were killed.

24th London Division, London

In Battersea Park stands sculptor Eric Kennington's memorial to the 24th London. Three soldiers stand close together, all facing in the same direction. It's a form used repeatedly in war memorials and very reminiscent of the iconic memorial to the commandos of the Second World War, at Spean Bridge near Fort William. Kennington himself repeated the form at a memorial to the Missing of the Aisne Battlefield, near Soissons.

In the case of the 24th London memorial, it is said that Robert Graves – one of Kennington's close friends – was the model for one of the soldiers.

Animals in War, London

A unique memorial dedicated to every animal killed in the service of British and Allied armies – not just in the Great War but in every conflict. Designed by sculptor David Backhouse, carved by Richard Holliday and Harry Gray and built by Sir Robert McAlpine, it sits on the central reservation of Park Lane opposite a luxury car dealership. Two mules, one carrying ammunition boxes, the other loaded with parts of an artillery limber, walk towards a gap in the concave face of a huge crescent of blond-coloured stone engraved with buffalo, more mules, horses, camels and elephants. Through the gap, to the rear of the crescent, a dog, maybe a setter of some kind, looks back over its left shoulder as though urging the mules to follow. The lead animal, striding massively away ahead of the dog, is a shire horse, slightly larger than life-size.

... FROM THE PIGEON TO THE ELEPHANT THEY ALL PLAYED A VITAL ROLE.

The main inscription on the stone crescent says:

THIS MONUMENT IS DEDICATED TO ALL
THE ANIMALS THAT SERVED AND DIED
ALONGSIDE BRITISH AND ALLIED FORCES IN
WARS AND CAMPAIGNS THROUGHOUT TIME.
THEY HAD NO CHOICE.

It was unveiled on 24 November 2004 by HRH the Princess Royal, patron of the Animals in War Benevolent Fund.

East Chiltington War Memorial, Sussex

A 9-foot-high granite cross engraved with a 'crusader's sword' commemorates the names of nine men who died in the Great War. A war memorial committee comprising the great and the good of the area went out of their way to map the district, verify the names of the fallen and seek donations and subscriptions from every household in the area. Their effort was typical of the work required by any community, large or small, wanting to erect a permanent reminder of their lost loved ones.

Angmering War Memorial, Sussex

A 20-foot-high cross of Portland stone, made at the Carrara marble works in Worthing. Here was an attempt by a committee to meet the needs of every interested party. The first public meeting was held in 1919 and decided that '. . . our first duty is to those who made the supreme sacrifice, our second to those who came back, our last to ourselves'. The committee itself included relatives of three men killed in the war and representatives from local 'friendly societies'. The memorial was made to a design chosen by the committee and made from local materials.

Lowick War Memorial, Northumberland

The original war memorial committee, chaired by local land-owner General Sitwell, veteran of Gallipoli, ordered four blocks of undressed stone from the local quarry. Once assembled, the lump was engraved with the dates of the war – 1914–1918.

When the rest of the people of Lowick saw the thing – devoid of any element of design and with no space on it to place the names of their dead loved ones – they reacted with hurt and anger.

The general, a man unaccustomed to having his word and will challenged, was forced to resign, along with every member of his committee. Their successors gave General Sitwell six days to remove his memorial and promptly commissioned the present one, of polished Aberdeen granite on a base of Doddington stone. The original was moved out of the village altogether.

One of the names on the Lowick memorial is that of Thomas Hall Bruce, the youngest son of Andrew and Robina Bruce, of Beal Farm. By all accounts he was a quiet-living family man. Following the outbreak of war he served as a private with 12th/13th Battalion of the Northumberland Fusiliers. He died of influenza aged twenty-nine on 12 November 1918, the day after the Armistice, and is buried in the Rocquigny-Equancourt Road British Cemetery at Manancourt, Plot XIII, Row B, Grave 2. His name also appears in the roll of honour kept by Fenwick village hall.

Earlier in 1918, while at home on leave, he saw his son Thomas junior, born in July, for the first and only time. In 1948, Thomas junior was married to Attha. She's eighty-one years old now and remembers getting to know her husband's mother – hearing how hard it had been to bring up a son on a war widow's pension. Attha became interested in the Lowick war memorial after a visit to the site with her grandson. She wanted him to see his great-grandfather's name there and was upset to find it, like all the others, made almost illegible by time and weather. She campaigned for its restoration and has also sold poppies for the Royal British Legion.

Attha's Thomas served in the Second World War. He was captured at St. Valerie and spent five years as a prisoner of war. Attha said that while her husband backed the efforts of the Legion, he did not attend Remembrance Day parades.

19

With Eager Valour

In the north Somerset village of Mells, near Frome, the church of St Andrews sits against a backdrop of green fields. It was built in the fifteenth century, no different from scores of other churches in that part of the world.

The Horner family settled there some time in the first half of the sixteenth century. When Henry VIII dissolved the monasteries the Horners' share of north Somerset was increased by the acquisition of the buildings of the monastery and the land surrounding it. Though not accepted by the family, this is widely reputed to be the 'plum' pulled out by the Little Jack Horner of the nursery rhyme.

Inside the church, by the north aisle, is the parish memorial to the men of the village who were killed in the Great War. It is inscribed:

TO THOSE WHO FOUGHT IN STRANGE LANDS
AND DIED FOR ENGLAND THE MEN AND
WOMEN OF MELLS HAVE SET UP THIS STONE
IN LOVE AND GRATITUDE
1914–1919.

Beneath the inscription are the names of fourteen men:

RAYMOND ASQUITH   WYNDHAM HAMES
FRANCIS BABER   EDWARD HORNER
GEOFFREY BATES   ARTHUR LONG

OLIVER BURGE   HERBERT OLDING
STANLEY BURGE   FRANK PHILLIPS
EDGAR CHAMBERLAIN   LEONARD SILK
ALFRED GRACE   THOMAS WITCOMBE

The quotation below the names says:

THEY SOUGHT THE GLORY OF THEIR COUNTRY
THEY BEHOLD THE GLORY OF GOD.

The names are in alphabetical order, without rank or any other distinguishing feature. They are united in death. Elsewhere in the church, though, are other symbols that challenge the egalitarian objectives of the simple tablet.

In the Horner Chapel within the church is a huge and almost overpowering equestrian statue cast in bronze, by the sculptor Sir Alfred Munnings. It sits on top of a plinth designed by Lutyens, a family friend. The figure on horseback represents Edward Horner, eldest son and heir of the family. On the plinth, beneath the horse's tail, is the wooden cross that marked Edward's war grave until a regulation headstone replaced it.

A nearby stained-glass window describes how Edward was a lieutenant in the 18th Hussars, '. . . who was born on 3rd May 1888 and died on the 21st of November 1917. He was greatly loved at his home at Mells but with eager valour he left his heritage at the outbreak of war to fight in France'.

Edward was severely wounded at Ypres but recovered and returned to his regiment, '. . . and fell at last in Picardy whilst defending the village of Noyelles against the German Army in the Battle of Cambrai.

'Thus in the morning of his youth he hastened to rejoin his friends and comrades by a swift and noble death.'

He was twenty-four years old and is buried in Rocquigny-Equancourt Road British Cemetery, at Manancourt, Plot I, Row E, Grave 23.

Raymond Asquith, who appears first on the tablet only by dint of alphabetical order, was one of Prime Minister Herbert Henry Asquith's sons. He was married to Katharine Horner, Edward's eldest sister. Raymond's wooden cross is in St Andrew's church too, above an entrance to the Horner Chapel. At the time of his death on the Somme, on 15 September 1916, he was a lieutenant with the 3rd Battalion, Grenadier Guards. He was thirty-seven years old. Although shot and mortally wounded he tried to reassure his men by casually lighting a cigarette as he was carried away from them. He died almost as soon as he was out of their sight and is buried in the Guillenmont Road Cemetery, at Guillenmont, in Plot I, Row B, Grave 3.

Raymond was educated at Winchester College and his name appears on the memorial there. As the son of a prime minister, he is also name-checked on a memorial at the Houses of Parliament.

The church at Mells is a place where equality in death mixes with the proud demands of private grief. Regular working man Arthur Long also has his own memorial inside the church, paid for by his wife and other members of his family. His rank is listed as corporal on the brass plaque that tells how he was killed in action near Ypres on 13 May 1915. His body was never found. On the Commonwealth War Graves Commission website he is listed as Private Long, North Somerset Yeomanry. It says his name is on Panel 5 of the Menin Gate, among the 54,338 others listed there.

Outside in the churchyard is the grave of the war poet Siegfried Sassoon. The inscription reads:

SIEGFRIED

LORRAINE

SASSOON

1886–1967

R.I.P.

He died the year I was born. He was originally from Weirleigh in Kent and lived a life of easy privilege before enlisting on

2 August 1914, two days before the British declaration of war on Germany. He got his commission with the Royal Welch Fusiliers in May 1915. Two deaths in the war – his brother's at Gallipoli and that of his friend David 'Tommy' Thomas, shot and killed while out with a wiring party – had a profound effect on him. For a while then he was 'Mad Jack' – a nickname given him by his men on account of his appetite for high-risk sorties in search of Germans to kill to satisfy his hunger for revenge. A suitably dangerous raid on a German trench earned him the Military Cross.

Two bouts of illness – trench fever, soon followed by German measles – saw him invalided home to Britain. Back with the RWF by March 1917 he was at Arras and then the Second Battle of the Scarpe, where he suffered a shoulder wound. It was after this event that he made his 'declaration' of 'wilful defiance' – that he would fight no more. Only the intervention of his friend and fellow officer Robert Graves secured him a stay in hospital at Craiglockhart, in Edinburgh, rather than disciplinary proceedings.

It was at Craiglockhart that he met Wilfred Owen, in August 1917. The building is still there, part of Napier University. I went there for a few months in 1994 to finish my training as a newspaper journalist.

Sassoon recovered well enough to be passed fit for general service and was in Palestine with the 25th Battalion, RWF, by February 1918. Defiant no longer, he was subsequently posted back to France but suffered a head wound in the July of that year that sent him back to Britain once more. This time he was placed on indefinite sick leave, and this meant the end of his war. He left the army in March 1919, still angry with and isolated from a home front he believed had conspired to prolong the war and made a financial profit out of it.

He moved to Mells later in life to be closer to Monsignor Ronald Knox, who he hoped would instruct him in the Catholic faith. Knox died in 1957, ten years before Sassoon.

Like the chivalric idealism that drove its young men into the Great War, the village of Mells can seem hard to find now. It's tucked away at the bottom of a steeply sided valley, almost lost among the threads of minor roads. It's a lovely spot, cut through by a river.

There's something here too of a world lost bit by bit after 1914. In the church and churchyard of St Andrew's is a summary of all the Great War's grief – aristocrat, prime minister's son, ordinary working men, all caught up together by the same event and all dead at the end of it, their names on a plain stone.

The war poet is there too, survivor of it all. As an observer should, he has stayed on the outside right to the end.

20

The Handsomest Man in the World

According to legend, Patrick 'Paddy' Crossan, full-back for Heart of Midlothian Football Club in Edinburgh for the 1914/15 season, would tell anyone he was the handsomest man in the world. As the story goes, he could pass a ball but he could never pass a mirror.

Like many professional sportsmen in late 1914, he faced a dilemma. When war broke out, the Football Association had gone so far as to ask the government whether the professional game should be postponed to free up men for military service. The official reply was that it was up to them to decide the right course of action for themselves. The amateur sports of golf, rugby union and hockey had all stopped play as soon as hostilities kicked off. The RU was able to declare: 'It is the duty of every able-bodied man of enlistable age to offer personal war service to his king and country, and . . . every Rugby footballer of the present day comes within the scope of Lord Kitchener's appeal.'

Those making a living from their games faced an economic as well as a patriotic decision.

Kitchener's recruitment posters were everywhere, challenging men's pride from every angle. As well as more famous images – such as the little girl asking her daddy what he did in the war – there were others taking a different, more specific tack. By November 1914 there was one showing a wounded soldier standing over the body of a dead friend. His gaze was turned towards an image of a far-away football match being played in front of a packed crowd. 'Will they never come?' he asked. Stuck on the walls of football clubs around the country, these posters were hard to miss.

For every professional sportsman in the country it was a time of intense pressure. For the men of Hearts FC first eleven, the choice was especially badly timed. They were poised to lift the League Cup for the first time since 1897. They'd won eight games on the trot – one against the national side of Denmark – and they were without doubt the most successful squad in the country that year. But how much pleasure was left in the game when the *Glasgow Herald* newspaper was using its coverage of the November 1914 Old Firm clash to ask how much the fates of Rangers and Celtic really mattered when 'the greatest of all internationals' was being played in Europe?

Then local businessman and pillar of the community Sir George McCrae stepped forward to ask whether he might have permission to raise a new battalion for the Royals Scots Regiment. McCrae was an enigmatic figure. The son of an Aberdeen servant girl, he'd left school at fourteen, taken work as a messenger boy and then made a meteoric rise through the worlds of business and politics. Personal charisma allied with a modest and good-hearted nature made him the kind of man that others were likely to follow. His wish to create a new battalion was granted. On 24 November he was at Hearts FC making a rousing recruitment speech. The following day Crossan and every man jack of the first eleven enlisted in the new battalion, along with five Hearts reserve players. Alongside Crossan in 'The Sixteen' were Hearts favourites Ernie Ellis, a boot-maker before he turned professional footballer; full-back Duncan Currie, part of a footballing family that boasted a goalkeeping father, one brother who had played for Hearts and Bury and another who turned out for Leicester Fosse; and James Boyd, former coalminer and brother of Archie, himself a one-time goalkeeper for Hearts.

The Hearts directors, believed to have had money worries following the building of a new stand, may have encouraged the enlistment. The club was ready to pay 2 pounds a week to those who joined up – half their entitlement as footballers and something of a saving. In any case, the enlistment of the whole of the first team in Kitchener's Army would surely defuse any simmering bad publicity surrounding the club's financial fortunes?

Whatever the reasons, the stars marched away to war as part of a move the like of which the world of professional football had never seen. It's easy to imagine what happened next. Inspired by their heroes' actions, young men from across the city rushed to their local recruitment offices to try to sign up to McCrae's 16th Royal Scots. Other footballers joined too – professionals from rival Edinburgh side Hibernian as well as many from neighbouring amateur sides such as the Edinburgh and Leith Postmen and the Pumpherston Rangers.

By the time the battalion was up to strength the footballers were shoulder to shoulder with other sportsmen, as well as students, schoolboys, clerks, shop workers, labourers, artists, doctors and lawyers. This then was the cross-section of Kitchener's new army. It had examples of every kind of man, and because of the sheer pressure to join up it had scores who knew one another either as neighbours, friends, workmates, schoolmates or teammates.

Some of those who took part in the Great War sound vaguely familiar to everyone: the 'Accrington Pals' from east Lancashire, the 'Cardiff Pals', the 'Leeds Pals', the city transport workers who formed the 'Glasgow Tramways', the 'Grimsby Chums'. Many of them sound like old-time music hall turns, or characters from a half-remembered comic strip – and then you remember that they were soldiers.

They turned out in such numbers the authorities could hardly cope with them. The machinery of regular army life in 1914 was unprepared to deal with the deluge. Volunteers arrived at hastily extended or makeshift camps that often had no uniforms, rifles or kit of any kind with which to equip them. There were precious few NCOs or other officers to train them and no new commanders to lead them. Improvisation on an industrial scale became the order of the day. Kitchener had the recruits for his army and there would be no need for compulsory enlistment – the conscription initiated by the Military Service Act – until 1916.

The numbers generated by that conscription would never be noticeably greater than the force made up of those who volunteered at the start.

Successful though the 'pals' strategy undoubtedly was – from the point of view of rounding up the men required to fill the new armies – it was also flawed. For as long as the pals' regiments stayed hale and hearty they provided a focus of pride both for the men themselves and for the communities from which they'd been drawn. But when they went into action – disastrously on the killing fields of the Somme – whole neighbourhoods lost the best of their menfolk at a stroke.

In the aftermath of the Somme, individual battalions would never again have the local strength they'd had at the start of the battle. There was a deliberate move away from such aggregation of men related by blood, address or workplace. While some have argued that this only added to the dehumanising anonymity of the average man's experience of the war – cutting him off from everyone and everything he'd known before – it did at least prevent any repeats of tragedies like the decimation of the Accrington Pals and the Grimsby Chums.

The impact of such wholesale loss had not been taken into account – either that or no one in authority had predicted that the loss would be as all encompassing as it eventually was. It is best to believe that such an outcome was unimaginable for the top brass; the alternative, that all those men were seen as expendable, doesn't bear thinking about.

21

Her Wedding Day

Why do we remember the things we remember? Why do we forget the things we forget?

Mother's Day, 6 March 2005, 8.45 a.m. Radio 2 is playing in the kitchen – *Steve Wright's Sunday Love Songs* – and the boy band McFly are singing 'All About You'.

Trudi and Evie are dancing. Evie's dancing at twenty-three months is individual and strenuous. To an uninformed observer it probably looks like running on the spot while waving both arms and smiling, but it's dancing. She's still wearing her sleep-suit – a pink fleece all-in-one with a zip that runs from knee to chin.

She comes over to where I'm sitting in dressing gown and slippers at the kitchen table after a breakfast of poached eggs on toast. She stops beside me, smiles at me, then runs back to Trudi and looks up into her face. 'Well . . . you'll have to get him up,' says Trudi. 'Go and take his hand . . . go on.'

Evie comes back to me and takes my hand. Her hand is so small, perfect. I stand up, stoop and pick her up into my arms so I can waltz her. Trudi says, 'Well, that's the first time your daughter's got you up to dance.'

For a little while the three of us dance together. We laugh into each other's faces as we dance close.

Then Trudi breaks free and walks away towards the table, her back to me and Evie. I set Evie down – she keeps dancing and waving and smiling – and walk over to Trudi. I know she's crying and I turn her around and hug her. 'I just got caught by the moment,' she says over my shoulder, wiping her eyes with a tissue. 'Just being silly.'

We stand like that for a while. I smell soap and shampoo on the collar of her white towelling dressing gown. Evie is oblivious, still dancing, still smiling. 'And then it was her wedding day and she was getting you up to dance.'

Trudi's mind does this kind of thing. I think she becomes aware of the happiness of a moment and then time runs on at impossible speed, way beyond the happiness, towards the old age she dreads.

I think this is because moments are all we remember and the moments we remember are not enough.

22

A House of Memory

I visited the Scottish National War Memorial, within the walls of Edinburgh Castle, on one of the hottest days of 2005. The Royal Mile was heaving with visitors, as usual, and on the esplanade in front of the castle a squad of workmen were putting up the grandstand for the Tattoo. This sloping parade ground is dotted with memorials to various people, various wars. There are so many the place sometimes looks like a temporary store for memorials waiting to go somewhere else. Earl Haig is there on horseback, frowning over his moustache. History and tradition are so thick here, so infectious, it takes a conscious effort to stop me snapping salutes at passing tourists. I feel proud of the place, proprietary in the face of strangers, foreigners; as if its mine.

If the Cenotaph in Whitehall commemorates every soldier of every nation who died fighting on the side of the Allies, Scotland's national memorial is something different, maybe even unique. I've been a few times over the years, taking it in as part of this or that visit to the castle. When you're a Scot, as I am, you have to visit Edinburgh Castle every few years – there's always some new acquaintance or other wanting to make their first trip to the place. However many times I go to the war memorial, though, it always affects me the same way. It takes me by surprise.

A visit to Edinburgh Castle is usually pretty expensive, I have to say – enough to make a person think twice before treating two or three adult friends to the tour, for example. But when I told the lady in the ticket caravan that I only wanted to see the war memorial, she waved me through for free. She gave me a special ticket for the purpose marked Scottish National War Memorial, and I was passed from one friendly uniformed official to another, like a parcel, until I reached my destination. I almost felt duty bound to keep my eyes on the ground so as not to see any attraction I hadn't paid for, as I followed the path anti-clockwise through the Inner Barrier, the Portcullis Gate, beyond the Six Gun Battery, through Foog's Gate, past tiny St Margaret's Chapel and then round, clockwise now, into Crown Square.

The memorial's location on the summit of the Castle Rock is no coincidence. This spot, the highest point on Scotland's most famous landmark, was chosen to show the esteem in which the country would hold the memory of its dead.

The building itself – this is the crucial difference from the Cenotaph, it's a building not a sculpture – forms one side of the square. Originally it was the Billings' Building, used mostly as a barracks. Its conversion into Scotland's National War Memorial was overseen by architect-in-chief Robert Lorimer, and it was opened to the public on 14 July 1927. What Lorimer and his team of craftsmen achieved here is a war memorial like no other. It is a house of memory.

I think a lot about memory and remembering – how it starts, why we remember the things we remember, why we forget the things we forget. If you read a bit about memory you find out it was once revered as an art, almost as a form of magic. In the days before books and hard drives and all the other artificial ways of making sure things are not forgotten, students of memory were taught to use architecture as a store for what had to be remembered.

First you built a building in your mind – it might be a real place you were familiar with, such as the family home or the local church, or the product of your imagination; the point was to become so familiar with the place you could run round it in your mind in darkness or blindfold. Once you had the layout off pat you could fill it with things to be remembered – not the memories themselves but symbols to trigger their recall. If you needed to remember a speech you were about to give you would arrange evocative symbols at locations throughout your house of memory, the more vivid and striking the better. All you had to do was imagine walking through the house, seeing each symbol in turn and remembering the points you wanted to make. Whatever you needed to remember became part of an internal landscape; the memory came to life.

That's the theory. But I have to say, hard though I've tried, I've never made it work.

Adherents of the house of memory said the system did something else besides store things that were not to be forgotten. Two symbols stored side by side – symbols unconnected and representing two different memories – might occasionally conspire without the owner's knowledge to create a third. The third would be something else, something the owner didn't know he knew.

I don't suppose Lorimer had a house of memory in mind when he designed the memorial but I think that's what he made. Every carving, symbol and detail comes together as one story of Scotland's Great War: its history, its servicemen, its women. When the time came, there was room for the story of 1939–45. Houses of memory are like that – adaptable.

The symbols built into the fabric of the place might not make sense the first time you go; you might not even notice them all. Carved wreaths surround the badges of the armed services on the outside walls. The army's is laurel, representing victory; the navy's is laurel for victory combined with oak, for Britain; the air force's is rowan, a tree that grows in high places. A lot of what's going on is subtle, overlooked by the many and appreciated by the few. Elsewhere the sense of continuity, of continuing, everyday remembrance, is made obvious by new wreaths of poppies hanging from bronze hooks designed for the purpose. The writing on the message cards is still legible, not yet blurred by rain or faded by sunlight. People who come here are busy with remembrance.

However much you miss, you can't avoid the strangeness of some of it. Stand outside the main entrance and look up to the right. In a niche where you might expect to see a soldier maybe, head bowed, or an angel with folded wings, there's an armoured knight with a naked toddler at his knee. It's striking, almost shocking. You don't expect it. This is Mercy. Above the double doorway is a figure rising with a phoenix out of the flames. This is the Survival of the Spirit. Even in bright sunshine its face stays in shadow. Step through into the stone porch. On the left-hand wall in gold letters 6 inches high are words taken from Psalm 24: 'Our soul is escaped even as a bird out of the snare of the fowler: the snare is broken and we are delivered.'

The unexpectedness goes on and on. The symbols are not what I anticipated. Above the inner door is a carving of a pelican feeding her young with blood from her breast. This is about Sacrifice. There's a lot of animal imagery in here. Near the base of a pillar in the south-west bay is an engraving of a cage holding two canaries and, beneath them, two mice. It's called 'The Tunnellers' Friends' and marks the contribution of animals used to detect gas underground. Elsewhere are the heads of horse, mule, camel, reindeer and dog: 'Remember also the humble beasts that served and died.'

Inside, the memorial feels a bit like a church – but the main axis runs away on both sides rather than leading straight ahead. The roof is higher than the exterior suggests. The stained-glass windows designed by Douglas Strachan heighten the effect. They depict the nature of every kind of war service given by men and women: infantry, artillery, navy, air force, munitions workers, land girls, nurses – picked out in designs that look more modern than might be expected from work completed nearly eighty years ago.

Around the walls are twelve regimental memorials – The Queen's Own Cameron Highlanders; Princess Louise's Argyll and Sutherland Highlanders; The Highland Light Infantry; The Cameronians; The Royal Scots Fusiliers; The Scots Guards; The

Royal Regiment; The King's Own Scottish Borderers; The Black Watch; The Seaforth Highlanders; The Gordon Highlanders; The Royal Scots Greys. On the far left wall is the memorial to the air service and to the right that to the naval services, the Royal Artillery, the Tank Corps, the Royal Engineers, the Royal Army Medical Corps. All who served are marked with a memorial in this building.

More affecting still are the books. Below the memorials are leather-bound books containing the names of all of Scotland's war dead – from both world wars. The edges of the pages are worn and stained from the thousands of hands that have touched them. Periodically they have to be repaired – whole pages replaced when they are torn out and taken away as souvenirs. I expect a lot of people do what I do – look up my own name and wonder whether the dead namesakes are relations.

The focus of the whole place is the Shrine, directly opposite the entrance. Lit by more stained glass, it contains a Stone of Remembrance cut from green marble and engraved with the Cross of Sacrifice. The stone sits on an outcrop of the rock that breaks through the floor. The passage of many feet has worn it as smooth as glass. On top is an iron casket. It looks a lot like the Ark of the Covenant from the Indiana Jones films, complete with angels, but this is the holy of holies. A gift from the king and queen, it contains the roll of honour of all Scotland's Great War dead.

Most powerful of all is the sense of a story being told. The imagery is forceful. It's like listening to a foreign language. You get the meaning without understanding the words. The Scottish National War Memorial is a story. The symbols mix in new ways all the time. It's as relevant today as it ever was. It's as if this memorial knew that other wars were coming, was readying itself to receive them.

For all that it represents, the Cenotaph has always seemed empty to me. This memorial is full of people. It's quiet and sad. Visitors are taken inside, not left outside. The Cenotaph seems blunt; this place welcomes the hurt and tries to find a place for it.

23

'Have You News of My Boy Jack?'

Vermelles
France
24/9/15

My Dear Wife & Children
I am writing these few lines hoping they will find you & the
Children in the Best of Health.

I don't suppose you would be in very good spirits if you
knew at the time that I am writing this that there is going on
one of the most terrific bombardments of modern time. Shells
are bursting in thousands all around us. To morrow its to be
or not to be, Dear. Poor Dick Betteridge was killed by a Shell
this morning not long after I was talking to him. We charge
the German trenches in the morning and I expect their [sic]
will be a good many that will never return but we are going to
do our best Dear. If I go through it alright I will write as soon
as possible. We has [sic] three chances to be in France
Wounded & sent home to blyty [sic] & lastly to give our
Checks in. If I go under Joe must have my medals. Take great
care of them till he grows up. And please God if I am spared I
will give a German 2 Stabs for you & one for each of the
Children. I hope Dear Wife if I do not return that the
Children will grow up a Credit to you & if the government
keeps their promise they will not go hungry. Remember me to
All & Closing With my Fondest and best love to you & the

*Children I remain for the Present your True and Affectionate
Husband Ernie xxxxxxxxxX I wish I was there to give them.
For the Children xxxxxxxxxxxxxx Share them amongst
them. PS Greater Love has no man than to lay down his life
for his Wife & Children.*
Letter from Sergeant Ernest Richard Artus, 10th
Gloucestershire Regiment, at the battle of Loos, killed
26 September 1915

Sergeant Artus lived with his wife on Granville Street, off Poole Way, in Cheltenham.

Private David Hawling's wife Beatrice was pregnant with their first child. They lived on Nailsworth Terrace, in St Paul's.

These were two of the Cheltenham men of the 10th Battalion, Gloucestershire Regiment, who went into action for the first time at the battle of Loos on 26 September 1915.

The Hawlings' son would be born the following year and named David, like his dad. Beatrice gave the boy Loos as a middle name.

Cheltenham is an elegant Regency town, popular with tourists. It hit its peak in the middle of the nineteenth century when the wealthy made a point of visiting the spa there to take the waters for the good of their health.

There's a photograph of some of the men of the 10th lined up with their women and children on the platform of Cheltenham railway station. It was taken on 3 August 1915, and if it wasn't for the uniforms it would look like some kind of mass outing, maybe a day trip to the seaside for a whole street.

Private Hawling had a good job as a brewery foreman – he might have resisted the call to join up but off he went. He had a year's training with the 10th before his battalion went off to France.

The Allied top brass were in the mood to get things moving on the Western Front. The First Battle of Ypres had run out of steam in mid-November 1914. Denied any real forward motion, the Allies settled down into the soft earth. The lines of trenches emerging then – from the spadework of both sides – would become more or less fixed positions for the next two years and more. Unfortunately, the generals did not know this and set their hearts on advance.

By the high summer of 1915 plans were well advanced for a major Allied offensive. The British, for their part, would attack in the mining area of Loos to the south of Vimy Ridge. Sir John French, in charge of the British forces on the ground, planned to use poison gas against the German defenders. It was tit-for-tat – the Germans had already unleashed the stuff at the Second Battle of Ypres earlier in the year.

In the early morning of 26 September the gas was released towards the German lines. After a sensible pause, six divisions of the First Army followed it and had some early success – taking Loos itself. A reserve made up of the Guards Division and two inexperienced divisions of Kitchener's New Army was supposed to follow up and capitalise on the gains. But delays in passing the relevant orders down the chain of command meant that the reserve arrived late in front of the German positions. It was here that the Cheltenham men made their debut in the Great War.

A report from the Germans' point of view described the use of machine guns to repel the Allied attack:

> . . . with barrels burning hot and swimming in oil, they traversed to and fro along the enemy's ranks unceasingly; one machine gun alone fired 12,500 rounds that afternoon. The effect was devastating. The enemy could be seen literally falling in hundreds, but they continued their march in good order and without interruption. The extended lines of men began to get confused by this terrific punishment, but they went doggedly on, some even reaching the wire entanglement in front of the reserve line, which their artillery had scarcely touched. Confronted by this impenetrable obstacle, the survivors turned and began to retire.

After just a few hours the dozen British battalions that had been there at the start had been cut to pieces. Of 10,000 officers and men of the New Army, 8,000 were dead or wounded. By the time the British called time at Loos, more than 40,000 men were lost. The largest battle ever undertaken by the British army at that time had proven to be one of its bloodiest.

Rudyard Kipling's only son John, a lieutenant in the 2nd Battalion, Irish Guards, was among the dead. An early would-be volunteer, he had been turned down at the first attempt on account of his appalling eyesight. He made it into the service only because his father pulled some strings and got him a commission.

He had been in France for around six weeks when he was killed. His body was not found and Kipling senior, broken by the loss, spent the remaining twenty years of his life trying to find his son's remains.

In 1916 he wrote the poem 'Have you news of my boy Jack?':

'Oh, dear what comfort can I find?'
None this tide,
Nor any tide,
Except he did not shame his kind –
Not even with that wind blowing, and that tide.

Then hold your head up all the more,
This tide,
And every tide;
Because he was the son you bore,
And gave to that wind blowing and that tide . . .

Remains found in 1992 were said to be those of Lieutenant Kipling, though there is still controversy about the identification. They were buried in St Mary's ADS (Advanced Dressing Station) Cemetery at Haines, Plot 7, Row D, Grave 2.

(Kipling composed the wording used on the gravestones of soldiers who could not be identified at the time of burial, 'A

Soldier of the Great War/Known unto God'. He also chose the line 'Their name liveth for evermore', from Ecclesiasticus, which features on the Stone of Remembrance:

And some there be, which have no memorial; who are perished, as though they had never been; and become as though they had never been born; and their children after them. But these were merciful men, whose righteousness hath not been forgotten . . . Their bodies are buried in peace; but their name liveth for evermore. The people will tell of their wisdom, and the congregation will shew forth their praise.)

Sergeant Artus from Cheltenham was killed at Loos as well. So too was Private Hawling. During the whole of the war around 1,600 Cheltenham men were killed. In one day's fighting at Loos, the 10th Gloucestershire's first action, a total of forty-four died together. It was just fifty-three days since a crowd of them had had their photograph taken on the railway platform back home.

WOMEN

24

'I Should be Pleased if I Could Hear From You'

There dwells a wife by the Northern Gate
    And a careworn wife is she:
She breeds a breed o' rovin' men
    And casts them over sea.

And some are drowned in deep water
    And some in sight o' shore,
And word goes back to the weary wife,
    And ever she sends more.

And some return by failing light.
    And some in waking dream,
For she hears the heels of the dripping ghosts
    That ride the rough roof-beam.

Home they come from all the ports,
    The living and the dead;
The good wife's sons come home again
    For her blessing on their head!

Rudyard Kipling

The Old Pye Street flats, in London's Westminster, are unremarkable, typical of the kind lived in by the city's workers.

There's a stone plaque built into one wall. One of 279 Great War memorials in Westminster alone, it's been there long enough for the residents to stop seeing it. It has a simple cross on top and underneath the words:

LEST WE FORGET
IN HONOURED MEMORY OF
THE MEN OF THIS ESTATE WHO LAID DOWN
THEIR LIVES IN THE GREAT WAR 1914–1918.

Underneath those words are the names of fifteen men:

SERGT CALLAGHAN, T., WELSH GUARDS
PTE DEAN, H. T., AUSTRALIAN IMPL FORCES
PTE FIFIELD, J. W., R. IRISH FUSILIERS
PTE FIFIELD, J. P., R. INNISKILLING RIFLES
PTE KIRTLAND, J. A., MIDDLESEX REGT
PTE LITTLEFIELD, W., E. SURREY REGT
PTE MARSHALL, J. C., R. FUSILIERS
PTE MARSHALL, A., NORTH'D FUSILIERS
PTE MASON, S. J., GRENADIER GUARDS
RIFLEMAN MILLER, A., RIFLE BRIGADE
RIFLEMAN MOONEY, J., RIFLE BRIGADE
RIFLEMAN PENNINGTON, C. W., RIFLE BRIGADE
PTE SMITH, F. C., WESTMINSTER DGNS
SAPPER TEMPLE, C. W., R. ENGINEERS
PTE TOWNSEND, J., R. FUSILIERS.

Even with the truncated words for rank and regiment, the first names cut to initials, it's a long read. If you don't read them – if *no one* reads them – the plaque might as well be blank.

Over 5,700,000 British soldiers fought in the Great War. At least 850,000 of them were killed. That figure rises to well over 1 million when you add in men drawn from the rest of the Empire.

I try to imagine what that one big list would look like, the names of a million dead men gathered together on one roll of paper, stacked in one column. Because that's impossible, I try to read some of the names on the war memorials that I pass day to day. It makes me feel better.

Private Littlefield, W. – picked at random from around the middle of the fifteen names on the wall of the Old Pye Street flats, back in Westminster. The alphabetical order places him sixth in the list – beneath Private Kirtland, J. A., of the Middlesex Regiment, and above Private Marshall, J. C., of the Royal Fusiliers. Privates Kirtland and Marshall are only names until someone else notices them, follows their stories.

Follow Private Littlefield's name on the trail through national census forms, registers of births and marriages, the collections in the Public Records Office and the like, and you get to a man and a family; turns out the 'W' stands for William.

For William Littlefield, a gardener, 1912 was a good year. It would become memorable to most, of course, for two legendary tragedies – the sinking of RMS *Titanic* in April and the discovery of the bodies of the luckless explorers led to the South Pole by Captain Robert Falcon Scott in November. But back in the hustle and bustle of Westminster, twenty-four-year-old William was doing all right for himself.

He'd married his sweetheart, Alice Ezard, twenty-three, and the pair set up home in the Old Pye Street flats, a short walk from Horseferry Road. At the time the Littlefields moved in, the flats housed a well-established community of ordinary people – labourers, porters, coachmen, servants, charladies. It was a place for working-class families of the kind to be found all across the city. Unremarkable lives, but happy enough.

A respectable nine months later, in May 1913, the Littlefield's eldest son Thomas was born. Their second boy, William after his dad, was born in November 1917. By then, William senior had been dead for four months, killed in France.

The sixty-four-year-old Field Marshal Lord Kitchener had

been made secretary of state for war in the summer of 1914. Britain declared war on Germany on 4 August, and two days later Kitchener was asking Parliament for permission to make a whole new set of armies with 500,000 new soldiers. The national newspapers took up the call and the response was instantaneous. On 7 August mounted police had to be called in to stem the flood tide of volunteers outside the Central London Recruiting Office, in Great Scotland Yard. Some of those that first day were from the Old Pye Street flats – it was just a short walk for them.

William Littlefield, father of one, didn't go off to war at the first opportunity. Perhaps the pull of his new family was still strong enough to hold him back.

Nationally, though, it was a flood that wouldn't abate for months to come. Every droplet was a man. On a single day in September, more than 33,000 of them signed up. Before the month's end, Kitchener had enough for one whole army, around 100,000 strong. While the flow of men continued, he set about building a second army – then a third, fourth and fifth. Within three months of Parliament giving its approval to the idea, Kitchener had his new armies. It had been a recruitment drive without precedent, and nothing like it would ever happen again.

It showed no signs of slowing, either. By Christmas 1915, 2,466,719 men had volunteered.

As well as a story of names, the Great War is a story of numbers, uncountable columns of numbers. Totals of volunteers, strengths of regiments, of battalions, of companies. Nearly every book I read on the subject is peppered with references and footnotes linking to more numbers quoted in other books for other reasons. Later it's the lists of dead and wounded which catch the eye. In addition to saying that the death toll was 'unprecedented' and the like, they often assure you that accurate final figures will never be known. The unknowable total of dead is part of the legend. Read a few pages of the numbers churned out by the Great War and they become meaningless, like the same word repeated over and over. Meaning comes back when you manage to peer through the fog of numbers to see a single name.

Nearly two and a half million men signed up during 1915. William Littlefield, father of one, enlisted on 27 January the following year. The records say he was 5 feet 8 inches tall and weighed 139 pounds. He had hammer toes on both feet.

Perhaps it was the propaganda shaped to hurt the pride of any man not in uniform. No doubt it played a part. Kitchener's appeal, 'Your Country Needs You', had been irresistible to millions. Maybe Alice pushed him into it – so many of the posters around Westminster and all across the country told women like her that it was up to them to persuade any reluctant men of their duty. Maybe she pleaded with him to stay.

In any case, he added his name to the 1st East Surrey Regiment's roll and by 26 January 1916 he was in the thick of things at the front. He was twenty-nine years old, the same age as Trudi's younger brother Johnny is now, when he was killed on 2 July 1917. He is buried in the Orchard Dump Cemetery, at Arleux-en-Gohelle, Plot I, Row C, Grave 10. Alice was a nicely rounded five months pregnant with their second child when she got word. Army Form B.104–82B came in a buff-coloured War Office envelope (telegrams were for officers' families only). Deaths were commonplace by July 1917, and the bureaucratic machinery for letting families know was mindlessly, cheerfully whirring by then. In pro forma type it began, 'It is my painful duty to inform you . . .' It's hard to imagine Alice had to read much more before she knew that William wouldn't ever see his second child, William after his dad. Thomas and William junior would grow up as two of the 340,000-odd British children who lost at least one parent during the Great War.

Men who took part, even dead men like William Littlefield, were entitled to certain battle honours. Those who had signed up by 1915 were owed the 1914–15 Star, the British War Medal and the Allied Victory Medal, a trio known among their recipients as Pip, Squeak and Wilfred. Those like William who joined up later were not entitled to stars and got just the two medals instead, the less desirable double act dubbed Mutt and Jeff.

Families like Alice's that had lost a loved one were also supposed to get a bronze medallion, called the National Memorial Plaque, once the war was over. It was designed by the sculptor E. Carter Paxton and came with a scroll from the king. An accompanying note from His Majesty read, 'I join with my grateful people in sending you this memorial of a brave life given for others in the Great War.' Just about everyone except the king called them dead men's pennies. One woman in London's East End had thirteen sets of medals and thirteen dead men's pennies on display in her front window by the end of the war.

Nearly three years after the Armistice, Alice was still fighting for William's due. The letters she sent to the War Office reveal Alice, as nothing else could, as an ordinary woman of her class and time. The replies she got seem to suggest that by the onset of the 1920s the reality of the human tragedy had already been reduced, in part, to a wearisome admin job:

> *21B Peabody Buildings,*
> *Old Pye Street,*
> *Westminster*
> *8 Dec 1920*

Sir
I am writing to ask if you over look me as regards my
husband plaxk. I received my scroll months ago and oblige,
AJ Littlefield
Pte W Littlefield
8099
1st Battalion East Surrey Regt

'I Should be Pleased if I Could Hear From You'

War Office
8 Dec 1920

With reference to your letter I have to inform you that the memorial Barrage Plaque will be forwarded to you as soon as ready for issue.

21B Peabody Buildings,
Old Pye Street,
Westminster
12 Jan 1921

Sir

I am writing again as I did not have answer from my letter of 10/12/20 as regard my husband plaxk.
I received my scroll months ago. I should be pleased if I could hear from you and oblige,
AJ Littlefield

War Office

With reference to your letter of 12/2/21 I have to inform you that the barrage plaque in memory of your late husband will be forwarded as soon as ready for issue.
I should also inform you that your letter of 10/12/20 was answered by this office on 10/12/20.

21B Peabody Buildings,
Old Pye Street,
Westminster
17 Oct 1921

Sir

I have received the 3 medal and scroal but not plaque had they overlook me.
And oblige,
AJ Littlefield

A pension for a war widow like Alice was meagre. She'd been a charlady when she met William and so she remained, working at various addresses in Whitehall. Later she got a cleaning job at a new building, just across the river from her home. The Imperial War Museum, established in 1917, had been built as a commemoration of the conflict. In time it would house Corporal James McPhie's VC. In the meantime it needed cleaning, just like anywhere else.

Alice marched with the Suffragettes, adding her voice to the call for women's equality with men. By 1940 she was still living in the Old Pye Street flats, but at a different address from the one she had shared with William. On 10 November 1940, the day before Armistice Day, the block was hit by a German bomb. Alice died in a London hospital in 1944.

Thomas, William and Alice's eldest son, was killed in action in France in 1944, two weeks after D-Day. By then he was married as well, with a son and a daughter, David and Teresa.

Alice's life and legacy had been shaped by war.

25

They Think it Must be Him

There was always something faintly mysterious about the more distant branches of my dad's side of the family while we were growing up. Grandma, Grandpa and Aunt Margaret were the only ones we visited, but I'd gathered from overheard snatches of conversation that there were more relatives out there somewhere.

It was a surprise and also somehow no surprise when Dad and I arrived back from the swimming baths one Sunday morning to see that Mum had found one of them in the centre pages of the *Sunday Post* newspaper. She was waiting for us in the kitchen of 249 Annan Road, our first house in Dumfries, as soon as we walked through the back door.

She was holding the newspaper open for Dad and I could see the headline:

CAN ANYONE HELP ALEX TO FIND HIS FAMILY?

I have the snippet in front of me. It's about thirty years old now and age has turned it a dirty yellow colour. It's also brittle, like something that's been put in a tumble dryer at too high a heat. It says:

ALEXANDER PATERSON, of Ayr, was 26 and had just come through the First World War.

He'd enlisted in the Ayrshire Yeomanry, transferred to the Royal Scot Fusiliers, and served in Turkey and Egypt.

After demob, he returned to Scotland, married his childhood sweetheart, and got a well-paid job in Nigeria.

As his wife was expecting their first baby, it was agreed she'd stay on in Scotland until the baby was old enough to travel.

Then one day a telegram arrived.

It brought the tragic news Alex's wife and baby had been killed in a car accident in Scotland.

Shocked, he resigned from his job, cut himself off from all his relatives, and for five years gave himself up to aimlessly wandering and working his way round the world.

In 1925, he found himself in the Fiji Islands. He got a job there and worked until he was 75.

Then, in 1968, he went to live in the Pearce Home, an old folk's home in Suva, the capital of Fiji.

ALEX, now 85, deaf and almost blind, knows he'll never visit his homeland again, but longs to find his family if they're still alive.

He had a brother, George, who moved to Leeds after World War I.

His sister, Margaret, married Robert Oliver, who worked for Cooper, the grocer, in Glasgow.

Can anyone, anywhere, help an old Scot to forge a last link with the family he last saw nearly 60 years ago?

'That must be your mum's brother, surely?'

This was unbelievable. People like us didn't have long-lost relatives who turned up on tropical islands on the other side of the world. And who was this Great-uncle Alex anyway, might I ask? I'd never heard his name mentioned in my entire life, and yet here he was publicly advertising his membership of our clan in a Sunday newspaper! He'd been out there somewhere for a lifetime's worth of years without anyone back here being any the wiser. And Fiji? Where exactly was that? Near the Bahamas? We'd never been farther than Majorca (and then only once), and now it turned out that one of the family had been off to Africa and Fiji and who knew where else long before Dad had even been born. How had the family managed to lose one of its members – and such an exotic member at that – so completely for nearly sixty years?

Dad walked through the living room and out into the hall, to where the telephone sat. On the wall behind his head was a dark wood, hand-carved spear in the stylised form of a crocodile, and two circular fans made from some sort of stiffened animal hide. They'd been around as long as I could remember. Sometimes on rainy days I would take them down to play with.

Mum left me in the kitchen and went through to Dad, whose voice I could hear talking on the phone. He was reading the article out to someone. Judging by how loudly he was speaking, it was probably Aunt Margaret (Aunt Margaret was a bit hard of hearing and phone conversations with her could be a bit of a performance, since they had to be conducted at a fairly high volume).

I heard the phone being set back down in its cradle.

'They think it must be him,' he said.

26

A Lucky Family

The centrepiece of Huntingdon's Market Square is a memorial known locally as 'The Thinking Soldier'. As these things go it's unusual, a far cry from most. The plinth is traditional enough – pale stone set on graduated steps. The bronze figure on top – a helmeted soldier – is set in an unconventional pose. He half sits, half leans against a low wall. He is leaning forward, his chin supported by his left fist, his left elbow supported on his upraised left knee, the sole of his left boot back against the wall. There's a bit of Rodin's *Thinker* about it, but he seems uncomfortable – bent so far forward he seems about to overbalance. In his right hand he holds his rifle, bayonet fixed, butt on the ground by his right foot.

It was unveiled on the shining winter's morning of Armistice Day 1923. In his address to the assembled crowd, the mayor said: 'Let us trust and hope that our children, and our children's children when they look upon this beautiful statue of a soldier, portraying as I think, not so much of the fighting unit, but rather a soldier deep in thought, may turn their thoughts to those who have set such a grand example of duty nobly done.'

Huntingdon Women's Institute raised the money for the bronze and the base, and the work of assembling it was paid for by public subscription. The sculptor, who accepted no fee, was Lady Kathleen Scott, widow of Captain Robert Falcon Scott, Scott of the Antarctic.

He had died with his team in 1912, the same year William

Littlefield and Alice Ezard were married and moved into the Old Pye Street flats. His body and those of two other members of the team were found together within the collapsed remains of their tent on 12 November. Word of their deaths reached Britain the following March, and soon their story, narrated by Scott's last entries in the diary found on his body, was the stuff of legend. The uncomplaining way in which they had accepted their fates became the benchmark against which every British man's courage would be measured. The men who volunteered for service in the king's armed forces less than two years later would have felt the long shadow cast by Captain Scott and his men.

It's easy to lose sight of Kathleen in all this. Those who knew her in her youth remembered a free spirit, and she was successful enough as an artist to be financially independent. When Captain Scott was posthumously knighted, she became a widow of a Knight Commander, Order of the Bath. At the time of Scott's death, the couple had one son, Peter (later Sir Peter Scott, the famous painter, wildlife photographer and environmentalist). She was married for the second time in 1922 to Edward Hilton Young, and their son Wayland was born the following year. It was under the name of Mrs Hilton Young that she created 'The Thinking Soldier'. Among other works, including at least two busts of her first husband, she sculpted the statue of Edward Smith, ill-fated captain of the *Titanic*, which sits in Lichfield. Her biography, *A Great Task of Happiness*, was written by her granddaughter – the journalist and novelist Louisa Young.

The story of the Great War tends to be a story about men, millions and millions of them. Their massed ranks are to the fore in all of it, and it takes a great deal of effort to see past them to the women, who had their own stories. It's also far harder to find the women's memorials. War is something men do, rather than women, and it's a simple fact that far more men's names appear on war memorials than do women's. The women are there, though.

Almost one whole bay of the memorial in Edinburgh Castle is dedicated to women. A stained-glass window depicts land girls, munitions workers and nurses, and the east wall of the bay has on it the crests of all the women's units. An inscription reads: 'In honour of all Scotswomen who, amid the stress of War, sought by their labours, sympathy and prayers, to obtain for the country the blessings of Peace.'

But there are no women's names. The only individual named in the whole of the fabric of the Scottish National War Memorial is that of a man: Earl Haig.

Given the context, it's inevitable that women take a secondary role in the story of the Great War, but it's still unsatisfactory.

When I think about the war it's always my grandfathers I see, even though I hardly know what they looked like as young men. Grandpa usually appears in the image as Private Godfrey from *Dad's Army*, complete with medical kit and white armband, and my mum's dad is Edward Fox in *The Day of the Jackal*, wearing sweater and slacks. It's a confusing image, right enough.

Then I have to remind myself that somewhere in among all that, behind what was happening to Grandpa in France and to James in Turkey, was what was happening to the women who became my grandmothers. Remembrance like this is a conscious effort.

I have a photograph of my dad's mum, my grandma, as a young woman – I saw it for the very first time just this year. It's one of those straight-faced, formal line-ups that looks as if it required the participants to stand still for quite a while so as to avoid blurring the image. No one is smiling; they look as if they're having the photograph inflicted on them against their better judgement. It's as if they've just had some worrying news, but I suspect it's just trepidation at being in front of a camera in their best clothes.

Standing on the left of the shot is my Great-uncle Alex. He's in the uniform of the Camel Corps, identifiable because of the camel badge on his cap. Standing on the right is his brother, my Great-uncle George. The age of the photograph makes it hard to identify any one particular regiment, but he seems to me to be wearing the garb of an infantryman. George survived the war, moved to Leeds, married and had a son, George junior. Behind him in the photo a Union Jack flag hangs in folds.

Seated in front are their mother and father, my great-grandparents, Archibald and Eliza Paterson.

(This is why Paterson is my middle name. It's tradition in our family, as it is in many other Scots families, to keep names going by using them and reusing them in different combinations. My first name is Neil because my mum's maiden name was Neill, with an extra 'L'. Is that remembrance?)

At the centre of the photo is my grandma, Margaret Paterson. This is the part of the picture which is a revelation to me. I always picture Grandma as I knew her in life, as a tiny, white-haired old lady who wore glasses, walked with a stick and was so stooped she always seemed to be looking at the floor. Here she is as a seventeen-year-old girl.

Her hair is dark brown and if it isn't cut short it's tied up and back in a bun or a chignon of some kind – it's impossible to tell. In any case, the effect is to make her face look almost boyish. She wears a dark, formal dress and has what looks like a long watch chain around her neck. The watch itself is tucked into the belt of her dress.

There's nothing outstanding about this; it's hardly a surprise to learn that my grandma was seventeen years old at one point in her life. But these are personal revelations for me just the same. However obvious it seems, I think I have to come face to face with the fact that my grandparents were young before I can start to understand my own youth, my own middle age.

I asked Dad what Grandma did during the years of the Great War. He said she had worked as a secretary in the offices of a thread mill company called Coats, in Paisley.

It was hardly the tale of dangerous munitions work or the life of honest toil in the land army that I'd been hoping for. But they were a lucky family just the same. All of them survived, and that's all that matters.

27

The Devil's Porridge

However unexciting it may seem to me, my grandma's work in the mill was part of life on what became known for the first time during the Great War as the 'Home Front'. A lot of the books, a lot of writers, have overlooked the roles played by women in the years between 1914 and 1918. In *Women and the First World War* Susan R. Grayzel notes that John Keegan has dismissed the women's contribution as 'insignificant' and that Niall Fergusson has suggested the German blockade didn't matter because it affected only 'relatively' unimportant people like women.

The Great War had little physical effect on the Home Front. During the first three years of the Second World War, more women and children died than men. The Great War was fundamentally different, its visible effects inflicted primarily on the men fighting on the various fronts. Right from the start, though, women were involved, were affected.

From the first their idealised images featured in campaigns to encourage enlistment. Women were told to persuade their own menfolk, and all the men around them in the broader community, to leave their day jobs and get into uniform. Recruitment posters showed women looking proudly upon those men who were departing for the front, or looking askance at those staying behind. Men were being told it was their duty to leave these noble women behind and travel abroad to fight a good fight that would do honour to those at home.

There was also the notorious 'White Feathers' campaign initiated in 1914 by Admiral Charles Fitzgerald, which encouraged women to present white feathers – symbols of cowardice – to any man not in uniform. In fact it stopped only after one too many wounded soldiers in civilian clothes was publicly humiliated.

The writer Compton Mackenzie, a serving soldier, condemned the so-called Order of the White Feather. He wrote: '. . . idiotic young women were using white feathers to get rid of boyfriends of whom they were tired'.

The pacifist Fenner Brockway said he was given enough of the things to make a fan.

Private Norman Demuth, 1st/5th Battalion, London Regiment, said:

Almost the last feather I received was on a bus. I was sitting near the door when I became aware of two women on the other side talking at me, and I thought to myself, 'Oh, Lord, here we go again.' . . . one leant forward and produced a feather and said, 'Here's a gift for a brave soldier.' I took it and said, 'Thank you very much – I wanted one of those.' Then I took my pipe out of my pocket and put this feather down the stem and everything and worked it in a way I've never worked a pipe cleaner before. When it was filthy I pulled it out and said, 'You know we didn't get these in the trenches,' and handed it back to her. She instinctively put out her hand and took it, so there she was sitting with this filthy pipe cleaner in her hand and all the other people on the bus began to get indignant. Then she dropped it and got up to get out, but we were nowhere near a stopping place and the bus went on quite a long way while she got well and truly barracked by the rest of the people on the bus. I sat back and laughed like mad. (Quoted in Max Arthur, *Forgotten Voices of the Great War*)

Publican's son Arthur Pratt from Moreton in Marsh was fourteen when he started work in a mill in Soho. In 1911 he was promoted to the role of machine man, and by the time war broke out he was well established in a reserved occupation. One of the thousands of recipients of a white feather, he enlisted early in the war. He was wounded at Gallipoli, recovered and was later killed at Gaza. His neighbour Frederick Rumsby was a carpenter in the local mill. He married a local girl, Margaret Pugh, a milliner, and in 1908 the couple had a son, Victor. Like Arthur, Fred was given a white feather and, though he too was in a reserved occupation, his services urgently needed at the mill, he went off to Marlow, where he signed up to the Worcester Regiment. Transferred to the Hertfordshire Regiment, he died of his wounds in a field hospital at Bailleul on 25 September 1917.

By the end of the war, men in reserved occupations – as well as wounded soldiers not in uniform – had to wear government-made badges saying they were serving 'King and Country'.

It was while the level of volunteering by young men continued through 1914 and 1915 that women began to be affected directly. Industries providing the materials for war were suffering severe labour shortages, and it was into this vacuum that women were steadily drawn.

It wasn't as though women, particularly working-class and lower-middle-class women, had been living easy, work-free lives before August 1914. For a start there was the endless, back-breaking, unpaid domestic work of women, utterly devoid of anything in the way of labour-saving devices like washing machines or vacuum cleaners. Wives and daughters were the engines of households, and they were no strangers to ceaseless, thankless toil. Domestic service too had always employed women – often in harsh conditions and always for little money. Women's work at the time was uniformly unskilled and no thought was given to their training or advancement. Whatever work they did have, they were often expected to give it up when they married. Even in the teaching profession, a traditional employer of women, marriage meant the end of a woman's career.

It has been suggested that it was this atmosphere of repression which radicalised women – and that it had already driven them well along the road to emancipation and the vote before the Great War came along to complicate matters.

Although war did not introduce women to the workplace – or to the notion of work – it drew them into industries that would previously have been men-only closed shops.

Britain was in every way unprepared for a war of such voracious appetites as the Great War. The rapidly increasing global scale of the conflict coupled with the likelihood that it was going to last for years rather than months forced the country and its population to learn new ways of feeding a new monster. It has been estimated that as many as 2 million women and girls eventually replaced men in various spheres of employment between 1914 and 1918. By the end of the war many would have become accustomed to the independence and to the spending power that the new sources of employment had brought them. They had been changed in ways that were irrevocable.

Shortage of ammunition for the fight was a serious problem right from the start, and by 1915 it was threatening to undermine the whole of the British war effort. Existing munitions factories in places like Sheffield and Newcastle expanded to cope with the seemingly endless demand. Leeds began a munitions industry practically from scratch, and at His Majesty's Factory Gretna, on Scotland's Solway Firth, 'the greatest munitions factory on earth' was created. At full strength it employed over 20,000 people from every corner of the Empire, 9,000 of them women. War correspondent Arthur Conan Doyle visited the place and described the process of combining explosive nitroglycerine with nitro-cotton – to make cordite – as 'stirring the devil's porridge'.

If the lot of the working woman had been hard before the start of the war, it didn't get easier any time soon thereafter. For one thing, the industries into which they were inducted tended to be inherently dangerous, or at least unhealthy. The Flying

Corps and the Royal Naval Air Service would unite in 1918 as the Royal Air Force. But in the early years of the war, the fledgling flyers busied themselves forging the traditions of armed flight. Even this provided a source of danger for women workers: early aeroplane wings had to be coated in varnish and the toxic fumes it produced made illness and unconsciousness an occupational hazard.

The explosive trinitrotoluene (TNT) being packed into the artillery shells permeated the bodies of the women working with it, turning their skins so yellow they were known as 'canaries'.

Munitions worker Mrs M. Hall said: 'After each day when we got home we had a lovely good wash. And believe me, the water was blood red and our skin was perfectly yellow, right down through the body, legs and toenails even, perfectly yellow. In some people it caused a rash and a very nasty rash all round the chin. It was a shame because we were a bevy of beauties, you know, and these girls objected very much to that' (quoted in Max Arthur, *Forgotten Voices of the Great War*).

During 1916, 181 of the so-called 'munitionettes' were diagnosed with toxic jaundice, and fifty-two of them died. The following year there were 189 cases and 44 of them died. Things had marginally improved by 1918 when there were just 34 reported cases and 10 deaths. Mrs Hall said:

> Yet amazingly even though they could do nothing about it, they still carried on and some of them with rashes about half an inch thick but didn't seem to do them any inward harm, just the skin. The hair, if it was fair or brown it went a beautiful gold, but if it was any grey, it went grass-green. It was quite a twelve-month after we left the factory that the whole of the yellow came from our bodies. Washing wouldn't do anything – it only made it worse.

The TNT was packed into the shells by 'monkey machines' that used heavy weights to provide the necessary compression.

Explosions were a constant risk and deaths at work were far from unusual.

Another munitions worker, Mabel Letheridge, said: 'The shells were very heavy and we had to kneel down in front of the machine. When you stood up you felt that you hadn't got any knees and hadn't got any back, except one aching mass. That was from all the carrying, the long hours and the weight.'

The Barnbow munitions factory at Crossgates, in Leeds, started filling shells in 1916. Employing over 16,000 people at the height of production, it was among the largest in the country. On 5 December 1916 an explosion killed thirty-five women workers, a fourteen-year-old girl from Castleford and a sixteen-year-old from York among them. The blast killed seventeen-year-old Edith Sykes as well. Her big sister Agnes might have died alongside her, but had stayed at home that day, having been taken ill with a dose of the flu.

Owing to the importance of the work at Barnbow to the war effort – and its sensitivity – the disaster was quietly covered up and media coverage of it suppressed. The work of filling shells was back under way in the same room in which the accident had happened before the end of the same day.

Given that Edith's family considered she'd been killed in action, her brother borrowed a gun carriage from a nearby barracks and had it used to transport Edith's coffin to the funeral. It was as close to full military honours as he could manage.

Only recently, some ninety years after the tragedy, has a memorial been raised to remember the deaths of those 'Barnbow Lasses'.

It became increasingly commonplace to find teenaged girls working in dangerous conditions. Because the requirement for unskilled labour was high, it made economic sense to use younger and younger women. That wasn't to say their employment went without opposition. Trade unions in particular were worried about the long-term effect on men's wages of employing women, particularly younger women.

Although some of the right noises were made about equality of pay and conditions for women, the reality was often different. One Croydon factory paid a woman 12 shillings and sixpence a week to replace a man who had received 3 pounds for the same job the week before.

Still the women came and worked, and sometimes died in the course of it. Memorials at Whitkirk, Chapel Allerton and Pontefract carry the names of the Barnbow women, but the discoveries of women and girls' names on memorials of the Great War are still few and far between.

Brunner, Mond and Company opened for business at Crescent Wharf in East London's Silvertown area in 1894. To begin with it produced soda crystals, but when war began the government demanded the place be adapted for the production of TNT. The management objected – the surrounding area was too densely populated for such an enterprise to be safely contained, they said. Undaunted, the government's Explosives Supply Department insisted, and production of high-grade TNT got under way in September 1915.

On the night of 19 January 1917, people living in nearby homes became aware of a red glow in the sky. Looking out of their windows, they saw that fire had taken hold of the factory. While they picked up their children and ran for their lives, leaving all their belongings behind, firemen from the Silvertown fire station directly opposite the factory set about fighting the blaze. Just before seven o'clock, with many firemen inside the place, the biggest explosion ever to have taken place in London blew the factory apart. The shock wave from the blast was felt across London, and the flames from the fires could be seen from as far away as Maidstone in Kent and Guildford in Surrey. Neighbouring factories, streets, homes, the fire station – all were destroyed either by the blast or by the fires that followed it. A *Stratford Express* reporter wrote: 'The whole heavens were lit in awful splendour. A fiery glow seemed to have come over the dark and miserable January evening, and objects which a few minutes before had been blotted out in the intense darkness were silhouetted against the sky.'

Nearly 17 acres of Silvertown were laid waste, including hundreds of homes and tens of thousands of properties, at an overall cost of £1.2 million. Insurance claims ran into many more millions of pounds. In all, seventy-four men, women and children were killed and nearly a thousand injured.

Because the blast happened in the evening, the factory was relatively empty of workers at the time. Catherine Hodge was the only woman worker killed – and hers is the only woman's name on the memorial that commemorates the loss of life.

28

Never to Return

Great-uncle Alex had almost disappeared, but not quite. While I listened, Dad was telling Mum how Grandma was pretty sure the man in the *Sunday Post* was her missing brother. Aunt Margaret had relayed the newspaper article's contents to her while Dad read it all out over the phone.

'But who is he?' I asked.

Dad pointed to the crocodile spear and the fans.

'Uncle Alex sent those to Grandma,' he said. 'From Africa. Years and years ago.'

I looked at them again, as if for the first time. Why didn't I know this? Why had no one told me before? It was as if I'd never really noticed what they were before – even when I'd played with them. It had never occurred to me that they had *come* from somewhere. They were just ornaments balanced on nails hammered into the wall. They were just some of Mum and Dad's stuff.

I reached up and took the crocodile spear off the wall again. Knowing what I knew now, I felt obliged to handle it like a priceless family heirloom.

From Africa. Years and years ago.

But it was just what it had always been. It didn't look different, it didn't smell different and it didn't feel different. There was nothing to suggest it had ever been anywhere but in our hall.

And in the way of children, I moved on from that brief fascination. There was a follow-up story in the *Sunday Post* to report a successful outcome for Alex's search. I remember there was an exchange of letters and photographs. They showed another ancient man, white haired and frail, wearing black glasses. All but lost too, far away on the other side of the world. After a while, it all went quiet again.

I think that having satisfied himself that he did still have relatives on the other side of the world, Great-uncle Alex's enthusiasm for the quest ebbed away as quickly as it had come. It must have been enough for him simply to know we were there.

Soon enough it seemed he went back to taking us all for granted, in that way of families; and we him, perhaps. The letters stopped and so too the phone calls. His brief resurfacing at an end, he sank back below the surface, never to return.

29

Mrs Barbour's Army

The war revolutionised the industrial position of women. It found them serfs and left them free.

Millicent Fawcett, leading feminist, founder of Newnham College, Cambridge, and president of the National Union of Women's Suffrage Societies from 1897 to 1918

In the summer before the war, women already provided the bulk of the labour force in several lines of work. Around 60 per cent of workers in hospitals, the clothing trades, the production of linen and silk, and education were women. The national census of 1911 recorded that some 30 per cent of all women were in paid work of some kind.

Prior to August 1914, however, their presence was negligible in the shipyards, the dockyards, iron and steel production, coal-mining, stone quarrying, the building trades, the transport industries and a whole host of other work looked on as suitable only for men. There were exceptions – women chain-makers demanding the minimum wage had marched in chains through the streets of London in 1911 – but the mass of women did not hold down jobs in heavy industry.

All that changed – some of it rapidly – once Britain began to haemorrhage men to the fighting fronts. Right away large houses throughout the land began to 'release' their domestic staff, theoretically for war work. There was a collapse of parts of the service sector as attention was turned to the production of goods required by the armed forces. Dressmaking shops and laundries began to lay off staff and the services of charladies were less and less in demand.

This caused all manner of problems for families at the start of the war. For while many traditional female jobs were becoming harder and harder to find, the industrial alternatives were not yet fully into gear across the country. In households that had already lost their young men to service in the armed forces – and were suffering the drop in wages that sometimes went with it – the loss of the women's jobs as well caused short-term hardship. Where the woman was the only breadwinner, the first weeks and months of the war must have been especially difficult.

Once the war effort was fully under way, life on the Home Front actually improved in many practical ways. For a start, the push to keep the armed forces equipped, fed and watered meant there was virtually full employment. With the slack of unemployment quickly taken up by voluntary enlistment in the armed forces and later by conscription, coupled with the creation of new jobs in the steadily growing industries of war, people back in Blighty had much to be thankful for, strange to say. There was generally plenty of food too. In 1917, coincidentally the year of one of the biggest harvests on record at that time, a form of voluntary rationing was introduced, but it never bit deeply. The pre-war seasonal fluctuations of the economy – plentiful work in spring and summer, shortages in autumn and winter – were also largely smoothed out during the years between 1914 and 1918.

It was not all as egalitarian and even handed as some of this might make it seem. At the beginning of the war women were not the first choice to fill the breach left by the men. Serious consideration was given first to importing manpower from the imperial colonies (subsequently written off as too pricey) and also to employing thousands of male refugees who had fled Belgium in the face of the German invasion.

Britain's women even had to fight for the opportunity to join the war effort. And fight they did. Mrs Pankhurst was one of those behind the 'Right to Serve' march, which won the support and backing of David Lloyd George.

Even when the Establishment faced up to realities, and opened the doors of industry to the available female workforce, it was hardly a world of equal opportunity into which they walked. For the most part, women exchanged one kind of menial, unskilled, low-paid work for another. They were employed at the lowest levels in factories, generally paid less than the men they replaced and even the men they worked alongside. Furthermore, their jobs lasted only as long as the war. Regardless of the efforts they were required to put in, it was always the plan that they would surrender their jobs once the war ended and the men returned. For that reason there was little effort put into providing training for the mass of the women workers. Young male apprentices, too young for war service, would be granted promotion and steadily increasing levels of responsibility, while women were generally used only to fill the gaps at the bottom of the employment ladder.

For all that, women made shells and bullets and the weapons to fire them, they pulled coal and drove the trams. They worked on the land to keep up food production. One team of women navvies built a shipyard. There was a minority that managed to learn new skills as well – in the building of aircraft and in trades like welding and engineering – and the inter-war years saw skilled women represented in the expansion of light engineering and the clothing industries.

The Great War – and British women's contribution to it – is often cited as the reason the vote was extended to them, if only partially, in 1918. But the campaign for women's suffrage was already well established before the war, and making headway. High-profile and often militant though their pre-war efforts had been, most of the Suffragettes quietened their call for the duration of the fighting. That said, in the workplace itself the militancy and demands for equality and fair treatment were given free rein.

Names like Mary Macarthur, Margaret Bondfield and Julia Varley became familiar – and these women would continue to be active in Labour and trade union politics from then on.

In the Govan area of Glasgow another name, that of Mary Barbour, came to prominence between 1915 and 1916, when profiteering landlords started to hike the rents on their properties. Thousands of people were pouring into industrialised areas to work in munitions and the rest of the trades needed by the war effort. This meant areas already overcrowded, and populated in the main by poor working-class people, were put under even more pressure than usual.

It being an ill wind that blows nobody any good, the situation was soon exploited by those in control of the housing. Working people already struggling in the face of overcrowding faced rent increases of anywhere between 14 and 23 per cent at a time when the cost of living was already going steadily upwards. Pensioners, wives and mothers of men fighting for their country suffered eviction and the confiscation and sale of their belongings to meet arrears. As 1915 wore on, more and more summary evictions were taking place – until working-class housewife Mary Barbour decided enough was enough. Forming the South Govan Women's Housing Association, she led the women of the area in active resistance. She encouraged her neighbours to form tenants' committees and to join forces when it came to resisting the sheriff's officers sent to carry out evictions. In many cases this amounted to nothing more complicated than packing so many people into the closes at the entrances to the flats that the sheriff's officers simply could not get in to do their jobs.

Barbour's tactics were soon taken up across the munitions and other industrial areas of Glasgow, and the whole affair came to a head in November with one of the largest public demonstrations ever seen in the city. At the height of the 'Clydeside

Rent Strikes' in 1916 every one of the city's munitions districts – Partick, Govan, Shettleston, Ibrox and Parkhead and others – were affected. More than twenty thousand tenants were withholding rent by the end. The campaign begun by one woman had won the support of the Independent Labour Party and its demands had reached the ear of Lloyd George's coalition government. The so-called 'Mrs Barbour's Army' – thousands of ordinary women alongside male shipyard and engineering workers – marched on the sheriff courts to demand action.

In order to bring the situation back under control the government had to completely modernise the antiquated housing laws, bringing in legislation that not only stopped the landlords' rent hikes in their tracks but forced rents back to pre-war levels, where they stayed for the duration of the conflict.

30

Loved and were Loved

It was almost exclusively men who fought in the Great War and mostly men who died. The bulk of the books about it are written by men and read by men.

Thinking about war always makes me think about the men in my family. Sometimes I believe this makes me ask the wrong questions – or forget to ask some of the right ones.

My dad and I have gone on short holidays together from time to time over the years, though it's a while now since the last one. It was in 2000, or 2001 maybe. We went on one of those battlefield tours you see advertised in the back pages of Sunday newspapers. My dad spends more time reading those bits than the news headlines. 'Seven nights in France and Belgium for eighty-nine pounds!' That kind of thing.

We got on a chartered coach in Dumfries in the wee small hours of the morning, along with maybe a couple of dozen old, old men. We were suppressing our laughter about the combined age of the group even before the driver put the key in the ignition, and we continued to find it strangely hilarious for the whole trip. There seemed to be about three thousand years' worth on that bus. I was the youngest by well over half a century and my sixty-something dad might as well have been a teenager. I can't for the life of me remember why it was so funny; you had to be there.

We set off into the night, down the inevitable M6 motorway, making for Dover and a ferry. There were lots of toilet stops.

The tour was to some of the battlefields and cemeteries of the

Great War. Dad and I are connected to the Great War and to each other, to some extent, by Grandpa. Because Dad's dad was there, we feel a certain ownership of part of the story. It's as if it's our right to be there, as if Grandpa claimed it for us, or something. It was a good trip. We visited the towns of Albert and Ypres and the Menin Gate, where some of the 300,000 missing are named.

At eight o'clock Ypres comes to a halt and a bugler sounds the 'Last Post'. It was just an ordinary weekday when we were there but the Menin Gate was crowded with people. Dad got talking to a local woman who looked to be about eighty years old. He always gets talking to someone, everywhere we go. She was smartly turned out, in a lilac-coloured tweed suit, crisp white blouse, good shoes. She had lived in Ypres all her life and had come to hear the 'Last Post' sounded at the gate almost every evening.

We went to Thiepval and to the preserved battlefield of Beaumont-Hamel where you can see the old trench lines rippling the grass. I know we were at Tyne Cot, but we visited so many of those tragically identical cemeteries on that trip I'm not clear in my memory about which was which. The tour was pretty comprehensive and we ticked off most of the big-name locations.

But in the way of these things, it's not the cemeteries or the memorials which I think of when someone mentions that trip; it's my dad. We had such a good time. It's hard to accept your dad as another man – he's your dad and that's that; the only known example of a unique sub-group of the male of the species.

But on trips like that one I catch glimpses. He misbehaves a bit when he's away with me. We drink a bit too much red wine and occasionally smoke green cigars that please him enormously and make me dizzy. We share twin rooms and he snores like a mighty beast of the jungle.

My favourite memory of the trip is actually on the ferry on the way back from Calais. It was a rough crossing and it took its toll on our fellow passengers. Ashen faces lay propped on rucksacks as people tried mind-over-matter techniques to spare themselves the unspeakable conditions of the toilets below deck. Dad and I were as happy as Larry.

Out of badness as much as anything else we sat down in the huge, empty cafeteria to enjoy a meal of deep-fried fish and chips, mushy peas and pickled onions washed down with miniature bottles of red wine and brandy. We carried ourselves throughout as though we were seasoned sailors. Whatever the reason, we were immune to the pitch and roll that sent our empties rolling off the table and on to the floor.

The point is that even when I visit the sites of the Great War, the story that affects me more than any other, I can't get close to it. The only thing the trip made me see was my dad, whom I already knew.

Every time I try to create a memory of the Great War for myself, all I see is family.

Maybe that's part of remembrance as well. If remembrance is to matter, that's part of how it starts. You have to notice as much as you can of what's happening, while it's happening. That's the point, I think. Otherwise who are we remembering? And why?

It's not just about my dad, this remembrance. One of the most popular poems from the Great War starts: 'In Flanders fields the poppies blow . . .' But that line doesn't make me think of the Great War, or anything like it. It makes me think about my mum. It ties in somehow to my earliest memory.

I'm about four or five years old and I'm riding my blue-and-red tricycle. It's a proper tricycle, the kind you don't often see any more, with a chain driving the back wheels and a box with a lid above the back axle behind the saddle where you could keep things like Action Man.

I'm at the top of a steep slope of pavement on a familiar route between our house in Masonhill in Ayr and the local library. In those days my mum seemed to get through books the way most other people got through newspapers, and we made a midweek visit to the library as well as the one on Saturday mornings, to keep the stocks topped up.

I'm not allowed out of my mum's sight so I stop at the top of the slope and look back, waiting for her to catch me up. She seems a long way away and my image of her is framed not by poppies but by cherry blossom.

Loved and were loved.

It must be spring because the trees lining the slope look ready to buckle under the weight of many plump clumps, branches bowed to breaking point.

Spring or not, it's a cold day and I am wearing a knitted balaclava that makes my ears itch.

A wind is blowing and the air is thick with dark pink petals. My mum is walking towards me through a blizzard of flowers.

31

One by One

Women's lives may well have been affected by gains made in the world of employment – however favourably, or superficial or short term. A seismic impact, however, was made on them by loss. Fathers lost sons and sons lost fathers. Brothers lost brothers. But surely the greater part of the burden of loss was borne by women?

The volunteers of Kitchener's new armies marched away from villages, towns and cities towards the great adventure. Those left behind inhabited a world made strange by absence. Honour rolls and street shrines kept the record of the missing, the names; but the young men were gone.

Inside the church of St John the Baptist in the Cotswold village of Great Rissington is a Great War memorial in the form of a stone tablet on a wall. It might seem unremarkable at first glance, like so many others on so many other church walls. Underneath the stone are photographs of five young men in uniform, all with the same surname. Brothers.

The Souls family lived in a cottage near the village school. Annie and William had six sons. William was a farm labourer, and if things had worked out differently his boys might well have followed him one by one into the job. As it was, the five eldest answered Kitchener's call and followed one another into the army.

Albert, the youngest of the five, and Walter were quickest off the mark, joining the 2nd Battalion, Worcestershire Regiment, in 1914. Kitted out and trained up, they were shipped to France in June the following year.

By September 1915 they were at Loos, along with Sergeant Artus and Private Hawling and the rest of the lads from Cheltenham. Unlike the Cheltenham contingent, Albert and Walter Souls survived the chaos of the gas and the efficient German machine guns. In fact the Worcestershire Regiment was afterwards praised for its gallantry.

Perhaps the effectiveness of the German guns affected Albert and Walter in some other way – in any case, they both transferred to the newly formed Machine Gun Corps in January 1916. Among the trenches by the pit-heads and slag heaps of the northern French town of Béthune they learned their new trade. Albert's death, however, was reported in the diary of the 5th Brigade Machine Gun Corps on 14 March. He is buried in the French extension of the Bully-Grenay Communal Cemetery, at Pas de Calais, Plot A, Grave 41.

The three other Souls boys meanwhile, identical twins Alfred and Arthur, and their brother Fred, had joined the 16th Cheshires.

Fred was killed at the Somme on 19 July 1916 and his body was never found. His name is listed among the missing at Thiepval. Walter was injured at the Somme too – taken for treatment at Rouen, where he died of a blood clot on 2 August. He is buried in the St-Sever Cemetery in Rouen, Plot B, Row 29, Grave 33.

Alfred, now with the 11th Cheshires, survived the Somme, Messines Ridge and the Third Battle of Ypres. His luck ran out at Ploegsteert Wood in April 1918. He was thirty years old and is buried in the Strand Military Cemetery, in Belgium, Plot 9, Row B, Grave 9.

Arthur died on the 25th of the same month, soon after hearing of his twin's death but not before he had won the Military Medal for his conduct during the fight to hold the Villers-Bretonneux plateau. He is buried in Hangard Communal Cemetery, at the Somme, Plot I, Row G, Grave 7.

Back in Great Rissington, Annie received the letters telling her how and when her five sons had died. (James Lazenby is the grandson of the man who was Little Barrington's village postman before the Great War. It was also James's grandfather's job to deliver mail to addresses in Great Rissington. When James's mother was seventeen her dad joined up and she had to take over his round. For the rest of her life she could describe in awful detail how it felt to deliver one dreaded letter after another, each announcing the death of a son, to Annie Souls.)

It was said that Annie never stood for 'God Save the King' again, and that her life in the village was made unbearable by gossips who reckoned she was living well on her pensions, one for each of her dead boys. She'd had to fight tooth and nail with the authorities to win the money to which she was entitled, but her neighbours resented it just the same. She moved to Great Barrington and there her surviving son, the only one who had been too young to join up, died of meningitis.

Every Remembrance Sunday in St John the Baptist church the names of the dead Souls brothers are read out one by one.

ALBERT SOULS,
aged 20, KILLED IN ACTION, FRANCE, 1916
FREDERICK SOULS,
aged 30, MISSING IN ACTION, FRANCE, 1916
WALTER SOULS,
aged 24, DIED OF WOUNDS, FRANCE, 1916
ALFRED SOULS,
aged 30, KILLED IN ACTION, FLANDERS, 1918
ARTHUR SOULS,
aged 30, KILLED IN ACTION, FRANCE, 1918.

The loss suffered by the Souls family was the greatest inflicted on any British family by the Great War.

Also read out on Remembrance Sunday are the names of the seven other Great Rissington men who died in the Great War. No doubt their mothers' and fathers' hearts were just as broken as Annie's. The loss of any child is too much.

It seems ironic that Annie's sons are still remembered, their names still recited with pride in the same village where spiteful gossip made their mother's life unbearable.

The memorial in the village of Reedham, in Norfolk, has on it the names of four members of the Hall family. James Hall, one-time landlord of the local Lord Nelson pub, married Ann John and together they had nine children in all. Six of them – Ernest, James, John, Susannah, Olive and Hilda – served in the Great War, and only Olive and Hilda survived.

In the same way that I found out about Corporal James McPhie, VC – hero of the broken bridge on the Canal de la Sensée near Aubencheul-au-Bac, remembered on the bench in Edinburgh's Princes Street Gardens beneath the memorial to the Royal Scots Greys – I looked for the Halls' children. It wasn't hard – again the website of the Commonwealth War Graves Commission made it no more challenging than looking up names in a phone book.

John Herbert, the youngest boy, joined the 1st Battalion, Coldstream Guards, Private 13817. Youngest son and first of the family to die in the war, he was killed on 4th March 1917, aged twenty-three. He is buried in the Sailly-Saillisel British Cemetery.

James was second to eldest and joined 'A' Battery, 107th Brigade, Royal Artillery, soon after the war started. On his enlistment papers either he or the recruiting sergeant switched his forenames so that he became 48051 Gunner Frederick James Hall. In the spring of 1915 he married Alice Lubbock, a Reedham girl, in the church at Colchester, where he was completing his training. He was killed on 23 June 1917, aged twenty-six, and laid to rest in Lijssenthoek Military Cemetery. Alice never remarried and lived with her mum and dad at Station Road, Reedham, until her death, aged forty-eight, in 1936.

The Halls' eldest boy, Ernest, known by the family as 'Nar' for reasons no one left alive can remember, joined the Royal Navy and was on the SS *Windsor Hall* when it was torpedoed on 17 January. He was twenty-eight and may have been married as well although his records don't make it clear.

When Susannah joined the Queen Mary's Army Auxiliary Corps (QMAAC) she, like her big brother James, changed her name. Taking her mother's name, Annie, she worked as a cook in D Company, service number 11900. After a time serving in England she was shipped to France in 1918. She survived the war but died of flu, aged thirty, on 23 March 1919. She is buried in the Terlincthun British Cemetery, in Wimille.

Like the Souls of Great Rissington, then, the Hall family of Norfolk was ripped apart by the war. When Ernest died the Bishop of Norwich was moved to write to the family: 'I grieve so deeply for you in your triple loss. They are together again but how you must miss them in your lonely home. May God comfort you by raising your heart where your treasure is.'

Olive and Hilda, both younger than Susannah, served in the QMAAC as well, and survived. Hilda received the British and the Victory Medal. When the Reedham memorial was raised, Susannah – known as Susie at home – was not included on it. It's not clear why – maybe discrimination on account of her sex or maybe by dying in 1919 she missed some cut-off date – but the omission was not rectified until 1995.

The Home Front was not to be completely spared from direct enemy action either. In addition to accidents in munitions factories such as Silvertown and Barnbow, there were times when the violence of war came to British towns.

During the morning of 13 June 1917, a squadron of German aircraft was spotted crossing the Essex coast and heading towards London. It was a Wednesday, and in the East End of the city, as elsewhere, work and school life were carrying on as normal. Eyewitnesses remembered it as a hot summer's day, the air shimmering with heat haze. The aircraft, around a dozen three-seater bombers, dropped their shrapnel and incendiary bombs on the unsuspecting streets below. This was the first daylight air raid ever suffered by a British city, the first instance of 'total war'. By the time it was over, 104 people were dead and 423 injured, 154 of them seriously. Most notoriously of all, eighteen of the dead were children killed in their classroom at Upper North Street School. A bomb had crashed through the roof and the upper floors of the building before exploding in the infants' classroom on the ground floor.

Three of the dead youngsters were buried at private family funerals, but on 20 June a combined service was held for the rest at Poplar parish church. One of the coffins held only parts of bodies.

The Bishop of London, who conducted the funeral, said: 'Never did we expect to have war waged on women and children.'

The coffins were carried on horse-drawn hearses and thousands of mourners watched them pass slowly along East India Dock Road en route to the East London Cemetery. Curtains were drawn in the windows of every house and flags flew at half-mast. Three hundred wounded soldiers were among those lining the route.

Nearly £1,500 was raised by a special commemorative fund and most was used for gravestones and a granite-and-marble memorial in the form of an angel. Unveiled on 23 June 1919, it has on it the names of all the children who died.

The Mayor of Poplar said: 'These boys and girls as truly suffered for their country as any men who have perished in the trenches, on the high seas or in the air.'

For the first time in any war in which Britain had been involved, people at home, women and children, were in harm's way.

On Uxbridge Road in Harrow Weald, in Middlesex, there's one of those Beefeater restaurants. It's called the 'Leefe Robinson VC' and it's named in honour of Lieutenant William Leefe Robinson, the first British pilot to shoot down a Zeppelin. This is his memorial. He is buried in the cemetery of nearby All Saints church, built by the Victorian architect William Butterfield.

On 9 August 1915, at Goole on Humberside, sixteen men, women and children died during a single Zeppelin raid. At least two whole families, the Acasters and the Carrolls, were wiped out, those killed ranging in age from eight months to seventy-eight years.

The Staffordshire town of Wednesbury was hit on 31 January the following year. Two Zeppelin airships, thought to have got lost while looking for the city of Liverpool, let go with their payload over the first built-up area they could spot and killed thirteen.

For a civilian population wholly unused to air travel, the airships were a terrifying prospect. Typically measuring around 180 metres in length, they could travel at over 130 kilometres per hour and carried as much as 2,000 kilograms of bombs. Owing to the primitive and unreliable nature of their on-board navigational systems, however, they often targeted the wrong places.

Walsall, near Birmingham, is another town thought to have been hit by mistake. During a Zeppelin raid on 31 January 1916, thirteen people were killed. Even today there are discernible signs of the raid in the form of clearly visible scars on the wall of the town's Coliseum nightclub, and the war memorial itself is built on the site of the first explosion.

Among the dead was Mary Julia Slater, the town's Lady Mayor, who had been travelling in a tram when the vehicle sustained a direct hit from one of the bombs. A bronze memorial portrait of Mrs Slater, commemorating her death, is on display in Walsall town hall.

As 1916 wore on, the airships increasingly targeted London and morale was taking a pounding along with the buildings and streets. Around 550 civilians had already been killed by the raids.

Twenty-one-year-old Lieutenant Leefe Robinson took off from the aerodrome at Sutton's Farm (later the legendary Hornchurch airfield of Battle of Britain fame) on the night of 2 September. A Zeppelin raid was under way over the capital when the young pilot set out alone in his BE-2 biplane in driving rain and low cloud. In fact he was facing what would prove to be the largest Zeppelin raid of the Great War, a fleet of twelve. Undaunted, he found the enemy and picked out a single ship, the *Schutte-Lanz II*. Having first fired a flare to warn the ground troops to stop their flak, he attacked the *S-L II* three times before finally bringing it down with incendiary rounds. Eyewitnesses hanging out of windows and crowding the rain-lashed streets below cheered as the monster fell in flames on to East Ridgeway, at Cuffley in Hertfordshire.

Three weeks later, two more Sutton's Farm aces, Flight Lieutenants Brandon and Sowrey, attacked another Zeppelin fleet over London and shot down one each. The might of the airships had been challenged and their raids soon stopped.

For Leefe Robinson there was a Victoria Cross, followed by service in France and elsewhere in Europe. He was shot down over France in 1917 and held as a prisoner of war. Weakened by his incarceration, he was in poor health by the time of his return to Britain. He visited his family for Christmas 1918 and while there contracted the influenza that killed him. He died on the last day of the year, aged just twenty-three.

A memorial at East Ridgeway, unveiled on 9 June 1921, marks the site of his greatest victory. There's another one at his old school, St Bees. The Leefe Robinson Restaurant, originally little more than a tin shack, opened on 21 June 1954. It was destroyed by fire in 1962 and rebuilt as a Berni Inn. Enlarged twice during the 1970s on account of its popularity, it had the honour of becoming the first Berni-to-Beefeater conversion in May 1991 following the takeover by Whitbread PLC.

Zeppelins in the night, air raids in broad daylight, infants killed in their classrooms, teenage girls killed by explosions in munitions factories. The Great War's reach was long enough to touch the world left behind by soldiers at the front. For the most part, however, the physical effects at home were slight in the scheme of things. It has been estimated by the Central Statistical Office that Britain suffered 8,389 civilian casualties between 1914 and 1918, compared to 63,635 between 1939 and 1945. During the Great War, damage to the landscape of Britain was relatively slight, while the Second World War saw whole swaths of cities laid waste.

For most people in Britain the world looked different for other reasons. Prisoners of war were put to work in towns and cities; wax-faced, wounded British soldiers clad in hospital blue sat quietly with their nurses in the parks. As battles like the Marne and First Ypres and Loos and the Somme took their toll, local sites of remembrance became more important. Street shrines that began as marks of pride, celebrations of men off doing their duty, were more and more becoming places of sad pilgrimage.

Many of those who did come back were changed – blinded, wrecked by poison gas, missing limbs, scarred and maimed. Those who had stayed at home had to accept the presence among them now of men physically and mentally damaged by what they had been through in France and other places. Some of the front's effects on returning soldiers were not immediately obvious. Mental and emotional trauma caused by shell shock and the rest of it was barely acknowledged, let alone understood. It led to the setting up of special hospitals like the one at Craiglockhart where Sassoon and Owen met.

For children there was the absence of elder brothers, fathers, uncles, neighbours. Family members went away, were replaced with photographs, letters, postcards. Sometimes there were medals later on. Often the men themselves would not return – or would return damaged. At school the only male teachers were older men. Young men were replaced by women – especially once the old rules barring married women from the profession were relaxed to help fill the gaps. Games in the playground featured 'Jerries' as enemies for the first time.

As the war continued, so the death toll rose. Again it's about numbers and statistics and estimates, but something like one man in ten under the age of forty-five was gone by 1918. Many of those had no known grave.

Different countries adopted different methods of informing the bereaved whenever someone was confirmed killed. In Australia a clergyman would deliver the message. In Britain the information was sent by post – telegrams for officer class and letters for the families of the rank and file. In France the mayor or his deputy would set out on foot to bring the news. This made every departure from the office by such men a cause for general alarm, their route followed anxiously, every pair of eyes praying they would be passed by.

In the confused and confusing atmosphere of war, mistakes were made from time to time.

Mary Morton Hardie, from Wishaw in Scotland, was a four-year-old in 1916 when the postman delivered the letter telling her mother that her father, George, was missing, believed killed.

Mary's mother, Mary Morton, later began a new relationship, and by the end of the war she was eight months pregnant. It was then that she received word that George was not dead but alive and relatively well, having spent the last two years as a prisoner of war.

In a panic, she and her new partner went on the run. George, however, was furious at the turn of events and embarked upon a court battle to get his children back. He later married someone else and little Mary spent six months in an orphanage, yet another victim of the war.

32

A Self-inflicted Injury

A pamphlet entitled 'A Little Mother' was published in 1916. According to its author, women were '... created for the purpose of giving life, and men to take it.'

It was a huge hit, selling 75,000 copies in its first week, and helped to underline the traditional role of women as nurturers, carers. With this in mind, the nursing profession was not only a popular choice for women wanting to make a useful contribution to the war effort, it was also a politically correct one. There had been a nursing profession in peacetime, but following the outbreak of war their numbers grew rapidly.

A pioneer in the development of the women's role in this field was Elsie Inglis, who studied medicine at the Edinburgh Medical College and the Glasgow Royal Infirmary before qualifying as a doctor. She took on a teaching post at the New Hospital for Women and later established a maternity hospital in Edinburgh staffed exclusively by women. She was also a staunch supporter of the Suffragette movement.

As soon as war broke out Dr Inglis began campaigning hard for the right to take female medical units over to the scenes of the fighting. Despite opposition, her first team was in France within three months, and by 1915 she had set up a two-hundred bed hospital. She was captured by the enemy in Serbia in April of that year, while working with one of her units, and freed along with her staff following intervention by American diplomats.

She was eventually taken ill herself, while working in Russia in 1916. She arrived back in England on 25 November but, despite treatment, died the next day.

In addition to doctors like Inglis, and professional nurses with medical training behind them, many women chose to serve with the Voluntary Aid Detachment. Set up in 1909, the VAD functioned as an offshoot of the British Red Cross and backed up the medical care provided by the Territorial Forces Medical Service. Women were trained in first aid and nursing and helped staff hospitals and convalescent care homes at home and abroad. As well as caring for the injured, VADs, as they came to be known, drove ambulances, performed clerical duties, staffed kitchens and worked as welfare officers. Many were there during the fighting in France, Italy and Russia, and in many other theatres of the war.

For many of them – often women and girls from sheltered middle-and upper-class homes – the culture shock of life in the war zones must have been stunning. Working in front-line locations, they were often in clear physical danger. The hospital at Etaples was shelled in May 1918, causing the deaths of many men and women. The trauma of the incident was such that four VAD nurses were sent home to Britain suffering from shell shock.

On Oliver's Mount, overlooking the seaside resort of Scarborough in Yorkshire, is a massive memorial, an obelisk. Built from local blond-coloured stone, it is visible on the skyline from all over the town. The obelisk is a traditional form for such a marker, pointing as it does towards heaven and God. It was paid for with money donated by the people of Scarborough and designed by the architect Harry W. Smith. As well as the names of servicemen – infantry, navy, air force – are those of four local VADs killed on active service:

McLAUGHLIN, M. M.
McLAUGHLIN, E. W.
SELLORS, E. P.
TAYLOR, E. E.

(The Scarborough memorial is unusually comprehensive in its listing of local dead. Also included are the townsfolk killed when the town came under attack by the German navy on 16 December 1914. Hartlepool and Whitby were also hit on the same day as the First High Seas Fleet showed British civilians how vulnerable they were. The attack came just after eight o'clock in the morning, and by the end of it the three towns had been pounded by more than 1,100 shells. In all 137 civilians were killed and 592 wounded. The Scarborough memorial has on it the names of twenty – nine women, eight men and three children – killed that day.

The children's names are:

BARNES, G. J.
RYALLS, J. S.
WARD, J. C. H.

These are jarring additions. Presented this way, like the adults with surname first followed by initials, it's harder somehow to see them for what they were.)

Perhaps more life-changing than the danger and the physical hardship was the exposure of the VADs to the physical reality of wounded men. Women and girls who might reasonably have expected to be shielded from the sight of men's bodies until after they were married found themselves cleaning and caring for men made helpless by illness and wounds.

'Throughout my two decades of life, I had never looked upon the nude body of an adult male,' wrote Vera Brittain, who nursed many of the wounded during the war. 'I had therefore expected, when I first started nursing, to be overcome with nervousness and embarrassment, but, to my infinite relief, I was conscious of neither . . . Short of actually going to bed with them, there was hardly an intimate service that I did not perform for one or another in the course of four years.'

Vera Brittain's work as a nurse is commemorated by a memorial in the church of St Martin-in-the-Fields in Trafalgar Square. Her autobiographical *Testament of Youth* is one of the most famous accounts of the effect the Great War had on the women, particularly middle-class women like herself, who found themselves drawn into a world they could scarcely have imagined in peacetime.

'I still have reason to be thankful for the knowledge of masculine functions that nursing gave me,' she wrote. 'And for my early release from the Victorian tradition which up to 1914 dictated that a young woman should know nothing of men but their faces and their clothes until marriage pitch-forked her into an incompletely visualised and highly disconcerting intimacy.'

The medical treatment available to wounded men near the front lines was often primitive, and nurses had to cope with assisting with operations, amputations and the like, carried out with little or no anaesthetic.

Many large properties in Britain, including stately homes, were donated or commandeered for use as hospitals and convalescent homes. Susan Marsh worked as a VAD during the war at Quex House, in Kent, home of the Powell-Cotton family. A plaque on one wall remembers how Quex, like so many other stately homes, was drawn into the war effort. Being so close to the English Channel, Quex was one of very few temporary hospitals back in Blighty that actually received casualties directly from the Western Front. On calm days, they say, it was possible to stand in the grounds and listen to the deep notes of the artillery bombardments pounding away in Flanders.

Susan's work would often have been harrowing, and always hard. Perhaps there were lighter moments as well, and opportunities to find out about the men themselves, the lives from which they had come. She kept an autograph book – and collected the signatures of those soldiers she helped to treat. Her own sweetheart was killed in the war and she never looked at anyone else again. She died a spinster.

At places like Quex House, young women like Susan found themselves working and mixing with men of all classes in ways that would have been unthinkable before the war. Many of them were profoundly changed by their experiences. Like women drawn into many other kinds of work by the war, they grew accustomed to freedoms and lifestyles to which they felt entitled after the war was over.

Baroness Elizabeth de T'Serclaes lived a life as filled with drama as her name might suggest. Born plain Elsie Shapter, she was no shrinking violet – but rather a woman with a reputation for a fiery temper, an appetite for riding motorbikes and, most scandalous of all, wearing breeches. She was married first to a Mr Knocker, but the union ended in divorce.

A singleton once more, she was in the ambulance service in Belgium at the start of the war, treating Belgian wounded. Despite the Belgian government having laid down a blanket ban on women serving in front-line positions, it seems someone made an exception for Elsie. In April 1916 she married her Baron and gained her title and *ad hoc* new name. She stayed at the front for the duration of the war and in March 1918, towards the end of a fortnight of constant enemy bombardment, found herself caught up in a poison gas attack.

She had been transporting wounded in her ambulance, but when she regained consciousness after the gassing, the vehicle was a write-off. Undaunted, she commandeered a passing lorry and got her wounded men to safety.

She later joined the WRAF and managed to come through the rest of the war in one piece. Back in the village of Ashtead, she named her house 'Pervyse' in honour of the front-line village in which she had served.

33

Patriotism is not Enough

Perhaps the most famous nurse of the Great War is Edith Cavell. Born in Swardeston in Norfolk in 1865, the daughter of a minister, she originally went out to Belgium in 1890 to work as a governess for a family in Brussels. Later she took a nursing post, the start of a career that would eventually elevate her to legendary status. She came home after five years but was back out again by 1907, and soon training young nurses.

They say she was a fairly humourless person, businesslike and self-disciplined.

Edith was on a visit to her mother's home back in Norfolk when war broke out – and she returned to her post immediately. Once the German army had occupied Brussels, almost every non-Belgian nurse was ordered to leave. Edith managed to stay and began working alongside Belgian women and those German nurses who were brought in to make up the necessary numbers.

Under the aegis of the Red Cross she treated servicemen of all nationalities. On the side, however, she was part of a network smuggling Allied soldiers out of Belgium and into neighbouring Holland, a neutral zone. Once there, they could be safely repatriated to Britain and sent back into active service. It is estimated that Cavell and her accomplices rescued around two hundred British, French and Belgian soldiers in this way. All this was forbidden by the Germans, of course, and Cavell would have known that she risked death.

The German authorities caught up with her in the summer of

1915, following the arrest of one of the network and the discovery of Cavell's name in paperwork relating to their work. She was arrested, held in solitary confinement and then taken to the national rifle range in Brussels where she was executed by firing squad on 12 October, still wearing her nurse's uniform. She was forty-nine.

Whether or not the Germans were legally entitled to do what they did, outrage at the act was felt deeply and expressed around the world. Apparently recruitment levels back in Britain were doubled in the weeks following Cavell's death, and the Allied view of the German people as monsters was assured.

She was buried within the grounds of the rifle range but in 1919 her body was exhumed and brought back for burial beside Norwich Cathedral. There is a memorial to her there. Beneath a bronze likeness of her head and shoulders a soldier, sculpted in profile, reaches up towards her with a laurel wreath in his right hand. A second memorial, near Trafalgar Square, has on it the words:

PATRIOTISM IS NOT ENOUGH.

This is part of what Cavell reportedly said to Stirling Gahan, the British chaplain in Brussels and her last English-speaking visitor: 'I know now that patriotism is not enough. I must have no hatred and no bitterness towards anyone.'

Reading about Edith Cavell (her brother apparently corrected reporters by stressing the first rather than the second syllable of the family name: '. . . it rhymes not with hell,' he said, 'but with gravel') it's noticeable how many seem to criticise her for a general stiffness of manner and a lack of humour. This observation seldom seems to be made about the men of the Great War. It's almost as though it wasn't enough that she was prepared to care for the wounded in occupied territory and sacrifice her own life in defence of their safety and liberty. She still manages a degree of personal failing simply by not having a properly documented back catalogue of witty asides and humorous anecdotes.

The marble statue in London is by Sir George Frampton and is often described as ugly. As the story goes, at its unveiling a general turned to Lady Asquith, a woman whose wit was widely reported, and said: 'The Germans will blush when they see this.' Lady Asquith is said to have replied: 'Won't the British?'

34

The Sense of Inevitability

I think I partly understand why Trudi cried when Evie got me up from the breakfast table to dance on Mother's Day. With Trudi, because she's more or less the same age as me (she's thirty-six now, I'm thirty-eight), I feel as if we're ageing at the same rate, travelling in the same vehicle.

For as long as it was just the two of us, the passing of time seemed manageable somehow, even reassuring. Having Evie, watching Evie, has made things different. There's a sense of the inevitable that comes from time spent with your own child, I think. Evie makes me see time differently. It feels as if Evie lives in a different time zone from ours, from mine. The difference makes it inevitable that her growing up will take her away from me. Time will keep passing for Trudi and me in the same old way and at the same old rate, rubbing along beside us. But it's inevitable that Evie is in a different time in ways I prefer not to dwell on. It's inevitable and I am powerless to stop or change it.

Evie's children will live in yet another time, partly separate, even if it overlaps with Trudi's and mine.

At the start of *The Go-Between*, L. P. Hartley said the past was a foreign country, and they did things differently there. If that's right then some of Evie's future will make a foreigner of me.

Some of the power of the story of the Great War is inevitability. It can feel like reading a book when someone's already told you how it ends. Every character, every person you're introduced to, is going to die. You feel that, deeply, even as you start. But still the story pulls you in, pulls you onwards. In fact you don't read on *in spite* of the inevitability, but *because* of it.

The inevitability of Evie is part of the pleasure of Evie. It makes Trudi and I pay attention to her.

When the characters on war memorials are reduced to names it doesn't matter so much. They're only names. But when you find out about them, and they become people with parents and addresses, ages and jobs, faces and children, the inevitability starts to weigh like a nagging doubt.

Edith Cavell's brother bothered to tell people that their name was pronounced to rhyme with gravel, with the emphasis on the first syllable. I like knowing this. It feels like a personal detail – the kind of thing you would normally know only if you actually knew the Cavells, spoke to them. I've known about Edith Cavell for years. I think I heard about her for the first time on *Blue Peter* back in the days when they told history stories like hers. But all this time I've pronounced her name, read it silently in my head, with the emphasis on the second syllable, to rhyme with hell – as her brother said not to.

I sometimes feel as if I shouldn't do this, shouldn't find out more about dead people from the Great War, but I can't help it. The story draws me in every time and it's the inevitability itself which is irresistible. Hartley said something else on the first page of his book, about an old magnet and its power to draw being weak, but still perceptible. I could go and look it up, but that's not the point of memory. You have to work with what you've got.

There was something of the inevitable about the Great War, of an old magnet's power, even as it started. Every other war memorial has on it something along the lines of: 'They shall grow not old, as we that are left grow old . . .' Laurence Binyon wrote that poem in September 1914 – after Mons and the Marne but before Ypres or Loos or the Somme or Passchendaele. Binyon seemed to be feeling unbearably sad about the whole affair almost before it had begun.

I couldn't possibly know for sure, but I think he wasn't alone in sensing the inevitability of what was coming. Once you get the sense of inevitability it changes things. Like a faint magnetic pull, it gently but irresistibly attracts.

35
Legoland

Regardless of what the author of 'The Little Mother' said about the right and natural role of women, there were those who marched to the beat of their own drum. Among those with a different understanding of their place in the order of things was Englishwoman Dorothy Lawrence.

Born in 1896, she was living in Paris at the outbreak of the war. Determined to find a way into the thick of things, she contacted the editors of several British newspapers offering her services as a war correspondent. Perhaps unsurprisingly, every one of them turned her down on the grounds that it was too dangerous for a woman. What Dorothy did next is better than fiction. Returning to England in 1915, she disguised herself as a man, adopted the name of Denis Smith and talked her way into the ranks of the British Expeditionary Force Tunnelling Company. She managed to hold things together for ten days at the front before she was either rumbled by her brother soldiers or gave herself up.

She was locked up in a French convent by the British authorities, who were so rattled by what she had managed to do that they would not release her until she signed documents promising to keep her mouth shut about the whole episode. Dorothy at least waited until the war was over before publishing her memoirs, *Sapper Dorothy Lawrence: The Only English Woman Soldier*, in 1919. She wrote: 'I wanted to see what an ordinary English girl, without credentials or money, can accomplish . . .

I'll see whether I cannot go one better than those big men with their cars, credentials and money.'

Sadly Dorothy's luck ran out. She was placed in an insane asylum in 1925 and remained there until she died in 1964.

Another woman who would have had an unusual take on 'A Little Mother' was British nurse Flora Sandes. Although already thirty-eight years old in 1914, this daughter of an Irish minister volunteered for service with a Serbian ambulance unit as the Austro-Hungarian Empire declared war on Serbia in July.

Although overrun by overwhelming numbers of Austro-Hungarians backed by Bulgarians, the Serbs inflicted huge embarrassment on their hostile neighbours by the manner in which they conducted their fighting retreat back into Kosovo and on through the Albanian mountains. By the time the Serbian government-in-exile had made it to Corfu, Sandes had switched from the ambulance unit to the Iron Regiment of the army itself. By November 1916 she was a sergeant-major and in that same year she managed to publish *An English Woman-Sergeant in the Serbian Army* to help raise funds for the war chest.

The end of the war found her still with the Serbian army, with the rank of captain and bearing the King George Star, the highest military honour the country could bestow. She married Yurie Yudenich, a former White Army general, and did not return to her homeland until after his death in 1941. She died at home in Suffolk in 1956.

The role of women in the Great War – even women like Dr Inglis, Dorothy Lawrence and Flora Sandes – has of necessity to be overshadowed by that of men. Sheer volume of numbers alone justifies weighting the story towards the male side. But this is not to dismiss or to slight in any way the efforts of the estimated 80,000 who served in the three British women's forces as noncombatants.

Katherine Furse joined the Red Cross Voluntary Aid Detachment in 1909 and following the outbreak of war headed the first

VAD sent to France. Although a trained nurse she proved also to be a skilled administrator and was quickly put in charge of the VAD Department in London. Frustrated by a bureaucracy that prevented her making the changes she wanted, she resigned her post in 1917. Almost at once she was offered and accepted the job of director of the Women's Royal Naval Service (WRNS), created in 1916. The Woman's Royal Air Force (WRAF) and the Women's Army Auxiliary Corps (WAAC) soon followed.

A total of twenty-three 'Wrens' died on active service during the Great War. In October 1918, Irishwoman Josephine Carr became the first of them when the mail steamer *Leinster* was torpedoed en route between England and Ireland. Her name appears on the memorial at Southampton commemorating all those British servicemen and women who have no grave.

Like millions of British women, my dad's mother played no active part in the Great War. She lived at home in Glasgow with her parents, worked in Coats thread mill in Paisley and waited for word from her brothers Alex and George. My mum's mum, Peggy McArthur, was too young to do anything but wait it out. She was only thirteen when the fighting started.

It's hard to find the women's story of the Great War, even when I look close to home. It's harder to find a connection to that story when the vast majority of the war memorials and most of the books are filled with men's names.

For those women who lived through the years 1914 to 1918 all the changes they experienced were triggered first by the disappearance of the men and then by their return. The disappearance created a short-lived world of new employment opportunities – and full employment at that – along with the freedom to explore the world outside their homes. For some, though, it meant little more than a change from one boring dead-end job to another.

Some alternations were relatively superficial – but still hugely significant in their own way. In terms of fashion, skirts got shorter and heels got higher. Up until the advent of war women had been shoehorning their bodies into 'S-bend' corsets and wearing bustles – the overall effect of which was to give them an exaggerated, almost cartoonish silhouette. Given that they could barely breathe in such outfits, let alone put in a full day's work in a munitions factory, changes were made initially out of sheer necessity and practicality. But once the changes were accepted, becoming the custom and the norm, there was no going back to the stifling fashions of the pre-war years. Women were cutting their hair too, into shorter styles that were practical as well as fashionable. For the first time they could go into pubs without being accompanied by men, smoke cigarettes and order meals in restaurants. The world was becoming new in many ways, some of them unexpected.

It had also been a world dominated by the wait for news of husbands, sons, fathers, brothers. For many it was a world shattered by loss, by men who did not return. I remember hearing in school history lessons about the number of spinsters who lived out their lives in cities such as Edinburgh. The level of volunteering was particularly high from districts like Morningside, and the subsequent death tolls left gaping holes in localised pockets of population. Many young women and girls lost teenaged sweethearts or young husbands – and the pool of available men of the right age was so depleted after the war they simply never found anyone else. They formed a blip in the census statistics right up to the time of my own childhood and youth.

Attitudes to sexual activity and behaviour had changed during the war. The necessities of war had invented new ways for men and women to spend time together. Women were out in the world more than they had been before, and a lot of the constrictions, the controls, of Victorian and Edwardian society became less effective – if they had ever been that effective. In some quarters it may even have been quietly suggested that women could boost morale by making themselves rather more sexually available than they might have done in peacetime.

Whatever the truth, it seems there was official concern during the Great War about the spread of sexually transmitted diseases. This is understandable in the context of a society that was trying to keep as many as possible of its young men fit and healthy – for the preferred purposes of putting them in the way of shells, poison gas and bullets. When you want your men fighting fit for active service, the last you thing you need is for them to lay themselves low with a dose of the clap.

With this priority in mind, in March 1918 Parliament passed an act making it illegal for a woman infected with a sexually transmitted disease to have sexual intercourse with a serviceman in His Majesty's army, navy or air force. The official opinion on the matter seemed to be that such diseases were a scourge knowingly inflicted upon unsuspecting Tommys by prostitutes and other ladies of uncertain virtue.

At a time before the wonder drug penicillin, STDs such as gonorrhoea and syphilis were difficult to cure and killing thousands of people every year. It was women who were blamed for this state of affairs, and following the new legislation it was theoretically possible for a woman with a venereal disease to be arrested for having sexual intercourse with her husband – even if it was her husband who had infected her in the first place.

There was such a stigma associated with the diseases that no one was likely to admit to having them. The armed forces knowingly colluded with the conspiracy of silence. Be warned: if you go looking for a relative's wartime records and find a vague reference to his being sent to hospital for a month, for no openly stated reason, and a note that his pay was stopped, then tread lightly. Obviously there are numerous possible explanations for such a state of affairs, but it's worth knowing that pay was stopped when a man was diagnosed with an STD (a self-inflicted injury) and not started up again until he was passed fit and well and able to return to duty.

On hearing that her husband was unwell, Birmingham woman

Ruth Evans wrote to her husband's commanding officer to ask what was wrong with him. The CO wrote back to inform her that the poor man was suffering from 'strain'. Ten years and three children later she found out he had been suffering from syphilis.

Any woman or girl prepared to have sex with a man outside marriage still ran the risk of being labelled an 'amateur prostitute' – and any woman who had illegitimate children was considered to be a very real danger to the moral well-being of the nation.

The return of the men at the end of the war was just as traumatic and unsettling for many as anything they experienced while the fighting raged. Women who had replaced men in various workplaces were often less than thrilled at the prospect of being ousted to make way for their return. Men promised a land fit for heroes were in no mood to accept unemployment as their taste of the new world. Jobs outside the home had opened up new worlds for women, and the freedoms that went with full-time employment were hard to give up. Men were just as determined that they would have their jobs back, and the ensuing resentment went a long way towards continuing the politicising and radicalising of women that had begun before the war.

The extension of the vote at the end of 1918, to property-owning women aged thirty or over, was hardly likely to fully placate anyone. It was only a step in the right direction. Despite their efforts throughout four long and hard years – and a contribution to the war effort the country could not have functioned without – women's overall position in the scheme of things had changed very little.

What *had* altered was the attitude of many women towards their circumstances, which had once seemed impervious to change. The world before the Great War was a Legoland of carefully shaped, regimented blocks, in which everything fitted. The experiences and opportunities that had opened up to women during the war years, their glimpse above the parapet, had shown them that the blocks could be moved around, that Legoland was not a world of permanent walls. The world could and would be made differently.

CLASS

36

Among Kings

On 7 November 1920 Brigadier-General L. J. Wyatt walked into the chapel at St-Pol, in northern France, where a number of freshly exhumed bodies lay on tables, covered by Union Jack flags. They were British servicemen killed in the war. Depending on what account you read, Wyatt, the general officer in charge of the troops in France and Flanders, either walked into the church with his eyes open or was led in blindfolded. There were either four, six or eight bodies on the tables, no one seems quite sure, but there's general agreement they'd been brought from British cemeteries at Aisne, Arras, the Somme and Ypres, four of the main charnel houses of the Great War. All the bodies had been removed from graves where the identity of the dead man was unknown – these were soldiers 'known unto God'. Wyatt selected one at random and it was put it into a waiting coffin. The rest of the bodies were reburied in the graveyard at St-Pol.

This is the most mysterious part of the most famous story of commemoration to come out of the Great War. Reading the many different versions of it, you spot a number of variations relating to key moments. Maybe the event was witnessed by very few but retold by many who cared so much about what they had been told they felt they'd been there too. That kind of thing happens a lot around actions of great pith and moment, and stories like these can easily change in the telling and retelling.

The whole story began in 1916 when the Reverend David Railton was serving as a chaplain to servicemen on the Western

Front. In the back garden of a house in Armentières he found a single grave marked by a wooden cross that had on it the words 'An Unknown British soldier'.

The sentiment of the marker stuck in his mind and four years later he contacted Dean Herbert Ryle at Westminster Abbey, to tell him about it. Ryle was intrigued enough at first and inspired enough by the end to start campaigning for a burial, in the capital, of another 'unknown soldier' who might represent all those who had been lost – those who, even if they had been buried somewhere, had been buried without their names.

The government eventually accepted the idea – on condition that he would be known as the 'Unknown Warrior', to allow for the inclusion of seamen and airmen. Once word of the plan was made public, every mother of a missing boy, every grieving wife, could imagine it might be hers that was coming home now.

That Unknown Warrior, selected with such determined anonymity at St-Pol, was carried across France with full battle honours. At the port of Boulogne the first coffin was placed inside a second that had been made from oak brought over especially from Hampton Court. A sixteenth-century crusader's sword was mounted on top and the whole lot was wrapped in a Union Jack – the same one used as an altar cloth throughout the war by the Reverend Railton, whose idea it had been originally. Taken aboard the French destroyer *Verdun*, the coffin was brought to England and put aboard a special train bound for London's Victoria station. On arrival, at Platform 8, the coffin was placed on a catafalque where it remained overnight under the protection of an honour guard. The following day, 11 November 1920, it was loaded on to a gun carriage pulled by six black, plumed horses and taken to Whitehall, where, at eleven o'clock, the newly completed Cenotaph was unveiled. A two-minute silence began.

In the years since 1920 the idea of a two-minute silence has become familiar, even commonplace. It's called for as part of memorial services marking tragedy after tragedy. We even *watch* two-minute silences on our televisions. Silence when it is called for now is seldom absolute. Traffic keeps moving through the towns and cities, people not involved in whichever sad proceedings are being commemorated keep about their business. The world groans round on its axis. I try to imagine the silence that followed Big Ben's eleventh toll at eleven o'clock on 11 November 1920. Buses pulled up to a halt; trains ready to depart stayed by their platforms; women on foot stopped in their tracks; old soldiers came to attention wherever they stood. I think maybe the sudden absence of noise that morning was a physical sensation; that the silence pressed in on the eardrums of the countless thousands in a way that made them feel as if they'd been dunked into deep water. The world stopped turning. Two minutes like those two minutes would add up to a long time, forever even. None would feel able to breathe, blink or swallow without drawing unwanted attention down upon themselves, condemnation even. Then, as abruptly as the silence had begun, it was over. Someone pressed the button marked 'play' and the pause was over; the world turned and bugles sounded the 'Last Post' and thousands of pairs of lungs exhaled in a death rattle.

Then to Westminster, where, waiting for him, were King George V; one hundred men who'd won the Victoria Cross and lived to tell the tale; one thousand women without a husband, or without a son; one hundred nurses wounded in service; and as many of the rest of Britain's population as could fit into the abbey. His coffin was carried inside by a party of pall-bearers that had among it Field Marshals Haig and French. Into the unknown warrior's second and final grave the king scattered French soil that had been exhumed along with his body.

Visitors to the grave today find it topped by a slab of black Belgian marble. Engraved on it are words composed by Dean Ryle:

BENEATH THIS STONE
RESTS THE BODY OF A BRITISH WARRIOR
UNKNOWN BY NAME OR RANK
BROUGHT FROM FRANCE TO LIE AMONG
THE MOST ILLUSTRIOUS OF THE LAND
AND BURIED HERE ON ARMISTICE DAY
11 NOV: 1920, IN THE PRESENCE OF
HIS MAJESTY KING GEORGE V
HIS MINISTERS OF STATE
THE CHIEFS OF HIS FORCES
AND A VAST CONCOURSE OF THE NATION

THUS ARE COMMEMORATED
THE MANY MULTITUDES WHO DURING
THE GREAT WAR OF 1914–1918
GAVE THE MOST THAT MAN CAN GIVE
LIFE ITSELF FOR GOD
FOR KING AND COUNTRY
FOR LOVED ONES HOME AND EMPIRE
FOR THE SACRED CAUSE OF JUSTICE AND
THE FREEDOM OF THE WORLD

THEY BURIED HIM AMONG KINGS
BECAUSE HE HAD DONE GOOD
TOWARD GOD AND TOWARD HIS HOUSE.

I can't read those words, or about the burial of the Unknown
Warrior, without feeling a tightening in my chest, a rush of blood
in my ears. The depth of feeling almost makes me feel foolish,
to be honest. But then that's me. That's precisely what all of it
was choreographed to do, and I've accepted over the years that
I'm genetically programmed to find ceremonies and symbols
relating to the Great War more moving than those of any other
historical event. The shapeless grief felt for a million and more

dead soldiers by who knows how many millions of people was, for a short while, focused pin-sharp on the body and grave of just one. Grief is heavy and the thought of all the grief of the Great War bearing down upon a single point, a singularity, makes me buckle, just for a moment.

It's hard not to feel cheated by all that too, even manipulated. Major-General Herbert Essame described the scene to be witnessed night after night at Victoria station in London during the four years of the war, specifically the allocation of trains to soldiers:

> There were six of them side by side at the departure platforms. Into five of them piled a great crowd of men with bulging packs on their backs to sit five a side in badly-lit compartments: these were the regimental officers and men returning to the trenches ... In sharp contrast the sixth train was brightly lit: it had two dining cars and all the carriages were first class. Obsequious myrmidons ... guided red-hatted and red-tabbed officers to their reserved seats. It was nearly 6.30 and the waiters in the dining cars were already taking orders for drinks ... The irony of this nightly demonstration at Victoria Station of the great gap between the leaders and the led, this blatant display of privilege was to rankle in the minds of the soldiers in the front line and to survive in the national memory for the next half century.

I read all that and I think about the Unknown Warrior. During his final journey he'd arrived at Victoria station, Platform 8. There's a good chance it's the platform he departed from more than once as well, before he was killed at Aisne or Arras or the Somme or Ypres. There's a memorial there now marking the spot where he spent the night of 10 November 1920 with his honour guard. In the scheme of memorials to the Great War, it's a recent arrival. It was organised by the Western Front Association and unveiled on 10 November 1998 by Frank Sumpter. Mr Sumpter was one of the pall-bearers in 1920, shoulder to shoulder with Haig and French. The words on the plaque say:

THE BODY OF THE BRITISH
UNKNOWN WARRIOR
ARRIVED AT PLATFORM 8
10TH NOVEMBER 1920
AND LAY HERE OVERNIGHT
BEFORE INTERMENT
AT WESTMINSTER ABBEY
ON 11TH NOVEMBER 1920.

It's right that a memorial should mark that spot and it's perfect that Mr Sumpter unveiled it.

But the Unknown Warrior travelled first class at our expense only once, dead and anonymously. He was treated royally only when it was impossible to know who he had ever been. The red-tabs Major-General Essame wrote about would not have allowed him to board their train in life. Only in death and without his name was he granted an upgrade.

37

The Bravest and most Gentle Fellow
in the World

Dream not of him that he is safe, being dead.
He sought no safety, living free from fear;
Nor count him happy that the day is here
Which sets a garland on the victor's head.
Say not of him that never tears were shed
For brighter promise, certitude more clear
Of that supremacy which men hold dear:
Say rather, others followed where he led
Say that with earnest eyes and will untiring
He sets another battle in array
Always the same glad confidence inspiring,
Ever the foremost in the perilous way,
No other guerdon of the night desiring
Than fronting danger at the dawn of day.

'Billy Congreve', by his house masters at
Eton, printed in the Eton Chronicle

Part of the little I know about what happened to my grandpa is that he was at the Somme and survived. This is a snippet of our family history but it might as well be a legend, a fiction, for all the detail anyone has been able to add. Beyond stating it as a simple fact to his family, it seems he never talked about it to anyone – or if he did they didn't repeat it, far less record it. The only corroboration comes from knowing that Grandpa's regiment, the Royal Scots Fusiliers, fought at the Somme between 1916 and 1918. He was there.

All of it is made that bit more difficult by what happened to the paperwork that once recorded the wartime movements of servicemen like my grandpa. One September night in 1940 an incendiary bomb smashed into a building on Arnside Street in Bermondsey in South London and exploded. It was early in the Blitz and Londoners were still getting used to seeing swaths of their city razed to the ground. That particular bomb, one of thousands dropped on London by Luftwaffe bombers that night, had hit the vast War Office Record Store. It held the service records of around 6.5 million men who had served in the British army between the late 1890s and 1920. All those particular eggs were in one basket.

By the time the blaze was put out only the records of 2 million people remained – less than a third – and most of those were charred and scorched by the flames, saturated with the water that put out the fire, or both.

The parts played in the Great War by the vast majority of servicemen like my grandpa were shrouded by the anonymity that comes from being one in a cast of millions. For those who won no special commendations for bravery, earned no mentions in dispatches, did not crop up in the regimental diaries, the only proof that they had been there at all lay in their service records telling when they joined up, where they went, where they fought. For every three people who had risked their lives and limbs in defence of the Empire, two had been all but erased from the record.

Those brittle fragments of lives that did survive were dried out and boxed by the thousand – stored for a time when the information they contained might be salvaged. Historians called the hoard 'the burnt documents'.

In 1996 volunteers from the Genealogical Society of Utah,

funded by £5.3 million from the National Lottery, set about the task of picking through the burnt documents.

On their website it says the Genealogical Society of Utah are '. . . dedicated to promoting the preservation of genealogical information throughout the world'. They are funded by the Church of Jesus Christ of Latter-day Saints – the Mormons. Followers of the Church, the Genealogical Society of Utah included, believe human relationships last for ever. With that in mind they try to ensure that the Mormon faith does not exclude people who inadvertently died before they had the chance to convert. Given that a blessing in a Mormon temple can make a post-mortem Mormon of a dead man or woman, the Church is leaving no stone unturned in trying to open the door to as many ancestors as possible.

In any case, 24 million spruced-up documents including medical, disciplinary and war records as well as private letters were made available to the public in 2002, at the Public Records Office.

My grandpa's service records, however, seem to have been among those lost in the fire of 1940. But I know he was at the Somme and I can never read or hear the name without wondering what happened to Grandpa there. For me, and for a lot of people, I think, when they talk about the Great War they're talking about the battle of the Somme.

Private Charles Kirman, 7423, 7th Battalion, Lincolnshire Regiment, old India hand, father of two, one-time bearer of good conduct stripes, turned up there too. Veteran of the retreat from Mons and all-round survivor, he made it out of that place with his skin intact.

Private William Cook, 15th Battalion, Highland Light Infantry, from Leadhills, second-highest village in Scotland, brother of James, was killed on 3rd July 1916. His body was never found. I looked him up in the leather-bound book on the shelf beneath the HLI memorial in the Scottish National War Memorial.

It's a strange feeling, leafing through the thick, parchment pages, scanning the names, looking for someone who must be there. I realised part of the feeling was expectation, almost excitement, and that made me feel bad. There he was: 'Cook, William 37740. Pte. b. Leadhills, Lanarkshire. Killed in Action F&F. 3/7/ 16 15th Bn.'

The 'F&F' is for France and Flanders. That's as far as he got. Because he has no known grave his name is one of the 73,103 'Missing of the Somme' listed on the Thiepval memorial, another of Lutyens's creations.

It's impossible to say anything about the battle that carries as much weight as the sound of the name: Somme. The word itself sounds like a single toll on a church bell. It resonates through all the years.

Near the village of Serre, not far from Serre Road Cemetery Number 1, there's a track leading to a place called Sheffield Memorial Park. Keep going, past Cemetery Number 3 and the track follows the line of the British front line as it was in 1916. There's a gate into the park, and inside, the shadow of a not-quite-silted-up trench is visible in the grass. It was from here that men of the 11th Battalion, East Lancashire Regiment, the 'Accrington Pals', attacked the German position on 1 July 1916, the first day of the battle. The Germans were well prepared – snug in their bunkers cut deep into the chalk landscape and protected on the surface by barbed wire filling any gaps between heavily defended villages and redoubts.

The 11th Battalion was first and foremost a pals' battalion. Captain John Harwood, mayor of Accrington, had put out a call for volunteers. Recruitment began in early September, and before the month was out it was at full strength – thirty-six officers and over a thousand other ranks. Half the men were from the town of Accrington itself, the rest from nearby Blackburn, Burnley and Chorley.

The Accrington Pals were in France by February 1916, ready

to take part in the Anglo-French push on the Somme, a huge assault designed to evict the German forces from strategically important terrain and take the pressure off the French forces at Verdun. A well-directed blow on the Somme might even break the German line itself. By now the pals' battalion had joined forces with the 12th, 13th and 14th battalions of the York and Lancaster Regiment. Subsumed though they were within the larger body – 94th Brigade, 31st Division – the pals continued to share a sense of identity born out of their connection to the same home towns.

The overall plan for the Somme offensive was massive in scale, on a 15-mile-long front. Success would depend in part on taking heavily fortified villages like Beaumont-Hamel, Fricourt, Thiepval and Serre. It was this last, Serre, which was named as the objective for 94th Brigade and its Accrington Pals. The attack was scheduled to start on 1 July, and for the week before the German lines were pounded with 1.5 million shells.

Stopping only to allow British troops to advance, this level of bombardment would continue throughout the summer.

The morning of 1 July itself began with yet another bombardment. Just before 7.30 a.m., with the man-made maelstrom still under way, the first of the British troops climbed out of their trenches and began to go forward. Minutes later the bombardment ceased and the bulk of the British forces, the Accrington Pals among them, set out across no man's land in long waves. The German infantrymen, having waited out the bombardment in shelters 30 feet underground, climbed out now and set up their machine guns. This was not in the script as the Allied commanders had written it. German soldiers, who were supposed to be dead and buried by now, were reassembling in perfect order behind lines of barbed-wire entanglements that had survived untouched as well.

As the British lines advanced towards them, so the machine guns mowed them down. Here and there, random as a lottery draw, pockets of the York and Lancaster Regiments made it all the way to the German front lines. But with no one arriving behind them to help press home the advantage, the reserve lying dead in long, heaped lines all over no man's land, they had no option but to pull out and head back to their original positions.

It had taken all of half an hour, and the attack on Serre was over. Of the 720 Accrington Pals of the 11th Battalion, East Lancashire Regiment, 584 were listed dead, wounded or missing.

Back home in Accrington, Burnley and Chorley, families had to turn first of all to newspapers to keep up with the pals' adventures. War reporting in 1916 was not the minute-by-minute stuff we take for granted now. Early reports suggested the first day at the Somme had gone well for the British army, that the Accrington Pals had been part of the successful capture of Serre itself. As the days wore on, the real story emerged bit by bit. One house after another drew its curtains until whole streets were in mourning. The toll for 1 July 1916 is a fixed point, a hub around which the story of the Great War revolves: 57,470 casualties; 19,240 dead; 2,152 missing. For most of us alive today, what happened on the Somme that day *is* the Great War.

Back in the Sheffield Memorial Park at Serre there's a wall built of Accrington brick. It marks the last place where they were relatively safe.

Private Paddy Crossan and the rest of the Heart of Midlothian Football Club are part of the Somme story too. The 16th Royal Scots, of which they formed part, were within the 34th Division at Contalmaison at the start of the attack on 1 July. The handsomest man in the world was wounded by a shell blast, his lungs wrecked by poison gas. He was one of the lucky ones. He made it home to Edinburgh, later opening a pub in Rose Street that bore his name right up to the 1990s. The man himself died in 1933, aged thirty-nine.

Private Henry Wattie was a one-time inside forward for Hearts and considered a huge footballing talent. Some of his comrades saw him fall in the first minutes. His body was never found and his name is listed among the missing, at Thiepval. He was twenty-three.

Private Ernie Ellis, the former boot-maker turned Hearts favourite, was a family man. Married to Isobel, he had a daughter he didn't live to see, born after he sailed for France. He was killed in the attack on Contalmaison that first day, and although he was given a burial, the grave was lost in the confusion of later fighting. Like Wattie, he is listed only at Thiepval. He was thirty.

Sergeant Duncan Currie, he of the footballing family, died on 1 July as well. He was twenty-four.

By war's end, seven of Hearts' first eleven were dead. As well as Wattie, Ellis and Currie, the club lost Lance Corporal James Boyd on 3 August 1916, as that same battle wore on towards the winter that would call a halt; Sergeant John Allan was the last Hearts player to die in the war, during the battle of Arras, aged thirty; Corporal Tom Gracie and Private James Speedie were also among the fallen before the end of it all.

July 1st tore the heart out of the 16th Battalion. Sir George McCrae himself would later face criticism from some who said that he stayed safely behind the lines while the men he had called into harm's way were dying in no man's land. This was fiercely denied by survivors who remembered seeing him at the front rallying his soldiers while shells and bullets flew.

A huddle of survivors of the opening push, combining men of the 11th Suffolks, 10th Lincolns and the 15th and 16th Royal Scots, had to hold a position within the German front lines for almost a day before they could be relieved. McCrae was said to have joined them there. He survived the war but his health was ruined. He died in 1928, aged sixty-seven. His funeral procession was watched by tens of thousands of Edinburgh folk.

Of the twenty-one officers and nearly eight hundred men of the 16th who fought on 1 July, twelve officers and over six hundred men were dead or missing by the end of it.

Today the clock tower near Edinburgh's Haymarket railway station is the memorial that commemorates them. It was unveiled in 1920. A recently erected memorial stone at Contalmaison itself marks the sacrifice of all the men of the 15th and the 16th Royal Scots.

Writing about McCrae's battalion, Jack Alexander says 1 July 1916 was Edinburgh's blackest day since Flodden in 1513.

At the battle of Flodden, on 9 September 1513, the Scots king James IV himself was killed while leading his men from the front. English infantrymen armed with bills – 8-foot-long wooden shafts topped with curved, axe-like blades – cut him to pieces. As well as the king, the fighting is said to have claimed the lives of twelve earls, thirteen lords of Parliament, the Archbishop of St Andrews, the Dean of Glasgow, the abbots of Kilwinning and Inchaffry, the Bishop of Caithness and the Isles and a clutch of clan chiefs. Uncountable numbers of ordinary soldiers died as well.

I met a military historian once who said the slaughter at Flodden – meted out hand to hand by men armed with bills, spears, swords and axes – may have been more traumatising for its survivors than the Somme. In any case nothing like it had ever happened to Scotland before – hardly a noble family survived intact and more than one lost every man among it. While he lived, James was the most popular and successful of the monarchs of the House of Stuart. Rather than being seen as nothing more than England's poor northern neighbour, under James Scotland had positioned itself at the heart of European culture. The loss of such a king and of so many of its aristocracy damaged Scotland's psyche in ways that took a long time to recover from. Some would say the damage inflicted on the mind of the nation, on its sense of self, was permanent.

The Great War too was a conflict that took an enervating toll on the upper as well as the lower classes.

Each stratum of British society responded to the demands of

the war in its own way and for its own reasons. While service in the ranks offered relief for working-class men from the trials of unemployment or of low-paid, menial work, it was the *destiny* of parts of the upper classes, and for profoundly different reasons.

The lower classes were motivated in large part by a sense of duty, yes – but also by pragmatism and the opportunity to walk away from unsatisfactory civilian lives. Those of the upper classes, particularly men from families harbouring proud trad- itions of military service, were born on to rails leading inexorably into the conflict. Many of them could not have avoided it if they had tried.

There cannot be many better examples of that system, that obedience to tradition and to honour and duty, than Major William la Touche Congreve, VC, DSO, MC, the 'Billy Con- greve' remembered in the sonnet at the start of this chapter. The son of Walter Congreve, later Major-General Sir Walter Congreve, VC, KCB, MVO, he was born in 1891 and went to school at Eton.

His father had collected his own Victoria Cross during the Boer War when, though wounded, he rescued a fellow officer while helping save the guns of the 14th and 66th batteries of the Royal Artillery. His men knew him as 'Old Concrete'. Billy's mother Celia La Touche was awarded three medals for bravery while serving as a nurse during the Great War, one of them the French Croix de Guerre. What else was there for their son but a career in the army?

Billy Congreve joined the Rifle Brigade, eventually rising to the rank of major. Soon after his arrival in France, in 1914, he was made aide-de-camp (ADC) to Major-General Hubert Hamilton. Although this made him a 'red-tab' – one of those whose rank made it possible for them to avoid the wet work of the front – Billy earned a reputation for getting his hands dirty, doing his own reconnaissance work and entering no man's land time and again when he felt the situation demanded it. He was awarded his DSO for the capture, single-handed, of four German officers and sixty-eight men on 27 March 1916.

He was married on 1 June, to Pamela.

He was at the Somme from the start, though his division did not fight on the first day. Still carrying out his own reconnaissance work, he was in and out of no man's land on numerous occasions. On the morning of 20 July 1916, at Longueval Ridge, he was shot and killed by a German sniper, the bullet passing through his neck and throat.

Billy's service had been outstanding, perhaps unique. He was commanded by his own father – who was himself commander-in-chief of XIII Corps of the Fourth Army – and his younger brother Christopher John visited the front lines dressed in his Boy Scout uniform, the youngest British visitor to the war. His bravery in the days leading up to his death earned him a posthumous VC. He also received the Croix de Chevalier. He was the first man ever to have been awarded all three British medals for bravery – the Victoria Cross, Distinguished Service Order and Military Cross.

Informed of his son's death, Old Concrete said only that he had been a good soldier. His friend and fellow officer Field Marshal Sir Henry Wilson said:

> I don't think there was ever anyone like him; he was absolutely glorious, and even when he was A.D.C., all the men knew and loved him – which is unusual. His friendship has done more for me in many ways than I can say; it was the most priceless thing I had. He was the bravest and most gentle fellow in the world, and I can imagine the smile with which he greeted the 'sudden turn' when the bullet got him.

Billy Congreve was twenty-five years old when he died. How could so much have been done by someone in twenty-five years? His life story wouldn't work as fiction, it's too implausible. The words written by his friend are perfect, still pin-sharp, so that it hurts to look at them. There's a photograph of Billy in uniform, a head-and-shoulders snap. If it's possible to glean any sense of a person from a photo, then Billy does look gentle, kind. He also looks younger than twenty-five (not the usual effect of these photos – they normally dispense with any trace of youth, leaving men in place of the boys they so often were), with fine features and neatly side-parted, light brown hair.

When I was twenty-five I was still mooching around wondering what I wanted to be when I grew up. What was I doing with my time? Where else would life have taken Billy Congreve if the sniper had missed, if he'd survived the war? And he's just one man among millions who died, tricked out of life by random fate. Would the world be different now if they'd stayed in it, touched it for the better? Or is perfection like theirs made only of short life and endless death?

Billy's Victoria Cross is on public display in the Royal Green Jackets Museum. He's buried in Corbie Communal Cemetery Extension on the Somme, in Plot I, Row F, Grave 35.

There's a memorial to him, and to his father who outlived him, in the pretty Norman churchyard of St John the Baptist at Stowe, by Chartley, in Staffordshire. The tablets bearing their names were designed by Lutyens.

38

A Born Aristocrat

Service during the war – brave deeds, sacrifice – could elevate a man to a status that had otherwise been denied him. Whatever the identity of the Unknown Warrior, anonymous death in war conferred on him, in that death, honours the king himself could hardly have taken for granted.

War can change, or appear to change, anything; even the centuries-old routines and rules of tradition, of rightful place in the scheme of things.

Charles Fryatt was born in 1872 in Southampton. By 1892 he was serving with the Great Eastern Railway as a seaman on the company's steamships. He was steadily promoted through the grades and was master first of SS *Colchester* on its runs to Antwerp, and then of the SS *Newmarket* to Rotterdam. By the time war broke out, bringing the dangers of unlighted coastlines, mines, enemy aircraft, warships and the dreaded German U-boats, Captain Fryatt was a veteran of the GER 'Continental Service'.

On 2 March 1915 he and his crew of the SS *Wrexham* outran a U-boat that chased them nearly all the way to Rotterdam. The management of GER were so impressed by their captain's skill and nerve that they presented him with a gold watch. On the back it was inscribed: 'Presented to Captain C. A. Fryatt by the Chairman and Directors of the G. E. Railway Company as a mark of their appreciation of his courage and skilful seamanship on March 2nd 1915.'

But as if that wasn't enough, the good captain was at it again later the same month. On 28 March he spotted a second U-boat looming in front of his ship, this time the SS *Brussels*. Fearing that his vessel was about to be torpedoed, he ordered a collision course that forced the U-boat into an emergency dive. Soon after his safe arrival at Rotterdam, he got a second watch, this time from the Admiralty. It had on it: 'Presented by the Lords Commissioners of the Admiralty to Chas. Algernon Fryatt Master of the s. s. 'Brussels' in recognition of the example set by that vessel when attacked by a German submarine on March 28th 1915.'

Captain Fryatt's subsequent fate is sometimes attributed to those watches. It has been suggested that he had either one or both of them with him when the German navy finally outran him. Overnight between 22 and 23 June 1916, while en route from the Hook of Holland to Tilbury in Essex, the SS *Brussels* was captured by a whole flotilla of U-boats and escorted to Zeebrugge. It is not clear whether or not the Germans immediately knew who they had captured. Some have suggested it was only when Fryatt was searched that one or other of the incriminating gold watches was found. In any event Fryatt and his crew were taken to Rublaben prisoner-of-war camp outside Berlin. Later they were brought back to Zeebrugge for interrogation. But while the crew were eventually returned to the POW camp, Fryatt was convicted of sinking a U-boat – the one he had charged at the previous year – and executed by firing squad on 27 July.

Like the shooting of English nurse Edith Cavell the year before, the summary execution of Captain Fryatt caused outrage around the world in countries unsympathetic to the German war effort. He had been, after all, a merchant seaman – a civilian – and not a member of the Royal Navy. Back home in Britain his execution was judged to have been illegal. In death, he became a national hero.

After the war, on 7 July 1919, Captain Fryatt's body was brought home to England aboard the British destroyer *Orpheus*. In what was almost a dress rehearsal for the funeral of the Unknown Warrior the following year, a special train met the coffin at Dover and carried it with full honours to London. A horse-drawn gun carriage transported it to St Paul's Cathedral where members of the royal family and senior representatives of the government and the armed forces attended a memorial service. Four of Fryatt's fellow GER captains acted as pall-bearers.

The following day a second special train returned the coffin to Dovercourt station. Thousands lined the route then taken to All Saints church in the town, the funeral procession accompanied by the bishops of Barking, Chelmsford and Colchester, senior military men, local worthies and a marching band. Captain Fryatt was buried in the churchyard in a spot chosen for its view out over harbour, from which he had once sailed.

A memorial stone paid for by GER marks his grave. Unveiled by GER chairman Lord Claud Hamilton, it is inscribed:

IN MEMORY OF
CAPTAIN CHARLES ALGERNON FRYATT
MASTER OF THE GREAT EASTERN STEAMSHIP, BRUSSELS,
ILLEGALLY EXECUTED BY THE GERMANS
AT BRUGES ON THE 27TH JULY, 1916.
ERECTED BY THE COMPANY
AS AN EXPRESSION OF THEIR
ADMIRATION OF HIS GALLANTRY.

Death in war, at the hands of a murderous enemy, made Captain Fryatt the focus of the kind of ritual at which British society was expert. That it was prepared to treat one merchant seaman, albeit a captain, as deserving of the highest honours was a fact that underlined the notion of equality in death. Every man or woman who laid down his or her life in the service of king and country rose straight to the top of the class, as it were, regardless of their background.

But this was still an aspect of social behaviour over which the Establishment could retain control. Great Eastern Railways had even written to the government to say an elaborate funeral for their captain might be good for morale. Rituals like Captain Fryatt's funeral were hardly about changing society itself. If anything they served to underline just how much of the pre-war status quo the Establishment hoped was still intact.

Some changes *were* real, and could neither be denied nor resisted. For many people, the war altered the way they saw the world. For them, old certainties were challenged and sometimes removed altogether.

On Stockcroft Road in the town of Balcombe in West Sussex is a building called the Victory Hall. Rather than erecting a stone tablet, or a cross of granite, or a plinth topped with a soldier in mourning, the people there opted to remember their lost loved ones with a building. The hope seemed to be that a village hall, somewhere that would be of use to generations of villagers, might be more likely to keep people reminded of those who had given their lives for that community.

It was built in 1923 with donations from people living near by and with a large donation from local landowner Lady Gertrude Denman, who was also a prime mover in bringing the hall into existence. It is inside the Victory Hall, however, that the visitor comes face to face with the real act of remembrance at Balcombe. A series of frescoes covers the walls – the painted figures based on real Balcombe people. They were made by Major Neville Lytton, squire of Crabbet Park and commander of 11th Battalion, Royal Sussex Regiment.

Lytton was a born aristocrat and in the years before the war enjoyed a life of privilege. He was a practised horseman and a championship tennis player. He and his wife, Judith, had a real tennis court built on their estate to help raise the standard of their game.

Arguably, however, it was painting which was closest to his heart – and it was the sketches he made while a serving officer in France that formed the basis for the works he would create at Balcombe Victory Hall after the war.

The coming of the Great War changed everything for Lytton. Already inspired by the soldiers he had seen training in the area, he was soon persuaded to encourage the estate workers to enlist. In the aftermath of Kitchener's call for volunteers to fill his new armies, local MP Colonel Claude Lowther had been empowered to raise battalions of Sussex men. Lytton became part of the recruitment campaign and travelled around his patch in a hired car to try to persuade the men of the area to follow him into the war. He knew many of them personally – had employed some of them on his land – and the force he raised became part of the 39th Division.

While Lytton survived the war, including fighting in and around the area of the Somme in 1916, many of his men did not. The time he spent with them persuaded him of the quality of the ordinary man, the common man. His experiences convinced him that the time of 'squires' like himself, ruling over little kingdoms, was coming to an end. The practicalities of war also took a heavy toll on his home life. Separation and eventual divorce from his wife proved costly and led to the sale of a lot of his land at Crabbet Park. When he returned to England after the war, he had to take on paid work as an artist and writer just to pay his bills.

Lytton had changed in many ways by the time he came to the Victory Hall to create the frescoes. Perhaps he was lucky in that he seemed to have the wit to adapt to a world that was changing whether he wanted it to or not. He saw that the ages-old connection between the aristocratic landowner and the people who occupied that land was being severed.

In 1914 he had toured his demesne, rounding up soldiers in much the same way that his medieval forebears might have done. By the turn of the twentieth century the relationship was more like that between a parent and his children – each was dependent upon the other somewhere along the line. Lytton saw that after 1918 his 'children' did not need the same relationship any more because the war had made them grow up, while the role of the aristocrat had just grown old.

There are two main frescoes at Balcombe – the war panel and the peace panel. Lytton appears in the peace panel as a flute player – a pastime he enjoyed in real life – and Lady Denman is pictured in among likenesses of men who worked on the estate. The images are intended to show a community living in the countryside, but no longer dependent upon 'the big house'. The war panel, with its shattered trees, dead and wounded soldiers, both British and German, tells a story of tragedy and futility. In context, 'Victory Hall' may be a misnomer.

Just as its benefactors may have hoped, the hall has been well used over the years. Gradually the frescoes – true frescoes formed of paint applied to wet plaster and therefore especially vulnerable to the ravages of time – grew dirty and marked. During one bad rainstorm water came in through the roof and left its own trail of damage. Money was made available for six weeks of clean-up and restoration in the summer of 1986, and experts came in and worked their magic on Lytton's originals. The year after the painters finished, craftsmen repaired all the damage and wear and tear to the hall's ceiling and cornices.

The scenes Lytton painted on the walls of the village hall were glimpses of the future he believed was coming. He considered it inevitable that as the twentieth century marched onwards, the aristocracy and the lower classes would have to accept that the old world was susceptible to change, and that their positions within it were no longer fixed.

39

The Love of a Father

The Bream cenotaph occupies a site looking out over the Forest of Dean. It was unveiled in 1921 and has the names of twenty-one men on it:

A. BROOKES
A. DODGSHON
E. EVANS
P. FROWEN
H. L. HOWELLS
T. JONES
W. T. KEAR
J. KENT
E. KILBY
L. LODGE
E. LUCAS
L. MAYNE
J. MATTY
G. NELMES
W. H. PEARCE
A. E. THOMAS
H. WALSEY
A. WATKINS
D. WILKS
E. WORGAN
G. WYNN

There are at least 36,000 memorials to the Great War in Britain. Think what *all* the names on *all* the memorials would look like, on a single stone. How long would it take to read them one by one?

No seniority is implied by the order of the names at Bream; only the unwavering run of the alphabet sets each in its place. Second from top – A. DODGSHON – is Angus John Charles Dodgshon, lieutenant, 2nd Battalion, 5th Gloucestershire Regiment. Historian Ian Hendy has hunted down the stories behind all the men on the memorial – the Second World War included – but the story of Lieutenant Dodgshon stands out. Like that of Major Billy Congreve VC, it has more tragedy woven through it than credible fiction would allow.

The bare facts of it are familiar enough – at least in terms of stories about young men called into service in the Great War. He lasted five weeks with his regiment in France before being killed near Arras on 10th November 1917, a year and a day before the Armistice. He was twenty-two. The Commonwealth War Graves Commission lists him as the son of John and Ada Dodgshon, born at Bream but with an address of 10 Campden Hill Square, Kensington, London.

He is buried in the Sunken Road Cemetery at Fampoux, Plot I, Row D, Grave 27. The village of Fampoux was taken by the 4th Division in April 1917, lost to the Germans at the end of March 1918 and finally retaken by the Allies at the end of August. The cemetery contains 196 burials and sits at the summit of the sunken road to Bailleul, on the east side.

Lieutenant Dodgshon was a rich man's son, as the London address might suggest. His father, John, was called 'the Colonel' by the people of Bream. As befits a man of military bent, he set up a rifle club for the local men and boys and was chairman of the village meeting in 1915 that called for volunteers to fill the newly created Forest of Dean Battalion. But for all that, it seems he didn't want his only son to go to war.

Angus was on the fast track leading to France. With a public school education behind him, and Cambridge University in front, he was nineteen when war broke out. Training with the Officer Training Corps came next instead of matriculation. He was commissioned first as a second lieutenant with the 2nd/5th Glosters and then promoted to captain towards the end of 1916. The rest of his battalion were in France by May of that year, but Angus stayed behind. Despite asking to be sent abroad, he had failed a medical board and been recommended for 'Home Service only'. The board members were swayed by a line from a private doctor saying Angus had suffered 'nervous exhaustion' following a motorbike accident some years before. Hendy believes Angus's father was behind the certificate that kept the boy back.

Whatever the truth, he was passed fit for service the following year – despite two letters from his father to the secretary of state for war asking for a second opinion. He joined his unit at Arras on 8 October and was killed the following month.

If John Dodgshon was pulling strings to keep his only son safe, who could blame him? He backed the call for volunteer battalions, was ready to watch other men's sons go off to war – what else could a man called 'the Colonel' do? But your own son is your own son.

Like all wars, the Great War made no allowance for social privilege, and in the end the love of a father provided no shield.

40

A Bird was Singing

Just before ten to seven on the morning of 22 May 1915 Signal-men James Tinsley and George Meakin were chatting together in the signal box at Quintinshill. It was a perfect morning, calm with a clear blue sky. The chances of a lovely early summer day seemed better than good.

It was more or less business as usual on a stretch of railway line in Dumfriesshire, just north of the city of Carlisle and the English border. We know as much as we do about the early part of that morning, in that otherwise nondescript setting, because of the one detail of the scene that was out of place.

Signalmen James Tinsley and George Meakin were so caught up in their chat that neither of them remembered the empty coal train parked on the southbound line. It was actually headed north, a local service, and only meant to be on the southbound side temporarily. If either man had remembered to clear the southbound line they would likely have enjoyed the rest of 22 May, and Quintinshill would be as forgettable now as it was then. Quintinshill isn't even a place. It was just a signal box in the middle of nowhere – one that no longer exists.

Neither of them remembered and they just kept chatting.

At 6.49 a.m. the troop train carrying Private Peter Stoddart and the rest of half the 1st Battalion, 7th Royal Scots Regiment, collided with the coal train at an estimated speed of 80 miles per hour. The troop train was made of timber and about as capable of withstanding a high-speed collision as a row of cricket pavilions. More than 200 yards of train and men were reduced to less than 70 in about the same length of time it took for Signalmen Tinsley's and Meakin's chins to drop towards their chests.

Chat over.

They looked out of the signal-box window to see the tangled wreckage of both trains lying, zigzag fashion, across the northbound and southbound tracks. Gas canisters slung beneath the carriages of the troop train, fuel for the interior lights, had ruptured on impact. The gas had ignited and exploded as it came into contact with the red-hot coals of the locomotives' steam engines. What remained of both trains was on fire.

The troop train had left Larbert station around dawn, en route for Liverpool docks, where the men were supposed to board ships bound for Gallipoli. There were nearly five hundred men on board and most were probably asleep as the train rattled and swayed through the Dumfriesshire countryside.

Peter was interviewed about the accident by a newspaper more than seventy years later. He remembered waking up at the moment of impact. When his world stopped tumbling and screaming, he realised he was trapped in the wreckage by his foot.

As he lay there in the first few seconds of the aftermath, and as Tinsley and Meakin looked on in wonder, a northbound express passenger train out of London collided with the carnage. Peter had heard its whistle blowing as it came on. 'I think I prayed,' he said. 'The express hit us and I lost consciousness.'

He came to lying on the embankment below the tracks, blood pouring from a head wound. A bird was singing. Peter remembered it as a lark. Another survivor, an officer of the Royal Scots, gave evidence at the accident inquiry. He said his clearest memory of that first moment was hearing the song of a blackbird.

Why do we remember the things we remember?

Peter said he looked up then, straight into the face of one of his friends. His friend was laughing like a madman, but when Peter stretched out his arms towards him he realised he was

20. Alice Littlefield with the couple's eldest son, Thomas.

21. Private William Littlefield with Thomas.

LEST WE FORGET
IN HONOURED MEMORY OF THE MEN OF
THIS ESTATE WHO LAID DOWN THEIR
LIVES IN THE GREAT WAR 1914-1918

SER.	CALLAGHAN. T.	WELSH GUARDS.
PTE.	DEAN. H. T.	AUSTRALIAN IMP. FORCES.
PTE.	FIFIELD. J. W.	R. IRISH FUSILIERS.
PTE.	FIFIELD. J. P.	R. INNISKILLING FUS.
PTE.	KIRTLAND. J. A.	MIDDLESEX REG'T.
PTE.	LITTLEFIELD. W.	E. SURREY REG'T.
PTE.	MARSHALL. J. C.	R. FUSILIERS.
PTE.	MARSHALL. A.	NORTH'D. FUSILIERS.
PTE.	MASON. S. J.	GRENADIER GUARDS.
RIFLEMAN	MILLER. A.	RIFLE BRIGADE.
RIFLEMAN	MOONEY. J.	RIFLE BRIGADE.
RIFLEMAN	PENNINGTON. E. W.	RIFLE BRIGADE.
PTE.	SMITH. F. C.	WESTMINSTER DGNS.
SAPPER	TEMPLE. L. W.	R. ENGINEERS.
PTE.	TOWNSEND.	R. FUSILIERS.

R I P

22. Not forgotten: the men of the Old Pye Street flats in London, who died in the Great War. Private William Littlefield's name appears sixth from the top.

23. Accrington Pals Regiment, photographed near Hyndburn Park School in Accrington in 1914.

24 and 25. 'Strong heart still beats loudly': Walter Tull, professional footballer, officer and gentleman.

26 and 27. The artist of Balcombe: Neville Lytton, squire of Crabbet Park, and (back row, second left) with brother officers of the 11th Battalion, Royal Sussex Regiment in France.

28. 'With eager valour': the statue of Edward Horner by Sir Arthur Munnings, in the Horner Chapel in St Andrew's Church, Mells.

29. Lieutenant Colonel Sitwell, chairman of the committee responsible for choosing the original Great War memorial (below) for the village of Lowick, in Northumberland.

30. Banished: Sitwell's 1920s memorial in the location chosen for it after the village demanded its replacement with, right, 31. a recently erected monument of more traditional design.

32. A land fit for heroes: unemployed ex-servicemen march in support of the Great Railway Strike, September 1919.

33. The Iolaire Memorial on the cliffs above the Beasts of Holm, near Stornoway, Lewis.

34. The empty tomb: Sir Edwin Lutyen's original, temporary cenotaph made of wood and plaster board, on display in Whitehall in July 1919.

35. The journey of the Unknown Warrior: the unidentified body is sent on its way.

36. Now in England, the coffin is borne towards its special train to London.

37. In Westminster Abbey, the 16th century crusader sword prominently displayed.

THIS MONUMENT IS ERECTED IN GRATEFUL
MEMORY OF THOSE MEN OF MARCH WHO
AT THE CALL OF KING AND COUNTRY
LEFT ALL THAT WAS DEAR TO THEM
THEY MADE THE SUPREME SACRIFICE
THAT OTHERS MIGHT LIVE IN FREEDOM.
LET THOSE THAT COME AFTER SEE TO
IT THAT THEY ARE NOT FORGOTTEN.

38. 'Let those who come after see to it that they are not forgotten': the memorial in March, Cambridgeshire.

looking only at his friend's severed head, eyes and mouth wide open.

Men who had survived the first crash were killed in the second as they struggled clear of the wreckage and the fire.

Peter climbed back up the embankment to see whether he could help anyone. 'Engines were piled on top of each other, carriages telescoped and overturned, fire breaking out everywhere, and hundreds of men still trapped in the wreckage.

'It was hell. Waving arms, waving legs. Fire had broken out all round. I put my head in my hands and sobbed.'

Wounded men still alive were trapped in the burning wreckage. Fire engines from Carlisle took three hours to arrive at the scene. Peter saw an officer of the Royal Scots shooting those dying men and boys he could reach with his service revolver, cutting short their hopeless agony.

Peter was found first by a woman from a nearby farm who did what she could to dress his head wound. Later he was put on a train to Carlisle with two other wounded men. It was just a regular passenger service and they were unaccompanied on the trip. By the time it arrived in the city the other pair were dead.

The express train from London had been steel framed and the casualties on board were relatively light. Of the nearly five hundred soldiers who had boarded the troop train at Larbert, however, 227 were killed and 246 injured. It is still the worst rail disaster to have taken place anywhere in the British Isles. All but a handful of the passengers were men of the Royal Scots. Out of a total of 485, 215 died – 3 officers, 29 non-commissioned officers and 182 men of other ranks.

Surviving members of the regiment were part of the attacks on Gully Ravine and Achi Baba at Gallipoli. Their greatest single body count of the war – 42 per cent of all losses – happened at Quintinshill before they were even out of Scotland.

Tinsley and Meakin were later found guilty of manslaughter and sentenced to eighteen months each in jail.

The bodies of the dead soldiers were taken to Edinburgh, many of them so badly burned their families were not allowed to open the coffins. Many could not be formally identified. They were buried together in the Rosebank Cemetery in Leith. It took three hours for the hearses to pass through the city streets. Large bronze plaques above the mass grave bear the names of the dead.

At Larbert station there is another commemorative plaque. It reads:

QUINTINSHILL RAIL DISASTER
22ND MAY 1915
IN MEMORY OF
THE MEN OF THE 1ST/7TH BATTALION
THE ROYAL SCOTS LEITH TERRITORIAL BATTALION
WHO LEFT LARBERT STATION ON THEIR WAY TO
THE FRONT TO FIGHT FOR THEIR COUNTRY
BUT WHO MET THEIR DEATHS IN A RAIL DISASTER AT
QUINTINSHILL OUTSIDE GRETNA

'AT THE GOING DOWN OF THE SUN
AND IN THE MORNING
WE WILL REMEMBER THEM'.

At Quintinshill itself you can find traces of where the signal box once stood. Near by a memorial stone overlooks the scene of the crash. It was unveiled on 21 May 1995.

Two brothers, James and Robert Sime, Privates 636 and 1388 respectively, of 40 Dalmeny Street, in Leith, died together in the crash. James was the elder at twenty-three; Robert was twenty-one. Their parents' names were Robert and Janet.

By the time William Cook, from Leadhills, Scotland's second-highest village, disappeared at the Somme in 1916, never to be seen again, his younger brother James was already dead. One of a handful of Highland Light Infantrymen travelling on the troop train, he was killed alongside the Royal Scots at Quintinshill.

James and William died more than a year and many a mile apart, and they are kept apart too by seven other Cooks on the same page of the same leather-bound book in the Scottish National War Memorial. James's entry comes first. It reads: 'Cook, James 7980, Pte. b. Leadhills. Died Home 22/5/15, 8th Bn. (T.)' 'Died Home'. It would sound almost comforting if you read it without knowing that he died in a burning train wreck.

The brothers Cook are together on the Leadhills war memorial, with no names in between. It is a roughly hewn granite plinth topped with a Celtic cross. On the shaft of the cross is an engraving of a broadsword, the years 1914 and 1918 picked out on either side of the hilt. Altogether there are seventeen names. It sits by the side of the B7040 road, enclosed by a waist-high wrought-iron fence, opposite the Hopeton Arms Hotel. On the day I went to see it there were eight terracotta bowls of fresh spring daffodils arranged around the base.

In the newspaper interview about the crash, Peter said his scalp was still pitted with pieces of grit from the burning train. His daughter could feel them when she washed his hair, he said. She didn't like it. My grandpa carried a piece of shrapnel buried behind his left ear until the day he died. I used to be allowed to run my finger along the submerged edge of it when I was a little boy.

I wonder now how much of the Great War stayed behind in the bodies it touched. In years to come, they will dig up old men's graves from time to time, to make space for new. In some of them, in among the bones and the teeth, the buttons and wedding rings, the keepsakes and artificial hip joints, they will find bits and pieces of other metal.

Those fragments are part of the Great War too, parts of another way of telling the story. And if it were all gathered together, what would it look like?

41

Not Forgotten

Like the Devil, remembrance is in the details. Before someone can properly be remembered, they must be noticed, appreciated for who and what they are. It's not enough to bother to recall a person's name after they're gone. Without knowing the details – noticing the details in the first place and remembering them – a person is lost and forgotten while they're still alive.

I believe I performed a miracle, of the everyday kind, when I was about fourteen. I believe it changed my life because it made me start to pay attention. It's when I started to try to notice what mattered to me and to remember it.

We were living in a house on Victoria Terrace by then – our second house in Dumfries and the one that's still the family home. There's a plaque beside the front door that says J. M. Barrie lived there for a while, in the years before he wrote *Peter Pan*.

It was a midsummer evening, about seven o'clock, and Dad came back in from the after-tea walk with Mack, our dog. 'I've lost my wedding ring,' he said.

Mum looked at him.

He'd been complaining it was slipping off his finger in the towel sometimes when he washed and dried his hands. Either his fingers had got thinner or the ring had stretched somehow – who knew? But now it had fallen from his hand . . . outside.

Before he could say anything else, and before Mum could speak, I stood up from where I'd been sitting in front of the telly. 'I'll find it,' I said. I had no doubt I could do what I'd said.

I ran downstairs (the house is what estate agents call a maison-ette, or a duplex, being the first and second floors of a three-storey terraced house) and out into warm air. I knew where Dad and Mack had been – it was where we always took him, along Huntingdon Road to its dead end and out on to the acre or so of rough ground that served as the car park for a weekly cattle market. At that time of year, it was waist high with thick, coarse grass.

I walked slowly out into the sea of green, looking down towards my feet. After a couple of minutes, and having done no more than meander through the grass in a big, lazy 'S', I saw a gold ring lying six inches in front of my right foot beside half a red brick. It was no surprise to me at the time (though the memory of it is a thrill, twenty-four years later) and I bent and picked it up, recognising it at once (Dad's wedding ring was not a plain band of gold, but what would normally be described as a signet ring – red gold set with a smooth, square, dark green bloodstone flecked with red. On the inside of the band, I knew, was the inscription of the date of their wedding, worn now almost to the point of illegibility).

I can't describe the feeling as I ran home with it. Dad met me on Huntingdon Road in our car (a dark brown Saab 900 Turbo, registration DSD 769V; men my age can always reel off the makes and number plates of the cars our dads had when we were little boys). I don't know why he'd decided to drive along what was just a five-minute walk from the house, but there he was. He had the driver's window wound fully down and I ran up to him, the ring in my right hand, thrust out in front of me at arm's length.

As I dropped it into his outstretched palm he looked at me as if I'd pulled off the greatest conjuring trick in the world.

Years later, long after I'd left home for good, Dad told me he had lost the ring again. Precious things can be lost and found and lost again. I wasn't there to look for it that final time and it stayed lost. I know it's out there in the world somewhere. Someone else has probably found it by now, but in every way that matters it's still lost because it's lost to its real owners. It's part of my family's story. It has some of our words on it and it's missing.

But it's not forgotten, and neither is the part of my family story it represents. I remember it. It's my dad's wedding ring and I remember what it meant to my mum and dad.

I think that's the start of remembrance.

42

Not One Street in Leeds

It is a force totally different from that which has hitherto left these shores. It has been drawn almost exclusively from the better class of artisans, the upper and lower middle classes . . . the people of this country will take an intimate personal interest in its fate of a kind which they have never displayed before in our military expeditions.

David Lloyd George, War Memoirs

The Accrington Pals; McCrae's Battalion – these were not by any means the only pals' battalions to come to grief at the Somme. The battle was a killing field for the young manhood of town after town. One after another, the pals' battalions were broken on the wheel of the Somme.

Bradford, Barnsley, Durham, Hull, Leeds, Sheffield – all had their battalions of pals. Raised in the main from among the middle classes, they were the embodiment of the aspirational values of the communities from which they had come. They had not had their position in society handed to them on a plate like men of the upper classes – rather they had striven and worked to rise up and better themselves and their families. Their privileges, such as they were, had been hard won, and when the war came they were among the first to volunteer. Here, after all, was an opportunity to show how much they believed they mattered, how much they could demonstrate their commitment to a nation on the up.

The men of the Leeds battalion were typical of the breed. It was first and foremost a club, and a fiercely selective one at that. It was not by any means enough just to be from Leeds – a man had to be of the right sort, middle class to the core, well educated and part of the city's thriving business community. One veteran recalled how the pals turned him away because he had bad teeth. Like the rest of the pals' battalions, the Leeds was composed of men who had known each other all their lives, gone to school together, got their first jobs together, joined up together, trained together.

Thomas Arthur Raymond Ellicott Willey was an articled clerk in his father's firm of solicitors. Like the rest of them, he enlisted with the 15th Battalion of the West Yorkshire Regiment, the Prince of Wales' Own. As a second lieutenant he led part of the first wave over the top on 1 July. We can picture him confidently shaking hands with his fellow officers, smiling at the sight of his men waiting patiently for him to blow the whistle so their triumphant stroll across no man's land could get under way. He was cut in two by a shell within the first few minutes and his body was never found. His childhood friend and fellow officer Lieutenant John Gilbert 'Jackie' Vause may have seen him fall. In any case, Jackie was reported among the dead that day as well. His body was never found. He and Thomas are listed among the 72,103 names on the walls at Thiepval.

The Leeds Pals lost thirteen officers that first day; two more died of their wounds later on. Of the other ranks, 209 died on 1 July, and twenty-four more succumbed in the following days and weeks to wounds received that day. It was said there was not one street in Leeds passed over by the cull.

Whole armies that had taken two years to create from among the finest men of their generation were almost wiped out within hours. In the weeks and months to come, the Germans made a savage defence of every town, every village, every farmhouse on the Somme. When the fighting stopped for the winter, the Germans fell back to their specially prepared defences on the Hindenburg Line. The respective positions of the opposing forces would not change in any way that mattered until 1918.

43

The Old Order

Battles like the Somme were not the only ones fought during the Great War – and those battlefields were not the only places where boundaries and territories were challenged and sometimes permanently redefined.

Behind the popular image of a nation uniting to defend itself against the enemy it is easy to find stories of social and political unrest. Strikes and other militant behaviours were still employed during the war. The fact the country needed twenty-four hour, seven-day industrial output did not always deter workers from withdrawing their labour and standing toe to toe with the bosses when they felt their needs demanded such action.

In February 1915 some nine thousand workers on Clydeside, in Glasgow, went on strike demanding a wages hike – and the employers gave in. Alarmed by this and other incidents, the government took action. The notorious 'Treasury Agreements' signed away independent union rights and the Munitions Act made illegal any action that might cut output – including strikes. A Clydeside munitions worker was jailed for three months in 1915 for 'slacking and causing others to slack'.

Even so, defiant militancy continued to provide powerful leverage for those in control of it, and the increased status won by the common working man during the war would contribute to the improved lot of many of them in the years thereafter.

The middle class numbered 1.7 million members in 1911. By

1921 the total had risen to 2.7 million as a result of wartime economic prosperity.

If the industrial, urbanised world was being changed by the war, so too was the world of the countryside. Rich landowners had traditionally dominated society and had exercised most of the nation's political power. As taxation on land rose between 1914 and 1918, those in possession of it increasingly felt the pinch. Death duties became a recurrent burden for the landed gentry as the war took its toll on the aristocracy of the officer class.

Land values rose sharply, after generations of relative sluggishness, and many landowners cashed in on the boom time. Over 500,000 acres of Britain were up for sale by 1919. Those who had been tenants before took the opportunity now to become landowners in their own right. The face of the countryside – unchanged and unchanging for generations – was altered for ever. The old order was being replaced.

During the war years, there was a clear divide between those who served in the armed services and those who stayed at home. It was every bit as much a division between men as any line drawn according to the traditional understanding of 'class'. Those men in the 'reserved occupations' faced their own fights, their own struggles and their own dangers.

The shipyards of the Clyde were one of the vital engine rooms of Britain's – and the Empire's – war effort. It was there that most of the warships were built, and the importance of the yards elevated the status of the thousands of workers employed there for the duration. Here was a reserved occupation of the first rank, and the men of the shipyards found that on occasion their work gave them something close to equality with those risking their lives in the trenches at the front.

In Elder Park in Govan, an area on the south bank of the Clyde that was once the beating heart of shipbuilding in Glasgow, there is a memorial with the names of thirty-two men on it. The dedication says:

SACRED TO THE MEMORY OF
THOSE NAMED WHO LOST THEIR LIVES IN
H.M. SUBMARINE K-13
IN THE GARELOCH, 29TH JANUARY 1917
AND ERECTED BY
THE OFFICIALS FOREMAN AND EMPLOYEES OF
THE FAIRFIELD SHIPBUILDING AND
ENGINEERING CO. LTD.

Those in the know say the K-class submarines were ahead of
their time. They were larger than most other subs, equipped with
boilers and funnels to give them enough speed to keep up with
the warships they were designed to accompany. For all that, they
had a reputation as death traps. They even inspired a joke –
supposed to be a quote from a K-class submarine captain spoken
during sea trials: 'I say, Number One, my end is diving, what's
your end up to?'

Of the thirty-two men who died during the *K-13*'s sea trials
in the deep waters of the Gareloch, seven of them were civilians.
In a reserved occupation they may have been, but they died the
same death as the fighting men of the Royal Navy who drowned
alongside them.

44

A Welsh Dragon

The coalminers of South Wales were another group among the working class whose work was deemed as vital to the war effort as any fighting in France. Militancy, refusal to kow-tow to management, was not wholly curbed by the war or by legislation, and the men of the valleys still came out on strike when they felt justified in doing so.

They downed tools in July 1915 after the government rejected a Miners' Federation demand for a wage rise to meet the soaring cost of living. Despite reminders about the constraints of the Munitions Act, the miners held firm – confident there was no way to jail 200,000 men. They were right. The crisis was eased only when Lloyd George himself travelled to Cardiff and personally agreed to the miners' demands.

Such militancy did not, however, get in the way of enlistment. Men raised to stand up for themselves and for their rights saw no contradiction in demanding better wages and working conditions from the boss class one day, and stepping forward as volunteers for the king's army the next. And the urgency of the war – the necessity to keep the mines working and the coal coming whatever it took – occasionally gave those miners who stayed in the pits even more clout than they had wielded in peacetime.

The working men in some of the reserved occupations were, during the years of the Great War, something of a class apart.

Perhaps the hardships of the mines made the realities of trench life less of a shock for miners than for some of their white-collar comrades. The bulk of the work of the regular soldier was hard, manual labour – most of it done with pick and shovel. New trenches had to be dug; existing trenches had to be maintained. There was even modified mining work itself to be done – and on an industrial scale – in the form of tunnelling towards and underneath the enemy lines. Miners were physically prepared for the job of soldiering in a way that many men from the industrial towns and cities were not, especially those from the business and commercial sectors that formed many of the pals' regiments.

More telling even than the physical preparedness of the miners was their familiarity with risk and danger on an everyday basis. They came from close-knit communities hardened to loss from pit floods, cave-ins, explosions and the myriad range of injuries offered by working every day with heavy machinery. They breathed dust and fumes and stink every day, and had learned how to put to the back of their minds the constant threat of crippling injury and death.

Mining families had lived for generations with the daily possibility of losing fathers, brothers, uncles. They were no strangers to bad news. The wider British public came to know loss, to count death tolls. The mining towns were long practised in the art. It is estimated that between 1868 and 1914 one miner was killed every six hours and twelve more were injured every day.

Seams of the 'black gold' had been found all over South Wales in the 1890s and the Universal Steam Coal Company opened a mine at Senghenydd, at the end of a valley near Caerphilly, in 1897. By the time it closed thirty years later it had inflicted upon its community the worst mining disaster in British history.

It was among the deepest in the South Wales coalfield and yielded more than 180,000 tons of the best coal available anywhere in the country every year. On 24 May 1901 an accident killed eighty-two men and boys – all but one of the miners working underground that day. This was a bad one by any standards – unbearable. But mining towns did bear such events, and moved on – in a grim foretaste of the way other towns and villages throughout Britain would learn to bear tragedies, and move on from them, in the years to come.

On the morning of 14 October 1913 a massive explosion, caused, it is thought, by a build up of methane gas, ripped through the galleries and shafts of Senghenydd. The blast was heard 11 miles away in Cardiff. This time 439 miners died – not just Senghenydd men but fathers and sons from Abertridwr, Penyrheol, Caerphilly, Bedwas and Cardiff as well. Only seventy-two bodies were ever recovered. Over two hundred women were made widows that day, and over five hundred children left without fathers. Eight of the dead were fourteen-year-old boys. There have been greater death tolls in mines around the world over the years, but in Britain nothing as bad as Senghenydd has happened before or since.

These, then, were the training grounds from which the Welsh regiments were raised – places that knew only too well how quickly a population of men could be decimated. So used were they to loss, in fact, that they often didn't bother to raise memorials to their war dead. In the towns in the valleys, men died by the score and more all the time – it wasn't always something that needed engraving in stone.

It is a certainty that patriotism played its part in encouraging early enlistment among Welshmen just as it had everywhere else. Ironically, though, many of the miners may have believed that by following the colours they were leaving hardship behind. They came from a world where mines opened up to swallow boys as young as eleven, taking them right to the coal face itself as young as fourteen. They faced the prospect of desperate health risks, low wages and all-round physical hardship – not to mention the ever present threat of sudden death. For men and boys like these, who might never have the opportunity to travel far from their own valleys, the chance to join an army, march tall, breath fresh air under the sky and travel to far off places may have sounded

Not Forgotten

like a dream come true. Quite what they felt when they found themselves, in many cases, drafted into the companies tasked with tunnelling through mud and rotting corpses towards the German front lines at Ypres has never been fully documented.

By the time plans got fully under way to raise a Welsh army corps of two full divisions, recruiting sergeants from across the border had already harvested part of the crop into other regiments. The Devonshires, the King's Shropshire Rifles and the Cameronians among others had a Welsh flavour. In the end, the Welsh National Executive Committee, created in September 1914 to drive Welsh recruitment, raised a single division. Initially the 43rd (Welsh), it was renumbered the 38th (Welsh) by the spring of 1915.

The new armies created from 1914 onwards comprised millions of men from every conceivable background and class. Politics, nationalism, patriotism – all three were inevitably ingredients in the mix. In Wales the situation was complicated further by the involvement of one of that country's most famous sons, David Lloyd George – first in the newly created post of minister of munitions and latterly as prime minister. The greater calling to fight the German foe transcended even the potent demands of political militancy and Welsh nationalism, and nearly 300,000 Welshmen would be involved in the fight before the end.

Frederick Hugh Roberts had been a Senghenydd miner. On the evening of 13 October 1913 he enjoyed a night out with some pals. The details of the evening are blurred by time, but it seems highly likely that gambling, a game of chance of some kind, was involved. There was definitely strong drink. Fred was supposed to be on the morning shift at the Senghenydd mine the next day – but despite his wife's best efforts he stayed home to nurse a mighty hangover. And so it was the demon drink – or its aftermath at least – which kept him away from the disaster that killed 439 of his workmates.

Soon after the outbreak of the war, he turned his back on coalmining for the last time and signed up to the 16th Battalion, Royal Welsh Fusiliers. But the luck that had kept him safe from explosion and fire back home was powerless to protect him amid the maelstroms of the Somme. On 10 July 1916 he fell with all the others. He is buried at the Heilly Station Cemetery, Méricourt-l'Abbé, Plot II, Row B, Grave 7.

His name also appears, along with sixty-two others, on the Senghenydd War Memorial. A community already blighted and all but broken by heartbreak beyond reason found that it still had more lives to lose after all.

The Welsh National Book of Remembrance, inscribed on 12 June 1928 by Edward, Prince of Wales, has in it the names of 35,000 Welshmen and women who died in the Great War.

At Mametz Wood on the Longueval Ridge, where the 38th lost 4,000 of its men in the early weeks of the battle of the Somme, a Welsh dragon stands its ground.

45

6322 Private John Condon

Ireland was a country on the brink of civil war in 1914. Supporters of Home Rule were squaring up to those backing the continuation of the Union. With the temperature of the debate at boiling point full-scale conflict looked like a certainty – and it has been argued that bloodshed there was averted in 1914 only by the outbreak of war in Europe.

But Kitchener's call was heard just as loudly and just as clearly in Ireland as it was heard everywhere else. More than 200,000 of its men, from both sides of the political divide, chose to put their differences on hold and risked life and limb together in the service of a king and an empire.

Corporal Clifford, Lane, 1st Battalion, Hertfordshire Regiment said:

> We had an Irishman named Mick Flemand on one of our guns and he's out in no-man's land this night, two men with him, and a shell come over that killed two and never touched him. During the night, he stuck that, alone, and a German officer and a German sergeant come creeping to steal a gun. They thought they'd killed all three, you see. Mick, he's got a revolver, that day, he let them get right onto him and he shot them both dead. He was still there when daylight came. Two pals laid out and two old Jerries. He got the Military Medal for that. Poor old boy, he couldn't neither read nor write. He'd come from Ireland I used to read his letters for him. He come from Southern

Ireland, they had a terrible job there in 1916, didn't they? When he had his leave from France, he daren't go home, you know. There was a place in London where the likes of him went. He told us he'd be killed if he went home, being in the British Army, you see. (Quoted in Max Arthur, *Forgotten Voices of the Great War*)

The men of the South joined the 10th (Irish) and 16th (Irish) Divisions; the men of the North joined the 36th (Ulster). By the end, more than 35,000 were dead.

In the Great War they fought not as rivals but as Irishmen, and honoured one another while they did so. In the fight for Messines Ridge in June 1917, the 16th (Irish) and 36th (Ulster) regiments fought and died side by side. Catholics and Protestants are listed together on the memorial tower in the Irish Peace Park which occupies part of the ridge today.

The Ulster Tower, near Thiepval, is a replica of Helen's Tower on the Marquis of Dufferin's estate at Clandeboye, near Belfast. It was at Clandeboye that the 36th trained. On the first day of the Somme, the 9th Royal Irish Rifles charged out of Thiepval Wood and broke through the German lines, one of the few British successes that day. The tower marks the location of the German trenches they overran.

Back in Ireland, like everywhere else, they were building memorials in the towns and villages before the war was over. By 1919 there were calls for a national memorial to remember all of Ireland's dead – and a National War Memorial Trust established to get the job done. In 1923 the trust published *Ireland's Memorial Records* – eight volumes listing the names of every Irish man and woman killed in the war, along with those from other countries who died while serving in Irish regiments.

Plans for the war memorial itself initially foundered in a mire of politics – nationalists in the newly independent Irish Free State opposed several proposed sites – and the Memorial Gardens in

Dublin were not completed until 1938. Located on the southern slopes of the Liffey river they were designed by Lutyens and built by veterans of the war. A 30-foot cross and a Stone of Remembrance are the dominant features there.

Remembrance of Ireland's Great War dead has been fraught with complications. The Union Jack flag was and is a potent symbol loved and loathed in equal measures. Even the Flanders poppy – the bloom that loves disturbed soil and so flourished in the aftermath of battles, *the* symbol of remembrance – has been too political for many Irish people to accept.

Many towns are without a Great War memorial of any kind and uncounted names have never been commemorated. It was too painful for some to think of men fighting for the British army, a force that had been an enemy. They certainly didn't always go out of their way to remember or to celebrate the fact.

One of the most visited of Irish memorials is the gravestone of 6322 Private John Condon, at the Poelcapelle British Cemetery, in Belgium.

In the years before 1910 Condon lived at 2 Wheelbarrow Lane, off Wellington Lane, in Waterford, with his mother and father, John and Mary, his brothers Patrick and Peter and his sisters Katie and Margaret. His mother and his sister Katie both died of tuberculosis that year and young John was packed off to live with his Uncle Michael, a cobbler, in Kneefe's Lane. All the men in the family had manual jobs and John was employed in Sullivan's Bottling Stores.

On 24 October 1913, nearly a year before the outbreak of war, he turned up at an army recruitment office in the city. Captain J. P. T. Mackesy, JP, witnessed the paperwork as John joined up for six years' service with the 3rd Battalion, Royal Irish Regiment, Army Reserve. On 25 October he stood in front of a medical officer who gave him the regulation physical examination. The records show he was 5 feet 3 inches tall and weighed less than 8½ stone.

In June the following year he reported for training to the army barracks in Clonmel. He was mobilised on 7 August and joined the 2nd Battalion, Royal Irish Regiment, on 16 December. By March 1915 John was with his regiment in Belgium and on 24 May, during the Second Battle of Ypres, he was killed. His body was not recovered at the time.

Some ten years later a farmer tilling his field unearthed his remains. They were taken to the cemetery at Poelcapelle, where he was buried in Plot 6, Row F, Grave 1.

Sad though all this undoubtedly is, none of it is enough to explain why his grave receives more visitors than any of the others that lie there. It's not even a surprise to find that John's family learned he was in Belgium only when they received a letter telling them he was missing in action. Lots of men had their reasons for wanting to keep their business to themselves.

But Private John Condon was barely a man. He was fourteen years old when he died. I haven't seen any photographs and I don't know whether or not he looked older than his years. But he was 5 feet 3 inches tall and weighed less than 8½, stone, so you have to wonder. Apparently he fooled the recruiting sergeant in Waterford by taking on the identity of his elder brother, also called John, who was already dead by 1913.

He's generally accepted as the youngest Allied soldier to have been killed on active service in the Great War.

In 1922, John's father was sent his medals – the 1914–15 Star, the British War Medal and the Victory Medal: Pip, Squeak and Wilfred.

His grave receives hundreds of visitors every year and in Belgium he's revered as a hero.

46

'. . . I have Lost a Friend'

Equality in death: it's a phrase that's used a lot about the tragedy of the Great War. I'm not sure about it, whether or not it means much, in truth. It looks like equality, but maybe it's really something less grand. They can call you king when you're dead for all the difference it makes. Dead is dead; equality can be achieved only in life.

A memorial garden at Northampton's Sixfields football ground commemorates the achievements of a man who rose from poverty and a childhood spent partly in an orphanage to win success as a professional footballer. His achievements on the pitch were to be completely surpassed by how he conducted himself on the battlefields of the Great War.

Walter Tull was the grandson of a black slave. His father Daniel, a carpenter, came to Folkestone from Barbados in 1876, joined the local Methodist church and married a local white girl. Walter was born in April 1888. There were six children by 1895, when his mother died. His father remarried but died himself two years later, leaving Walter's stepmother struggling to cope. The Church arranged for Walter and his brother to be taken into care, a move that eventually brought the boys to a Methodist orphanage in London's Bethnal Green. Walter was ten years old. When he left school he began an apprenticeship as a printer. He was a keen footballer and played for a side in Clapton. In 1908 a talent scout representing Tottenham Hotspur spotted his abilities. Preston North End goalkeeper Arthur Wharton was officially Britain's first black professional, but Walter was the first outfielder. A sports writer with the *Daily Chronicle* called him a good player with 'a class superior to that shown by most of his colleagues'. It was a comment that would eventually be applicable to more than Walter's behaviour on the football pitch.

At a game against Bristol City in 1909 he was baited by the crowd on account of his colour – jeering, monkey noises, exactly what you'd imagine. The incident was traumatising – both for Walter and for Spurs. He never got fully into the rest of the season and was sold the following year to Northampton Town. He became a favourite there, and a star, turning out over one hundred times for the first team. When war broke out, he was close to signing for Glasgow Rangers, but chose the uniform of the 17th (1st Football) Battalion of the Middlesex Regiment instead.

He was a sergeant by 1916 and survived the First Battle of the Somme in which so many others fell. He briefly succumbed to trench fever, a disease carried by the ever present lice that thrived in the filthy conditions, and was sent home to recover later the same year. When he left hospital, he did not return to his unit. Instead he was sent to Scotland to train as an officer. This was unheard of for a black man. The *Manual of Military Law* of 1914 specifically forbade it. That Tull so impressed his superiors that they were prepared to break the rules for him says it all. He was commissioned as a second lieutenant in 1917, winning mentions in dispatches the same year for 'gallantry and coolness' under fire at the battle of Piave, in Italy.

Transferred back to France, he survived the Second Battle of the Somme. In the last spring of the war, at a place called Favreuil, he was ordered to lead part of an attack on the German trenches. He was shot during the first minutes of the charge, at the front of his men, and killed instantly. Despite murderous machine-gun fire his men made repeated attempts to get back into no man's land and recover their officer's body.

Their efforts were in vain, and Walter's body became one of the missing. His name is listed among the 34,738 on the Arras Memorial in the Faubourg d'Amiens Cemetery, on the Boulevard du Général de Gaulle, in the western part of the town of Arras.

His name disappeared from popular memory then, but has been brought to the fore in recent years by the creation of the Walter Tull Memorial and Garden of Rest. His memorial has on it the words:

THROUGH HIS ACTIONS, WDJ TULL RIDICULED THE BARRIERS OF IGNORANCE THAT TRIED TO DENY PEOPLE OF COLOUR EQUALITY WITH THEIR CONTEMPORARIES. HIS LIFE STANDS TESTAMENT TO A DETERMINATION TO CONFRONT THOSE PEOPLE AND THOSE OBSTACLES THAT SOUGHT TO DIMINISH HIM AND THE WORLD IN WHICH HE LIVED. IT REVEALS A MAN, THOUGH RENDERED BREATHLESS IN HIS PRIME, WHOSE STRONG HEART STILL BEATS LOUDLY.

Walter Tull demonstrated equality while he lived; claimed it. Rising above the poverty of his childhood and the prejudice he encountered on the football pitch, he secured the right to equality with the officer class through his own efforts.

Writing to Walter's brother to inform him of the death, his commanding officer said he had been popular throughout the battalion, that he had been brave and conscientious, that the battalion and company had lost a faithful officer, '. . . and personally I have lost a friend'.

That his qualities were recognised and rewarded in life surely mattered more than any equality in death?

47

A Worthy Son of his Father

Missing Over Eight Months

Mr G W Kirman of Mill Farm, Stallingborough, has received news of his brother, Private C H Kirman, late of Waltham and Brigsley, who was reported missing on November 2nd 1916. Until last week absolutely nothing was heard of him, and his wife and relatives had naturally suffered considerable anxiety. To their delight the news reached them last week that after eight months of hardship and suffering and great danger he had rejoined his regiment. No doubt behind these words lies a very thrilling story.

Grimsby Weekly News, *10 August 1917*

Old India hand Private Charles Kirman, survivor of Mons and the Somme, father of two, was shot for desertion at 6.09 a.m. on 23 September 1917; hardly the 'thrilling story' imagined by the *Grimsby Weekly News* reporter.

Transcripts of his court martial reveal that Charles was reported absent without official leave (AWOL) on 26 July 1917. His regiment was at 'the Railway Cutting' east of Blancy when he disappeared from the trenches without a word. Nothing was seen or heard of him until 31 July, when he handed himself in to men of the 2nd Battalion, 6th London Regiment, at Berneville.

On 16 August 1917, while he was under arrest for that first

offence, Charles took off for a second time. Around nine o'clock in the evening, while he was being taken to use the toilet, he bolted. Only the day before he had been told he was being sent on a sixteen-day tour of duty to the front line. Two days after he ran away, he turned himself in once more.

In a statement to the court martial Charles said: 'I have been out abroad in India 7 years and 4 months. I often suffered with malaria. I came out in August 1914 with the Expeditionary Force. My nerves are now completely broken down. I suffer with pains in the head when I am in the line. Sometimes I don't know what I'm doing.'

He called no witnesses and made no real defence. The court martial heard he had been AWOL once before – between November 1916 and March the following year. For that offence he had been sentenced to a year's imprisonment with hard labour, but later had it suspended.

Charles made a final statement – nothing resembling a plea in mitigation or an appeal for leniency, just a few simple facts about his time in France: 'I was wounded at la Basse in Nov. 1914 & again on July 1st 1916 at La Boiselle. I have been out about 18 months this time and about 4 months the first time.'

His words made little impact on the three men who constituted the court martial – Major R. P. Burnett, MC, of the 8th South Staffordshire Regiment, along with a captain and a lieutenant. In relation to the five-day absence in July he was convicted of the lesser charge of being absent without leave. For the subsequent two-day absence in August he was convicted of desertion and sentenced to death by firing squad, the order backed by Field Marshal Haig and duly carried out. He was thirty-two years old and is buried in the Ste-Catherine British Cemetery, Row F, Grave 1. The Commonwealth War Graves Commission website notes that he is remembered with honour.

It is not known how or when Charles's family were officially informed of his execution. Given that his widow would have received neither pension nor medals nor 'dead man's penny' after the war, she must have drawn the unavoidable conclusion sooner or later. She had his gravestone inscribed:

THOUGH DEATH PARTS
FOND MEMORIES CLING.

The Immingham War Memorial, in the village where Charles and his family had their home, sits on the green opposite the Market Buildings. It's made of Cornish granite and has on it the names of all twenty-eight of the village's men killed in the war. Charles is there with the rest, surname first then Christian name.

Back in Fulstow, where Charles was born, the villagers were initially keen to raise a memorial bearing the names of their seven dead. On being told than they could not include Charles's name – because of the manner of his death – the majority of them became so indignant at the slight they decided they would have no memorial of any kind.

And so it was and so it has always been. There has never been a service of remembrance in the local parish church, and although a village hall was erected to commemorate the dead of The Second World War, it makes no mention of the Great War.

By Remembrance Day 2005, eighty-seven years after the war ended, a memorial will be in place at Fulstow bearing the names of all ten Great War dead and five from the Second World War, including two women. Private Charles Kirman will be among them. Fulstow resident Nicola Pike first heard the story of the missing memorial in 1992 – in the pub, where all the best stories are told.

Impressed by the way the wartime villagers stuck to their guns and refused a memorial that left out one of their own, even if he had been shot for desertion, she set about bringing a long-unfinished story to a conclusion. On Remembrance Day 2005 all fifteen of Fulstow's dead from both wars, Private Charles Kirman included, will be represented by a modern-day villager, each the same age as the lost serviceman or woman at the time of their death. There will be a joint Methodist and Church of England service. A specially commissioned plaque will be unveiled. A space will be made for it on the outside wall of the village hall. Made of green slate, it will have on it each of the names, set in the order dictated by the dates of death, from first to last, either side of a depiction of a poppy:

THIS IS DEDICATED FOR THE MEN AND WOMEN OF FULSTOW WHO GAVE THEIR LIVES FOR OUR FREEDOM.

On the evening I spoke to Nicola on the phone, she and her family had just got in from the annual Lincolnshire Show. It had been a good day, and a long one. I could hear the voice of one of her little girls talking about 'Barbie' in the background. It was nice to hear Private Kirman's name being mentioned among the sounds of family activity.

I don't feel entitled to judge whether his death was wrongful or not. I've never been to war, never been under fire. I don't know how I would have behaved if I had lived his life. I do feel sorry that he died aged thirty-two because he couldn't cope with the circumstances in which he was placed by the war, and that he wasn't allowed to see his wife again, or to see his son and daughter grow up. 'This is a very small, close-knit community now,' Nicola said. 'It must have been even closer then.'

A total of 306 British soldiers were executed by their own side during the Great War for crimes ranging from murder and rape to cowardice, desertion, 'sleeping at post' or 'casting away arms'. From our perspective, some of them are hard stories to hear.

Opponents of rough justice say that men like Charles may have been suffering from any one of a number of emotional or mental traumas brought on by their experiences, and that the executions should never have taken place. Others say that in a time of war, when discipline was all that held a fighting force together, examples had to be made and justice enforced. They say it's misguided to revisit executions that were carried out at a time in British history when the death sentence was still firmly on the statute books.

There is a statue of a blindfolded boy soldier within the National Memorial Arboretum near Lichfield in Staffordshire. The figure stands near the River Tame at the eastern end of the site, as close as possible to the point where dawn first breaks. The memorial was sculpted by Birmingham art student Andrew De Comyn and represents every British soldier 'shot at dawn' during the Great War. Arranged behind the figure is an arc of 306 wooden posts, each with a plaque bearing the name of one of the dead men. Cypress trees in front of the statue represent a firing squad.

The larger-than-life-size statue is a likeness of Private Herbert Burden, service number 3882, 1st Battalion, Northumberland Fusiliers, shot for desertion on 21 July 1915. He was seventeen and had joined up aged sixteen after giving a false age.

The memorial was unveiled by eighty-seven-year-old Gertie Harris, daughter of 8871 Private Harry Farr. Harry had enlisted with the West Yorkshire Regiment, the Prince of Wales's Own, in 1914, but by the following year he was suffering from shell shock and had to be admitted to hospital. Apparently he shook so uncontrollably the nurses had to take turns to write his letters home. He recovered in time for the battle of the Somme but suffered a relapse and asked for more medical treatment, which was refused.

He was eventually convicted of desertion and shot by firing squad, on 18 October, aged twenty-five. Back home in Church Street, Hampstead, his wife Gertie received a pension for a while, but only by mistake. It was soon stopped. His name has since been added to the memorial at Thiepval.

In the French village of Bailleulmont, close to Arras, is a communal cemetery. Part of it is given over to the graves of thirty or so British Great War soldiers. Side by side in Row B, Graves

12 and 13, are Private 10495 Albert Ingham, aged twenty-four, and Private 10502 Alfred Longshaw, aged twenty-one, both of the 18th Battalion, Manchester Regiment.

Good friends back home, where they were clerks in the Salford goods yard, they joined up together and eventually found themselves at the Somme, via a stint in Egypt. They fought in the battle but deserted together on 16 October, making it as far as the port of Dieppe, where they tried to stow away on a Swiss ship. When they were discovered they were wearing civilian clothes and trying to pass themselves off as American citizens.

They were eventually handed over to a court martial, found guilty of desertion and both shot by firing squad on 1 December 1916.

Alfred was the son of Charles and Elizabeth Longshaw, and the family home was at Pendleton in Manchester. Albert's mother and father were George and Eliza, of Lower Kersal. To begin with, and for a long time thereafter, both families believed what the authorities had told them, that their boys had 'died of wounds'. Years later George Ingham found out that his son's fatal wounds had been inflicted by a British firing squad. He had Albert's gravestone at Bailleulmont changed. The personal inscription on it now reads:

SHOT AT DAWN
ONE OF THE FIRST TO ENLIST
A WORTHY SON
OF HIS FATHER.

When it came to executions for military crimes such as desertion, the British army under Field Marshal Haig was the most committed of the Great War's protagonists. Records show that the Germans shot fewer than thirty of their own men, and the Belgians were, by comparison to Britain, similarly restrained. The Americans shot not a single man and the Australians, despite pressure from Haig, also refused to carry out any executions. In fact the

British army brought nearly 40,000 of its servicemen to trial during the Great War, and for a multitude of alleged crimes. More than two thousand of these were initially sentenced to death, although nearly 90 per cent were reprieved.

Sergeant Joseph William 'Will' Stones was only 5 feet 2 inches tall. Officially he was too short to enlist, but the 19th Battalion of the Durham Light Infantry were glad to have him just the same. He survived the Somme, but towards the end of 1916 was accused of throwing away his rifle and sent before a court martial. In his defence he insisted he had not thrown the weapon away – a crime of cowardice punishable by death – but had used it to try to block the path of German soldiers pursuing him along a trench. Five defence witnesses, all of them officers, testified that Will was 'always brave and bold, the last man capable of cowardly action.'

He was found guilty and shot by firing squad on 18 January 1917. He was twenty-five, and is buried in Row D, Grave 1, in the St-Pol Communal Cemetery Extension.

His twenty-one-year-old wife Elizabeth, living in Wheatbottom, Crook, County Durham, approached the authorities about a pension for herself and for the couple's two daughters. She was told, 'The British Army does not give pensions to cowards.'

A campaign to win full pardons for some of the 306 has been under way since 1990. It is a difficult judgement call for anyone to make now. Spokesmen for the campaign, Shot at Dawn, have said than they do not expect pardons for those convicted of crimes like murder and rape. One soldier was shot for the imprisonment and rape of a mother and her daughter, followed by the murder of both with a bayonet. Shot at Dawn have said that the men shot for 'cowardice', 'desertion', 'sleeping at post' and, like Sergeant Will Stones, 'casting away arms' deserve to have their names cleared.

John Hughes Wilson and Cathryn Corns, co-authors of *Blindfold and Alone*, say it ought to be remembered that many of the British soldiers convicted of offences during the Great War were recidivists – repeat offenders, men who had been criminals in civilian life and just happened to commit further crimes while in the army. They have argued that such characters probably deserved whatever punishment was meted out to them. There are also those who simply made mistakes. Making a mistake in a time and place of war – the kind of mistake deemed to endanger the lives of other men – is always a bad move. In the case of a sergeant like Will Stones, the pay book he carried in his pocket made it clear to him that he would be shot if he 'cast away' his rifle in the face of the enemy. An experienced soldier like him would have known that his rifle was for shooting, bayoneting or clubbing the enemy – and most certainly not to be left behind to block his path or trip him up. He would have understood the consequences of his actions.

Maybe one side or the other in the debate will be proved right eventually. Perhaps too much time has gone by – every witness to every court martial is dead now, and what written evidence was available at the time is mostly lost. How can any of the cases be properly reinvestigated?

It's not hard to imagine that some of those who ran away, or were seen to have failed in some crucial way at some crucial moment, were just unlucky. No doubt a few were men and boys who never stood much of a chance of surviving army life anyway – the sort with the wrong sense of humour, who were no good at sports or games; the kind that were always bullied by their peers, inside the army or without. Perhaps they had enlisted in the hope of escaping from lives that were already unbearable – maybe they thought the army would provide them with the friends they had failed to make at home. From where we stand it is hard to judge them – or those who accused and convicted and executed them. We weren't there, we don't know the details of what happened, and we never will.

It will always be hard to read about frightened, sleepless teenage boys being shot at dawn by firing squads.

The last words attributed to one of them, spoken as he was being restrained at a wooden post with his hands behind his back at the dawn of his own execution, were: 'But what will my mum say?'

SURVIVORS

48

The Unexpected Guest

Many of those who came to look upon the war as waste and sham
did so, not at the time of the armistice, but through the lens of
penury and disillusionment that characterised the postwar
years for all too many of them.

Richard Holmes, Tommy:
The British Soldier on the Western Front 1914–1918

The Armistice brought the fighting of the Great War to an end
at eleven o'clock on the morning of 11 November, 1918. In
every way that mattered it was an arbitrary moment in time, and
in that way of arbitrary moments – like the scheduled departure
of a train – it was the wrong time for those caught on the wrong
side of it. There is a poignancy about the deaths that came in the
days and hours just before the calm of the ceasefire descended.

The BBC website hosts an 'interactive memorial' that remembers 863 men and women on the Allied side who lost their lives
on that final day. There's a soft-focus photograph of a landscape,
some Flanders poppies in the foreground. The site is animated
and random surnames appear, seven at a time. Click on one and
you find out a few brief details about a person: 'T. Duffy, 278th
Siege Bty, Royal Garrison Artillery, aged 25'; 'Frank Leslie Olive,
Private, 24th Battalion, Machine Gun Corps, aged 19, died of
wounds.'

Private Olive was the son of George and Alice, of West Ealing in London. He is buried in the Awoingt British Cemetery, Plot 3, Row D, Grave 3.

Eight hundred and sixty-three: getting on for a thousand of them, men and women who just missed the train.

War poet Wilfred Owen had enlisted with the Artists' Rifles in October 1915 and gained his commission into the 5th Battalion, Manchester Regiment, the following June. Injured in fighting and sent home in March 1917, in time for his meeting with Sassoon, he was back in the thick of it by August 1918. He was killed during a German machine-gun attack on 4 November. He was twenty-five. It's said the church bells were ringing out the news of the Armistice, near his parents' home in Shrewsbury, when the telegram was delivered to their door. He is buried in Ors Communal Cemetery, Row A, Grave 3. Only a few of his war poems were published while he was alive.

The Armistice made no difference either to Donald MacLennan, Fair Donald from the lonely island of Scarp, off the coast of Harris in the Western Isles of Scotland.

I asked about him while I was up there, but there didn't seem to be much information to be had any more. I gathered he did his time in the trenches but that at some point, towards the end of the war, he was taken ill with a stomach ailment. He was shipped back to Britain for hospital treatment but died on 15 November 1918, four days after the fighting stopped.

For those who survived, the coming of peace had to be greeted as the unexpected guest it was. Some met it with relief and joy; others could only look up in disbelief. Men who had been keeping their heads down, grinding on through the daily routines, had suddenly to look towards an uncertain future. As servicemen on active duty it had been little help to look too far ahead. Life at war was structured, regimented, and it had paid to just get on with the moment in hand without wondering what the long-term future might hold. The ending of the war took away those certainties – and the change would take a lot of getting used to.

Corporal Clifford Lane, 1st Battalion, Hertfordshire Regiment, said:

> As far as the Armistice itself was concerned, it was a kind of anticlimax. We were too far gone, too exhausted really, to enjoy it. All we wanted to do was go back to our billets, there was no cheering, no singing. That day we had no alcohol at all. We simply celebrated the Armistice in silence and thankfulness that it was all over. And I believe that happened quite a lot in France. It was such a sense of anticlimax. We were drained of all emotion. That's what it amounted to. (Quoted in Max Arthur, *Forgotten Voices of the Great War*)

There was hardly any sense of completion, either. To all intents and purposes the Allies had won the war by the time the Kaiser abdicated and the German republic asked for, and was granted, a ceasefire on 11 November 1918. The once mighty German army had been comprehensively defeated.

Many British soldiers felt cheated that final victory had been snatched out of their grasp just as it came within reach. They had spent years learning how to fight a modern war in a modern way. They had got better and better as time passed, and finally they had done what had to be done to get the job finished. They had defeated the enemy in every way that mattered, and now many of them wanted to chase the Germans all the way back to Berlin.

Never mind letting the Kaiser off – there was a lot of talk in the ranks of hanging him.

It was not to be.

The Armistice was treated as no more than a break in the fighting to begin with, and some could not find it in their self-preserving hearts to accept that it meant the war was actually over. That absolute certainty would not come until the signing of the Treaty of Versailles the following year – and it explains why around one in every four memorials to the Great War has it that the conflict lasted between 1914 and 1919.

Men who had joined up from the lower social classes as privates, and who had been promoted to positions of authority, faced an especially harsh new reality. In the armed forces they were *somebody* – leaders of men, who had earned and won respect and spent their days doing something that mattered. Such men realised – or were made to realise – that civilian life meant a return to circumstances they preferred not to remember. It was a long drop, from decorated officer in charge of scores of men to the sales counter of a city department store; or to the accounts office of a factory saying 'yes, sir; no, sir' to some pot-bellied, jumped-up nobody with a chip on his shoulder.

Some, particularly the conscripts, believed they ceased to be soldiers as soon as the hour of the Armistice was reached. They were wrong; and for many the process of demobilisation was long and tortured. Men at home on leave – perhaps naturally assuming they were home for good now the war was over – found themselves ordered to rejoin their units overseas as though the ceasefire had never happened. The war might be over, but the peace had to maintained and policed. For some it was too much to take, and there were mutinous riots in places such as Folkestone, and demonstrations in London.

The initial plan for demobilisation divided the men into groups – with those most likely to find work positioned at the head of the queue. Men conscripted most recently were likely to have retained connections to the civilian jobs they had left behind, which led to a tendency towards 'last in, first out'. This policy was obviously unfair – effectively penalising those men who had been away from home the longest – and was to all intents and purposes abandoned within weeks of its introduction. As 1919 wore on the process speeded up, but by February 1920 125,000 were still waiting for 'demob'. It was a long way back to the world left behind – if not in miles, then in time.

They were promised 'a land fit for heroes', but the reality was often different, and much less glamorous for most. The men may have changed, been changed by their experiences of war, but age-old enemies like unemployment were still there to be fought every day as they always had been.

The great and the good of Luton organised a party for 19 July 1919 to celebrate the signing of the peace treaty. Among other frills they planned a grand victory procession accompanied by brass bands and fireworks. There was to be a lavish dinner too, and most of it paid for out of the public purse.

Unfortunately for all concerned, the great and the good decided that a fixed number of veterans would be allowed – and all of those would have to pay their own expenses. On hearing about the plans the veterans attempted to organise their own do. The councillors promptly banned them from their venue of choice – Wardown Park – and the stage was set for trouble.

On the day, hordes of angry former soldiers confronted the leaders of the official parade. Trouble started on Upper George Street and the mayor was jeered as he tried to make his speech. There was more verbal abuse as the parade made its way to the town hall. Once the mayor was inside, a mob broke down the doors and vandalised the place. They calmed down when the pubs opened and many of the rioters retired for a drink. But later that night shops were looted and torched, and on a piano that had been dragged into the street someone began to play 'Keep the Home Fires Burning'. The trouble took days to settle down, and several of the rioters were given jail sentences.

Men who had survived a war, only to return home to a Britain where the fight for survival continued, even found some aspects of remembrance and commemoration hard to take. Armistice Day ceremonies in 1921 featured demonstrations by unemployed men – ex-soldiers all – carrying placards saying:

> THE DEAD ARE REMEMBERED
> BUT WE ARE FORGOTTEN.

In the trenches they had adapted to a world that was dangerous yes, but where they could rely on the tribal certainties of brotherhood – one where they could trust their fellow soldiers and know that they were trusted in return. The civilian world they came back to – in which their sufferings and sacrifices were soon meaningless, worthless, forgotten – must have seemed wholly lacking in the values they had become accustomed to during their time away.

For those who could find work, there were increased wages to enjoy. A man who marched away from a farm labouring job paying 13s 4d a week in 1914 returned to find it offered 46s by 1920. Average family incomes rose by 100 per cent during the four years of war – and although the cost of living had gone up by 75 per cent, the improvement was noticeable.

Against this background of improvement for some, those who could not find jobs were understandably angry. Having helped fight and win a war, they expected at least to return to the prospect of a living wage. Instead the country inflicted the disgrace of hardship and poverty upon men who had risked their lives in its defence. Ten years after the first anniversary of Armistice Day, veterans marched past the Cenotaph with pawn tickets on their lapels in place of their medals.

Thomas Whitham won the Victoria Cross at Pilckem, in Passchendaele, during the Third Battle of Ypres, on 31 July 1917. He came home to Burnley a hero, receiving a gold watch from the council as a mark of its respect. They even had his portrait painted.

Time passed and people's attention moved elsewhere. Thomas asked the council for a labouring job, but they turned him down. Like many veterans, he pawned his VC in exchange for some badly needed ready cash. Eventually he had to leave the area in search of a job, and it was while he was away working, in 1924, that he was injured badly enough to lose his memory. Cut off from his wife and their six young children, he died a pauper's death in the Oldham Royal Infirmary on 22 October 1924.

The council bought his VC from the pawnshop for £50 and put in on display in the local museum. It's still there.

Private Sam Harvey got his Victoria Cross at the battle of Loos in 1915 and died penniless in a hostel for the homeless in 1960. He had survived the charnel house that claimed so many, but was buried in a pauper's grave. Recently the Western Front Association set about organising a more fitting burial for Sam, but his VC has never been found.

If it was often hard for able-bodied veterans to find work, it was even more difficult for those who had been disabled by their injuries. By the time the fighting stopped some 1.2 million ex-servicemen were entitled to a disability pension – around a quarter of all who had served – and by the start of the Second World War there were still over 640,000 claiming money from the state for injuries suffered during the Great War. Predictably, it was often women who had to bear much of the burden, taking care of men permanently damaged. Many had worked through-out the war to keep their families housed, fed and clothed while their men were at the front. Now countless thousands of them had no option but to remain in the role of major breadwinner to support an invalid husband as well.

Unemployment was, not surprisingly, an even bigger problem for the disabled than for the able-bodied. On the streets of towns and cities throughout the land fit for heroes it became relatively commonplace to see disabled former soldiers begging for a living.

The King's Roll scheme was set up in 1918 to encourage employers to find places for men disabled by the war. Any company having a workforce comprising at least 5 per cent disabled men was entitled to put the King's Roll stamp on its letterhead – assuring it preferential treatment when it came to pitching for government contracts.

There were also some attempts to provide training schemes for the disabled, one of which taught boot-making. Perhaps predictably, all the efforts tended to make life easier for those less severely disabled. Those who had been damaged most suffered most. Philanthropic and charitable organisations were set up to try to help, and by 1918 there were more than six thousand registered, of which five hundred were still on the books by 1936.

Men who came back from the war with visible physical injuries were easier for the mass of the population to accept, understand. Those with mental illnesses brought on by the experiences of the front were another matter. By the end of the Great War, the British army had dealt with 80,000 cases of 'shell shock' alone.

The Maghull Hospital, near Liverpool, opened in 1878 as a convalescent home for youngsters from the city's workhouses. In 1914 it was sold to the then Lunacy Board of Control. Throughout the war it served as a military hospital specialising in the treatment of shell shock. New standards of care for mental illness caused by the war were established by the Knutsford hospitals. Each could take around thirty patients at a time, and men held there were treated more sensitively and with more dignity than those in conventional asylums. They were not, however, available to the majority.

Officers like Wilfred Owen and Siegfried Sassoon benefited from a standard of treatment for mental and emotional trauma that was in the main restricted to a privileged few. Owen arrived at Craiglockhart Hospital suffering from neurasthenia, the 'nervous debility' more commonly known at the time as 'shell shock'.

Craiglockhart Hospital had been taken over by the army in 1916 and was home at any one time to around 150 officers suffering from neurasthenia. The condition was little understood, and in many cases men were expected simply to 'snap out of it' under a regime of stern, uncomprehending discipline. At Craiglockhart, under revolutionary thinkers like Dr A. J. Brock, Dr W. Bryce and Dr W. H. R. Rivers, it was different. Damaged and wounded men were treated with a new level of understanding that was hard to come by elsewhere. And it was of course limited to the officer class only.

During his period of treatment Owen taught classes at a local school and edited the hospital magazine. When Dr Brock discovered that Owen was an aspiring poet, he encouraged him to carry on with his writing. The four months of his stay there are thought to have been among the most productive of his short life. Both 'Anthem for Doomed Youth' and 'Dulce Et Decorum Est' were written during his time in Edinburgh.

Sassoon arrived at Craiglockhart – which he nicknamed 'Dottyville' – about a month after Owen. Gradually the pair formed a friendship. Sassoon was the established writer of the pair but he spotted Owen's ability as a fellow poet. The works published during Owen's lifetime were helped on their way by Sassoon.

Rivers was not of the opinion that Sassoon needed to be 'cured' of anything. He was a man who had simply reached a point where he had seen enough killing and dying, and he wanted to see or cause no more of it; an understandable point of view perhaps, but one hardly likely to carry much weight with Sassoon's military superiors. Doctor and patient met regularly all the same. By the time Sassoon was discharged, back to active duty, the two had forged a bond that remained close until Rivers's death in 1922.

During the war the Lunacy Board of Control also took over parts of the Wandsworth and Napsbury hospitals for the treatment of servicemen. Supposedly cheery postcards of patients at Napsbury – often of men suffering mental illness – were circulated during the war as part of an attempt to boost morale, presumably by showing the care being offered to wounded men and their plucky refusal to be laid low. The practice was gradually phased out, and by the end of the war there was some appreciation of the need for sensitivity and understanding when it came to treating illnesses that did not display obvious physical symptoms.

Veterans also had to deal with the fact that the war they had just fought – specifically the battlefields themselves – had excited almost uncontrollable curiosity among the folks back home.

From London it was barely 70 miles, as the crow flies, to parts of the Western Front. When the allies detonated 1.5 million tons of explosives underneath the German lines at Messines, in 1917, the blast was heard in Downing Street. People who had either missed out on or avoided being sent there as soldiers now wanted to visit places like the Somme, Ypres and the Vimy Ridge as tourists.

As early as 1914 stunned observers on the Western Front were seeing civilians on the battlefields in search of souvenirs. In 1915 the travel company Thomas Cook had to go to the lengths of taking out an advert in *The Times* asking the public to stop making enquiries to them about the availability of tours of the Great War battlefields, 'until the war is over'. By 1919 that same company, along with many others, was making a healthy profit out of taking parties out to the erstwhile killing fields.

49

What if . . . ?

'Home at last!' they whispered, as glowed the shore-lights bright
'There lies the bay, and Arnish Light is gleaming through the night:
  Go, get your kit-bags ready, for the voyage now is o'er,
And grand will be our welcome on our well-beloved shore. Home at
last!'

  'Home at last,' they murmured. 'Our sorrows now are fled,
Ah! Sweet will be the pale-blue smoke of our peat fires burning red
  And won't we tell the stories of the dreadful years now past,
Of all our wild adventures now we are home at last. Home at last!'

They dreamed of lonely hamlets by the edge of the moaning deep;
  They saw the Harris Hills so still, in their purple-cradled sleep;
  And the brooding moorland called to them as a mother to her child;
Their hearts were in the heather, they heard the voice and smiled –
Home at last!

They heard the seagulls screaming where the blue sea breaks in foam;
  And the soft melodious ripple of the brooklet by their home;
  And their hearts were full of music, and fair dreams hovered near,
For there were the lights of Stornoway, and yonder loomed the pier.
Home at last!

  So near their home, and yet so far that never, never more
They'll roam the dreaming moorland, or by the lone sea-shore.
  Theirs be the calm of heaven, the peace the world denied,
After life's cruel tempest, the hush of eventide. Home at last!

                                    John N. Maciver, 'Home at Last'

257

William Hesketh Lever was born in Bolton, in Lancashire, in 1851. He was the first son of the family, after six daughters. His father was a wholesale grocer and took young William out of school and into the family business at the earliest opportunity. To begin with, the boy was put to work cutting and stacking blocks of sugar.

In 1886 he joined forces with his younger brother James to form Lever Brothers, based in Warrington, making and selling soap from vegetable oils. Together they made a fortune, and by 1888 William had built an entire town for his workforce, near Liverpool. He called it Port Sunlight, after his soap, and made it a model industrial town to give his employees good living conditions. It was the first product of the paternal attitude that would shape his thinking and business dealings from then on.

He took his ideas of social engineering to the Western Isles of Scotland when, in 1918, he bought the entire island of Lewis. His plan was to eradicate poverty, as he saw it, and to turn Stornoway into an industrial town. There would be a fish canning business on a grand scale – and he did manage to start the MacFisheries business that would eventually have outlets in towns throughout Britain. He spent huge sums of money on the dream – and in 1922 he was elevated to Viscount Leverhulme of the Western Isles for his troubles.

But the dream was not to be. There was large-scale opposition from the islanders themselves, even land raids. By 1923 the great philanthropist was so disenchanted he created the Stornoway Trust and simply gave 64,000 acres of the land back to the people and told them to get on with doing whatever they wanted. He moved on with plans for the neighbouring island of Harris and built a whaling station there, but little came of it. He died in 1925.

There is seldom a single reason for the failure of a grand idea.

But after the sinking of HMY *Iolaire*, enthusiasm for anything on Lewis, let alone a new business venture from an incomer, was hard to come by.

When those 205 seamen drowned in the early hours of New Year's morning, 1919, it was Lewis itself which stopped breathing. Men who would have returned the lifeblood missing from the island for four years were gone for ever. Lewis was wounded so grievously that morning it would never fully recover.

Instead of looking to the future, men with grappling irons pulled bodies from the waters around Holm and laid them gently on the grass above the high-water mark.

The *Scotsman* newspaper said on 6 January:

> The villages of Lewis are like places of the dead. No one goes about except on duties that cannot be left undone. The homes of the island are full of lamentations – grief that cannot be comforted. Carts in little processions of twos and threes, each bearing its coffin from the mortuary, pass through the streets of Stornoway on their way to some rural village and all heads are bared as they pass. Scarcely a family has escaped the loss of some near blood relation. Many have had sorrow heaped on sorrow.

The *Stornoway Gazette* of 10 January said:

> No one now alive in Lewis can ever forget the 1st of January, 1919, and future generations will speak of it as the blackest day in the history of the island, for on it 200 of our bravest and best, perished on the very threshold of their homes, under the most tragic circumstances. The terrible disaster at Holm on New Year's morning has plunged every home and every heart in Lewis into grief unutterable. Language cannot express the anguish, the despair, which this awful catastrophe has inflicted.

Soon there were lists of the confirmed dead, compiled for each district and village and hamlet in turn.

Shawbost, with a population of 913, lost nine men out of a total of twelve known to have been aboard the *Iolaire*: John Smith, married with three children under school age; Donald Martin, married with three children; Donald Nicolson, married with seven children; bachelors Angus Macleod, Roderick Murray, Donald Macleod, Donald Gillies, Donald Macleod, son of Peter, Malcolm Macleod.

Barvas had had only one man aboard, Donald Macleod, only son of Mrs Macleod, lost.

Laxay had five men aboard and lost four: John Macleod; Angus Mackinnon; Alexander Macleod; Angus Montgomery.

District after district, the lists go on and on. They are almost impossible to take in.

Before long there was anger on the island, mixed in with the grief. Bereaved families wanted to know whether the crew of the *Iolaire* had been drinking – it being Old Year's Night and all. Word spread too about how a lifeboat had had to be dragged from its store at the naval base by nineteen sailors because there had been no horse to pull it. There was much talk about how it had taken four hours or more for any doctor to reach and tend to any of the seventy-nine men known to have survived the disaster.

A full-scale inquiry was held in Stornoway and its verdict written up in the *Scotsman* newspaper on 12 February. In answer to the first rumour, every witness said every member of the crew had been sober. The inquiry did decide, however: 'That the officer in charge did not exercise sufficient prudence in approaching the harbour; that the boat did not slow down, and that a look-out was not on duty at the time of the accident; that the number of lifebelts, boats and rafts was insufficient for the number of people carried . . .'

None of it offered much comfort to the people of Lewis.

There was an old man from Breascleit, grieving for a son drowned, who dreamed at night of seeing a body floating in a bay he knew well. He recounted his vision to the head of the recovery team in Stornoway and when they went to the bay, just to put the old man's mind at rest, they found his son's body floating there.

Donald 'The Patch' Morrison, the man who had climbed the mizzen mast to escape the sea, outlived his brother Angus by more than seventy years. Angus had been demobbed first but had waited for The Patch so they could make their homecoming together. They are buried now side by side.

The effect of the Great War upon the world was too enormous, too far reaching, for any understanding.

On Lewis, the impact of the sinking of the *Iolaire* was too much to bear. Its effect on the island does, though, demonstrate the effect of the Great War – of which it was a part, a consequence – on a scale that can be just about understood today.

The tragedy was a *coup de grâce* of sorts. Throughout the four years of the Great War, the Western Isles had given and given and given again. The loss seven weeks after the Armistice of another 205 of its men, most of them from the same island, was one final wound too many. It has been said that the bereaved never confronted the tragedy in any effective way, never dealt with or admitted to the extent of their grief.

Nowadays we would talk of such an event as having caused 'post-traumatic stress' and efforts would be made to help a community like Lewis move on from the loss. This was never done, and many of the bereaved went to their graves without ever talking about what had happened. Maybe it was, anyway, too dreadful for any help.

Instead of being reinvigorated by the return of the best of its men, Lewis was eviscerated. In the years to come there would be root-and-branch emigrations to North America and Canada and other far-flung places. The heart had been taken out of the island in a way that not even the passage of time would restore.

John Angus MacLeod was born on Harris in December 1919.

He and his wife now live in Largs, on the Scottish mainland, but his younger sister is still on the island, in the old family home. John Angus and his family have always made regular returns to the place.

His father, John Morison MacLeod, was born on the island in 1878. A seaman from the first, he got his mate's ticket on the SS *Sheila*, the same boat that made the regular crossings between the Kyle of Lochalsh and Stornoway.

By the time war broke out he was in the Royal Naval Volunteer Reserve (RNVR) and soon transferred from the *Sheila* to troop carriers. During his time on active service he had to land men on the beaches at Gallipoli, among other places.

Custom dictated that as the eldest son of his family he would inherit the family croft. Since his younger brother would get the house, the other part of the deal laid down by the custom, he was aware of the need to sort out a place to live. With this in mind he had used some of his time away from the boats to gradually build himself a house, in the hamlet of Drinishader. By 1912, it was finished.

He had also used some of his time to court Seonaid.

Seonaid had been in no big hurry to marry. She had started out working in the Harris Hotel in Tarbert and soon realised that visitors to the island were short on choice when it came to places to stop for a bite to eat. In Tarbert it was the Harris Hotel or nothing. She opened a tearoom in a traditional stone-built villa and soon the place was doing a roaring trade. She served up cups of coffee as well, an exotic novelty in Tarbert in the years before the Great War.

One weekend in August 1918, when she was thirty-five years old, she travelled to Glasgow with her youngest sister to be married to John Morison MacLeod, there on a short leave.

Seonaid had made it clear to John Morison, by the way, that she had no wish for them to live in his house at Drinishader. It was in the middle of nowhere, she said. There was no real road to it – just a track that weaved and wound its way for 3 miles or more round the coast and across streams.

It was just as well. Having been in no real hurry to marry himself, John Morison had some years before allowed his middle brother to move in – middle brothers doing worst of all out of the custom of inheritance, and being entitled to neither croft nor house nor much of anything else.

And so it was that John Morison and Seonaid MacLeod planned to move into the tearoom. It was in a big house and there would be room enough.

By the middle of December 1918 he was back on the *Sheila* as first mate. On the night of the 31st, Old Year's Night as it is in the Western Isles, the *Sheila* was astern of HMY *Iolaire* at the Kyle of Lochalsh when the sailors boarded her.

He remembered the atmosphere among the waiting men that night – all high spirits and laughter, the returning soldiers and sailors looking forward to some drinks and some music once the boats got under way.

Not long before they were due to cast off, word came from the *Iolaire* that she was an officer short. Could the *Sheila* spare a man to help with the crossing?

The skipper turned to John Morison: 'Pack a bag and get over to the *Iolaire*,' he said.

John did as he had been told, picked up his gear and climbed ashore from the steamer. He had reached the foot of the gangplank on to the yacht when the missing officer turned up, just in the nick of time. 'It's all right, I'm here,' he said. 'You can get back on the *Sheila*.'

And so it was and so they died.

After all was said and done, Seonaid informed her husband that she thought it was time he gave up the life on the boats. He would never be as lucky again.

Sure enough, he turned his back on sailing for a living and instead opened up a grocery shop next door to his wife's tearoom. Later on he bought an old lorry and converted it into a mobile shop so he could take supplies to the outlying homes and villages.

He would wonder from time to time what might have happened had he been aboard the *Iolaire* that night. He had made the crossing from Kyle to Stornoway on board the *Sheila* more times than he could count, in daylight and in darkness. Had he been on the bridge, surely the navy skipper would have heeded his instruction to follow *The Spider* fishing boat's line into the harbour? Surely the lives of the 205 men would have been saved?

Maybe, but who really knows?

Back in Largs, John Angus reminded me of his own birthday – that he was not conceived until the spring of 1919, not born until the December. 'If my dad had got on the *Iolaire* that night, maybe you and I would not be having this conversation,' he said.

I told him about my grandpa – how it's family legend that a German 'whizz-bang' shell landed beside him on the Menin Road but didn't detonate. That was long before my own dad was a twinkle in Grandpa's eye.

John Angus and I had one of those 'what if?' conversations then. They're always strange, fun at the time but vaguely disconcerting.

But for a nick-of-time officer at the Kyle of Lochalsh and a dodgy German detonator inside a shell on the Menin Road outside Ypres, just who would have been sitting in the front room of that house on Brisbane Street in Largs that day?

I love stories like these. I love the connections they make between me and other people. John Angus is a good few years older than my dad, but through stories of our families in the Great War any distance between us is diminished to the point where it doesn't matter at all.

Today we think of the Great War as ancient history – the veterans of the Second World War are mostly in their eighties nowadays, never mind those men who fought between 1914 and 1918.

John Angus and I can get all the way back to 1918 in a single step.

Beside the main drag through Tarbert, on John Angus's home island of Harris, a memorial to some of the island's dead sits in a little garden. The road sits high and the memorial commands a grand view out over water and heather-covered hillsides. It's a quite impressive structure – a granite tower topped with crenellations that give it the look of a miniature keep. A Union Jack snaps in the breeze at the top of its flagpole. There's a panel on each of the tower's four sides, bearing name after name. You have to keep reminding yourself of the size of villages like Tarbert as the lists run on and on. Black Watch; Scots Guards; Camerons; Seaforths; Royal Navy; and a dozen more regiments besides. McAskills, McLeods, Campbells, McDonalds, McKinnons, Morrisons. All gone.

As befits a memorial in the Western Isles, the dedication is in Gaelic. I asked John Angus to translate it for me:

FAITHFUL UNTIL DEATH
THIS IS A MARK AND A MEMORIAL
OF OUR BELOVED SOLDIERS
IN PROTECTING OUR KINGDOM FOR US
UNDER THE HAND OF THE HIGHEST
WHO STOOD STRONGLY AND STAUNCHLY
AND FAITHFUL UNTIL DEATH
AS ALL OF OUR FOREFATHERS DID
FROM AGE TO AGE AND EVERYPLACE.

On the neighbouring island of Lewis, on a cliff top on Holm itself, high above the Beasts of Holm and the site of the wreck of the *Iolaire*, there is a memorial to her dead. In 1970 divers hunting for clams found the ship's bell and a plaque from one of its engines. They are kept by Stornoway Town Council.

An elegant tower dominates the skyline of all the approaches to the town of Stornoway itself. Rising out of the 300-foot-high knoll known as Cnoc nan Uan, it is both unmistakable and unforgettable. It had to be.

According to the 1911 census, there were just over 29,600 people living on the island of Lewis, in the Western Isles. More than 6,700 of the men served in the armed forces during the Great War. Some 17 per cent of them – 1,151 – were dead by the end of it. In terms of percentage of population, Lewis had lost more than twice as many men as any other part of Britain.

Against this already tragic backdrop, the loss of the men drowned on the *Iolaire* was too much more to bear. There were calls from every parish on the island for a fitting memorial to those who had died in the service of their country.

Lord Leverhulme was made chairman of a committee set up in 1920 to raise the necessary funds. He offered to double any amount raised by private subscriptions and donations, and with estimates for the construction work running as high as £20,000, a huge sum in 1920, it seemed clear they would need all the help they could get.

Artists and sculptors were invited to submit plans and ideas and J. H. Gall of Inverness was the man chosen for the job. In the end, the monument was completed for just a fifth of the estimated price and was unveiled to the public on 24 September 1924. It stands all of 85 feet tall, built of local Lewisian gneiss stone, and casts a brooding presence over the surrounding land.

Staircases in the central entrance chamber lead to four separate chambers above, each representing one of the parishes of Lewis. Bronze plaques bearing all the names of the dead lined the walls of each chamber. Two thousand people attended the opening ceremony, conducted by Lord Leverhulme, and the tower served its original purpose until 1975. The weather of the Western Isles, which had shaped and toughened the men who went off to war, had proved too much for the memorial made to commemorate them. Age had wearied *and* condemned it.

There were attempts to repair the damage in 1981 and 1982 and then again in 1990, but so far nothing has worked well enough to allow the tower to be reopened. The sixteen plaques bearing the names of the dead have been moved from their original positions inside the tower. Now they are mounted outside, where people can see them. Seats have been added as well, to give visitors somewhere to rest.

50

In Memoriam

On 1 July this year I bought *The Times* and the *Daily Telegraph* – what they used to call the quality newspapers. It was the anniversary of the first day of the First Battle of the Somme and I wanted to see the 'In memoriam' sections; I wanted to see who was being remembered.

There was nothing in *The Times*, not a single one (although they had remembered, on page seventy-two, that 1 July was the anniversary of the Somme *and* of the Battle of the Boyne in 1690, when the army of William III defeated that of James II).

I phoned the paper and asked whether they had done away with their 'In memoriam' section, but the lady on the other end of the line said there must simply have not been any booked for that day.

In the *Telegraph* there were nine: five for people who had died in other years and the other four remembering events in 1916. Under 'In memoriam' in a strangely pale, ghostly font, it said:

THEIR NAME LIVETH FOR EVERMORE.

And then there they were:

DISBREY. – 15812 Pte. Billy Disbrey. 11th Suffolks. Of Barton, Cambs. Killed at La Boiselle, Somme, July 1st, 1916. Remembered by his family.

JULY 1st 1916. – In memory of all who fell that day. 'Where once there was war, now peace reigns supreme, and the birds sing again in Mametz.' Friends of Lochnagar.

In Memoriam

KIRKWOOD. – Sgt. ALFRED KIA Somme 1916 and his brother CSM JOHN KIRKWOOD KIA, on 6th July, both with the Liverpool Pals KLR. Remembered by their nephew John Kirkwood.

WATKINS. – Corporal FRANCIS WATKINS M.M. Sheffield City Battalion 12th York and Lancaster Regiment, killed on the Somme July 1st 1916, aged 32 years. Remembered by his grandchildren. R.I.P.

Remembered after all this time. RIP.

On page two of *The Times* there was one of those little stories, a single-paragraph, single-column filler. It was headlined 'Veteran dies': 'One of Scotland's last veterans of the First World War has died at the age of 108. Bill Elder, born in Selkirk in 1897, fought in two battles at Ypres with the Royal Garrison Artillery and also survived the Somme. He later worked for the Duke of Buccleuch at his estate near Kettering, Northamptonshire.'

Survived the Somme. He was born around the same time as my grandpa, who survived the Somme as well. Just imagine. The Somme sounds like something inflicted upon men of the ancient past, like the fight for Troy, but some of the warriors are still here. I started wondering what Bill Elder made of the world of 2005, how it compared to the world of his youth and young manhood.

I wondered too what the men who did not survive the Somme would have said if they could have seen the stories in my copies of *The Times* and the *Telegraph* for 1 July 2005.

Another single-column filler on page two of *The Times* was headlined 'A line not toed': 'Raymond Perrett, 101, of York, the last crewman to run up HMS Victory's signal flags, on Trafalgar Day in 1921, has been told to wait 12 months for the NHS to clip his toenails. His family has been forced to find private care. 'You'd think they would take his age into account,' Mr Perrett's son, Chris, said.

Mr Perrett must have been born around 1904. He would have been fourteen or so when the Great War ended. The short-comings of a land fit for heroes do not always improve with the passage of time, it seems.

Elsewhere in the papers were stories that would have shown the men of the Somme that nothing, not their war nor any other, would bring an end to violence. In Israel, a place that didn't exist in 1916, the government had sealed off the Gaza Strip and was evicting Jewish settlers by beating them with batons.

Abigail Witchall, a pregnant twenty-six-year-old Surrey mother stabbed and paralysed from the neck down by an attacker while she walked home with her twenty-one-month-old son, was making progress in her long battle for recovery. She had some feeling back in her limbs. 'I'm in good hands and feel incredibly blessed,' she said.

The National Archives had released previously classified War Office files that revealed the results of a top-secret 1950s experiment to find the perfect string vest. Soldiers from the 1st Battalion, Royal Warwickshire Regiment, were subjected to the tests by men from the Directorate of Physiological and Biological Research at the Clothing and Stores Experimental Establishment in 1955.

Spread across two pages of *The Times* was an advert for Tom Cruise's latest movie, *War of the Worlds*. H. G. Wells wrote that story in 1898. Its readers could hardly have imagined that the war that would envelop the world in 1914 was going to be just as terrible as anything likely to be visited upon them by the inhabitants of Mars.

Soldiers pulling nervously on last cigarettes as they waited for the signal to climb out of their trenches and walk in lines across the no man's land of the Somme could have read about MSPs in Scotland voting to ban smoking in public places. In South Korea, the government was in crisis following the release of photos of naked soldiers in its army being physically abused and humiliated by their officers.

A man who was sexually abused from the age of seven by a Catholic priest, and who now suffered from schizophrenia and post-traumatic stress disorder that made it impossible for him to hold down a job, had been awarded £600,000 in compensation.

And so it went on. The *Telegraph* had a piece about teenagers risking rickets by spending too much time indoors. A professor from Newcastle General Hospital said their bodies were not receiving enough sunshine for the synthesis of vitamin D. Some of them were going outside for less than an hour a day.

A forty-one-year-old woman out shopping in Manchester was shot in the leg by a bullet fired from a gun dropped by a man walking behind her: 'The gunman was seen to pick up something but shouted, "It's a firework", before running off, stopping only to remove open-toe sandals that had hampered his escape from several pursuers.'

Scotland was preparing itself for an expected invasion by thousands of protesters keen to urge the leaders of the world's richest countries, meeting at Gleneagles for the G8 summit, to take all possible steps to end world poverty. And an American woman had had the web address of a gambling site tattooed on her forehead after selling it as advertising space on eBay for $10,000.

On the front page of *The Times* there was a little photograph of rugby player Jonny Wilkinson's hands, clasped in familiar style in preparation for a goal kick. Beside the photo was a quote from him saying: 'I feel like a soldier on the eve of battle.' It was a trailer for a story inside in which he talked about his nerves before the Lions' second match against the All Blacks in Wellington, New Zealand. He'd been talking to a couple of the team's security men, former Marines, about how they dealt with pre-battle anxiety. 'I have sometimes wondered what soldiers feel when they go to war,' he wrote. 'Do they feel anything similar to the way we feel . . . Don't get me wrong, I appreciate that my experience with rugby is not a patch in comparison.'

Had Jonny or the editorial team at *The Times* remembered

the significance of the date at the top of the page when they contemplated likening a rugby match to a battle?

(The content of the newspapers of 1916 was stunning enough for the men of the Somme. Those who survived the opening days could only marvel at print coverage that suggested it was all going jolly well, really, and that victory was inevitable.)

It was so depressing. On the BBC news on television that night there were reports of ethnic cleansing in Darfur in Sudan, pictures of walking skeletons in dazzling bright clothes, dying in the desert.

In Zimbabwe President Robert Mugabe was demolishing the homes of some of his poorest people.

All over the world there were final preparations for the Live 8 pop music concerts. Musicians like Bob Geldof and Sting would be saying what they said twenty years earlier at the Live Aid concerts – that it was wrong for people to starve and die in Africa when the governments of the rich countries had it in their gift to stop it.

And would those men who climbed out of their trenches on the morning of 1 July 1916 have been surprised to read those four 'In memoriam' messages? Could they have realised then that what they were about to do would be remembered with such sadness nearly ninety years later?

Remembrance – beyond anything commanded in breathless prose on war memorials – is in the details; like the thoughts spared for Private Billy Disbrey, and Sergeant Alfred Kirkwood and Corporal Francis Watkins.

Mention of their names means they are not forgotten.

51

An Endless River

The whole texture of British daily life could be said to
commemorate the war still. It is remembered in the odd pub-closing
hours, one of the fruits of the Defence of the Realm Act; the
afternoon closing was originally designed, it was said, to discourage
the munitions workers of 1915 from idling away their afternoons
over beer. The Great War persists in many of the laws controlling
aliens and repressing sedition and espionage. 'D'-notices to
newspapers, warning them off 'national-security matters', are
another legacy. So is Summer Time. So are such apparent universals
as cigarette-smoking, the use of wristwatches (originally a trench
fad), the cultivation of garden 'allotments' (Food Will Win the
War). So is the use of paper banknotes, entirely replacing gold
coins. The playing of 'God Save the King' in theatres began in 1914
and persisted until the 1970s, whose flagrant cynicisms finally
brought an end to the custom.

Paul Fussel, The Great War and Modern Memory

The Great War is distant now, far off in time. Its sounds and
voices have diminished to a few final whispers. A handful of
our oldest men were there and remember it as something real.
For everyone else it's the stuff of faded photographs, museum
exhibits and rows and rows of books.

The ceremony of remembrance, held every year on the Sunday
closest to 11 November, has become a ritual that's repeated

almost for the sake of repetition. The Queen and the rest of the royal family lay the same wreaths at the Cenotaph in Whitehall, in the same order and in the same places. Then all the rest of the wreaths are laid down too until there are heaps of poppies around its base.

Once upon a time it may have looked like blood pooling there, but not any more. The focus on the image has been made soft and blurred by age. There is no angry grief left for the dead of the Great War. They have no blood left to shed.

Watching the ceremony unfold now, the march-past of the veterans of other wars, the long lines of relatives, it's hard to concentrate on what's actually happening and what it all means. If they played a tape of last year's events instead, how long would it be before any of us noticed?

Even the impact of the set pieces of the war itself – First Ypres, the Somme, Passchendaele, Vimy Ridge – is dulled by time and by constant telling and retelling. It can be hard at times to make the players in the drama seem any more real than characters in *The Iliad*, or *The Odyssey.*

They have themselves become legends.

And as for the war memorials . . . Those stones have been weathered by the elements and smothered by the blanket of years.

An endless river has flowed dark and silent past the Cenotaph, and it has been made of people and time. Like rocks fixed in the path of that same river, the memorials of the Great War have been made as smooth as glass by its relentless passing; all their sharp edges are gone and they have lost their power to cut us.

While he was still head of the Imperial War Graves Commission, Fabian Ware said that if the Empire's dead of the Great War were to march down Whitehall four abreast, they would take three and half days to pass the Cenotaph.

Just imagine.

How many millions and millions of the living have walked past it by now?

Time makes everything smooth in the end. Brittle, broken points of pain and grief cannot last; they are made fragile by their sharpness. Our memories of hurt must lose their jagged edges, not because we forget, but because we love. This is part of what love does. This is the final gift to be had from having loved and been loved in return. 'It is the function of the brain to enable us not to remember, but to forget.'

I try to imagine what the grief of the Great War was like and what its ceremonies and memorials must have meant when the edges on the engraved names were still fresh and crisp and sharp.

I was in London on 14 July 2005 when the two-minute silence was held in memory of those who had died in the terrorist attacks on the city's transport network the week before. I was in a pub near Warren Street Tube station when twelve noon arrived. I'd known it was coming, the morning news had been full of it, but the arrival of the moment took me by surprise. I looked up from my newspaper and out through the window into the street. Hundreds of pedestrians had come to a standstill on the pavements. The traffic had pulled to a halt and the only motorcyclist I could see had taken off his helmet and bowed his head. The television was still on in the pub but all else was silent right enough. I walked out on to the pavement and stood for the remaining minute. I've never experienced anything else quite like it, and I expect most others on the pavements of London and other cities that day would say the same. Somehow the crowd sensed, as one, the arrival of 12.02 and began to move again, going about their business. Someone, a man I didn't see, let out a cheer, and it was briefly taken up as a shout of defiance, a challenge to an invisible foe. There was even a round of applause.

There was nothing routine about any of it. It was unlike any other two-minute silence I've ever known. It felt raw, like the long past Remembrance Days I've imagined, as though even a murmured conversation in the middle of it would have made the rest of the city flinch.

Remembrance of people newly dead, snatched away between one moment and the next just days before, made it feel as if death itself were watching the clock.

I have two stories I like to tell: 1. How I met Trudi the first time when I was nineteen and she was seventeen. 2. How I met Trudi for the second time, when I was thirty-five and she was thirty-three.

That's not quite right. I like to tell these stories again and again, but only when it's just Trudi who's listening, and taking her part in the telling. She enjoys them too and they are part of our private mythology. Every time we tell these stories to each other it reinforces our sense of who we are.

Everyone raises an eyebrow at the way a child likes to hear the same story over and over, or endlessly watches a videotape of the same television programme. There's something about the appetite for repetition which makes grown-ups smile. They smile as if the child's doing something only children do – something they'll stop doing once they're old enough to crave constant variety.

But really it's easy to see where they're coming from: familiar is comforting and comfort is everything.

Familiar rituals need not always be dulled by their repetition. From time to time they are made new by circumstances and events. History is always being made new by the passage of time. It comes around and around. This is part of how we continue to remember, and why we must.

52

Scarp Burial Ground

Donald John MacLennan of Scarp died when his ship, HMS *Duchess of Montrose*, was torpedoed and sunk off the coast of Dunkirk on 18 March 1917. He was thirty-two.

Around the same time, a naval frigate had come to the Sound of Scarp to drop off an emergency supply of food to the islanders. It had been bad weather for weeks and no crossings were possible from Hushinish in the open boats.

When Donald John died he had been married to Margaret, from Govig on Harris, for a matter of a few weeks. She never remarried, but lived a long life just the same.

The bodies of Donald MacLennan and Donald John MacLennan were returned to Scarp for burial. Fair Donald had been back in Britain in a military hospital for some time when he died of a stomach illness. Donald John too had somehow made it all the way back to the home of his fathers.

They are buried in a tiny cemetery on a knoll of high ground that commands a view out over the sound towards the empty mountains of Harris. Scarp's surviving exiles are still being returned to the island in death. The little open boat that took me across is occasionally called into service to carry a coffin over for a final homecoming. There are a few recent gravestones near those of Fair Donald and Donald John.

Most of the burial ground is taken up by graves marked only by large beach pebbles, each about the size of a child's skull, and as white. It must have been the way of things here for the longest time.

The standard-issue Commonwealth War Graves Commission headstones marking the graves of Donald and Donald John seem almost incongruous, as though they have turned up here by mistake. But of course this is where they belong. They are not side by side but separated by a few of the beach-pebble graves.

WR/339099   PIONEER
D. MACLENNAN
ROYAL ENGINEER
15TH NOVEMBER 1918
AGE 44

D. J. MACLENNAN
DECK HAND   R.N.R.   4527/SD
H. M. S. 'DUCHESS OF MONTROSE'
18TH MARCH 1917
AGE 32.

So this is death? It couldn't be more final than here. There are still a few journeys to be made, still a few of Scarp's exiles out there in the wide world, hale and hearty. But one day, and if the weather permits all the crossings of the sound at the right times, they will all be here in this little cemetery. And when that day comes, who will have brought the last one?

Scarp's only permanent residents now are the sheep and the dead. Holiday-home owners come and go but only the sheep and the dead are here to see them arrive and left behind when they go.

In accordance with the rights of all war dead, Donald and Donald John are entitled to be remembered with honour. But in Scarp Burial Ground they are short on visitors these days. It's all fenced off with posts and wire, the grass is long and tangled and my footsteps left a beaten trail that looked to have been the only disturbance for years. This place is even off limits to the sheep.

When all the people of Scarp are gathered together, laid out beside Fair Donald and Donald John and the rest, who will visit them then?

Who will remember them?

53

6.49 a.m.

Friday, 1 July 2005.

This house in Falkirk is empty just now, all except for me. Trudi and Evie are on holiday in Spain with Trudi's mum and dad, at their house near Barcelona.

The weather map on the TV this morning said it would be 34 degrees down there today. Trudi is four months pregnant with our next child, but she says she's still enjoying the heat. Evie is slathered in Factor 60 sunblock from dawn till dusk and covered head to foot in white cotton. She has developed a liking for siestas.

Every day I've been getting mobile-phone texts from Trudi about what's going on out there: 'E has been like a doll today in her long skirt and with her new flamenco baby. People smile at her in the street.' Apparently she's been asking after me as well, remarking on my absence from the scene: 'Poor Daddy. Away.'

They're due back next week. This will be the longest I've gone without seeing them since Evie was born. I can't wait.

Aboard the *Iolaire* on the way to Stornoway in the Western Isles of Scotland, it's ten to two in the morning of 1 January 1919. The Arnish light is behind them, along with 1918. The war is over.

In the air around a cork bridge across the Canal de la Sensée, near Aubencheul-au-Bac, on 14 October 1918, German machine-gun bullets are thick like flies. The bridge is coming apart and British soldiers struggle towards the far bank. There's death-or-glory work to be done by Corporal James McPhie.

In the forward trenches of the Somme near the villages of Fricourt, Beaumont-Hamel, Serre and Thiepval, it's nearly 7.30 in the morning of 1 July 1916. They're handing out footballs to kick and pass across no man's land once the whistles blow. There will be prizes for those who make it first to the German lines. The Accrington Pals are ready for the off.

Paddy Crossan, hero of Hearts FC, has no mirror to look in but he's still the handsomest man in the world.

At Thiepval Wood the men of the 9th Royal Irish Rifles await the signal to charge towards the German positions. Up and down the Allied lines it's the same. Whole armies stand, ready to step out into legend upon a day like no other. 'Gentlemen . . . when the barrage lifts.'

It's the morning of 26 September 1915, near Loos, and the men from Cheltenham are on tenterhooks, ready to start their war.

At Quintinshill in Dumfriesshire, near the border between Scotland and England, the sun is burning off the last of the clouds. It should be a perfect day. The railway tracks thrum and jangle, electric with a train's approach.

It's 6.49 a.m. on 22 May 1915 and in the woods near by a lark and a blackbird sing.

Acknowledgments

My biggest debt of gratitude is owed to Rupert Lancaster, my editor at Hodder. Despite my many and varied anxieties, he displayed an air of calm confidence throughout and never seemed to doubt that the project would come to fruition within the terrifying timescale that encompassed the creation of *Not Forgotten*. I also need to thank Hugo Wilkinson for his support and assistance.

I am of course immensely grateful to the production team at Wall to Wall Television, responsible for coming up with the *Not Forgotten* television series in the first place, and to which this book is an accompaniment. Series producer Victoria Watson was another who listened patiently on the phone while I wittered and fretted. A huge thank-you also to all of Victoria's team, namely Alex Finch, Olivia Howes, Matthew Hinchliffe, Alex Graham, Dan Clifton, Ian Leese, Zoe Watkins, Victoria Greenly, Nick Barratt, Lucy Heathcoat-Amory, Peter Scott, Naji Abu-Nowar, Jessica Chen, Elizabeth Pascoe and Claire Rebak.

The stories of life in the Western Isles I heard from John Angus MacLeod were an inspiration for much of what was written here – and I must thank him here too for lending me books from his own collection that were vital to the completion of all of this.

Many thanks also to Donald John MacInnes who went out of his way to track down details and family histories that I would otherwise have found impossible to trace on my own.

Andy Robertshaw at the National Army Museum was, as always, a unique source of knowledge and detail. Thanks yet again.

Georgina Binks at the National Inventory of War Memorials

was a pleasure to talk to and her insight into the importance and relevance of the resource held by the NIWM gave me invaluable help.

Thanks as usual to James Gill at PFD for chasing everything that needed chased and sorting out everything that needed sorting out.

The help, support and encouragement provided by all those named here was first class all the way. Any and all mistakes or omissions are mine alone.

Photographic Acknowledgements

With permission of the Berwick-Upon-Tweed Record Office: 29. Getty Images: 2, 12, 13, 31, 33. Reproduced courtesy of the Gloucestershire Echo: 7, 8. Crown copyright, reproduced courtesy of Historic Scotland Photographic Library: 20. Docklands Museum: 15. Martin Hornby: 28. Imperial War Museum: 1 (Q79991), 19 (Q105864), 34 (Q109517), 35 (Q111468), 36 (Q31492), 37 (UK NIWM 3472). Jo Morrison (*www.triharps.kel.com*): 32. Knebworth Estates (*www.knebworthhouse.com*): 26, 27. Mail Publications: 6. Private collections: 3, 9, 10, 11, 16, 17, 20, 21, 22, 30. Courtesy of Robert and Tony Robinson (*www.pals.org.ok*): 23. Royal Engineers Library: 4. Science Museum/Science and Society Picture Library: 14. Summer Fields: 5. Phil Vasili: 24, 25. Keith Waldegrave: 18.

Bibliography

Alexander, J., *McCrae's Battalion: The Story of the 16th Royal Scots*, Mainstream, Edinburgh, 2003

Arthur, M., *Forgotten Voices of the Great War*, Ebury Press, London, 2003

Barnes, B. S., *Known to the Night*, Sentinel Press, Hull, 2002

Barnes, J., *Metroland*, Picador, London, 1981

——, *Something to Declare*, Picador, London, 2002

Beckett, F. W., *Discovering British Regimental Traditions*, Shire Publications, Princes Risborough, 1999

Block, Howard and Hill, Graham, *The Silvertown Explosion: London 1917*, Tempus Publishing, Gloucestershire, 2003

Borg, A., *War Memorials from Antiquity to the Present*, Leo Cooper, London, 1991

Brittain, V., *Testament of Youth. An Autobiographical Study of the Years 1900–1925*, Gollancz, London, 1933

Brown, Dr J., quoted in J. Moir Porteous, *God's Treasure House in Scotland. A History of Times, Mines and Lands in the Southern Highlands*, Simpkin, Marshall and Co., 1876

Bushaway, B., 'The obligation of remembrance or the remembrance of obligation: society and the memory of world war', in J., Bourne, P. Liddle and I. Whitehead (eds), *The Great World War 1914–45, vol. 2: Who Won? Who Lost?*, HarperCollins, London, 2001

Carew, T., *The Vanished Army: The British Expeditionary Force 1914–1915*, Kimber, London, 1964

Clarendon, E., *The History of the Rebellion and Civil Wars in England Begun in the Year 1641* (facsimile of 1888 edn), Clarendon Press, Oxford, 1992

Cohen, Deborah, *The War Came Home: Disabled Veterans in Britain and Germany, 1914–1939*, University of California Press, London, 2001

Corns, C., and J. H. Wilson, *Blindfold and Alone*, Orion, London, 2005

Craddock, Dave, *Where They Burnt the Town Hall Down*, The Book Castle, Dunstable, 1999

Not Forgotten

Crowley, J., *Little, Big.*, Bantam, London, 1981

Denton, K., *Gallipoli: One Long Grave*, Time/Life Books, 1986

Dyer, G., *The Missing of the Somme*, Hamish Hamilton, London, 1994

Essame, H., *The Battle for Europe 1918*, Batsford, London, 1972

Fairweather, Leslie, *Balcombe: Story of a Sussex Village*, Balcombe Parish
Council, Balcombe, 1981

Fiorato, V., A., Boylston and C. Knusel (eds), *Blood Red Roses: The
Archaeology of a Mass Grave from the Battle of Towton, AD 1461*,
Oxbow Books, Oxford, 2001

Fussel, P., *The Great War and Modern Memory*, Oxford University Press,
Oxford, 1975

Grayzel, S. R., *Women and the First World War*, Longman, 2002

Grieves, K., 'Neville Lytton, the Balcombe frescoes and the experience of
war, 1908–1923', in *Sussex Archaeological Collections*, 134, 1996

Hay, I., *Their Name Liveth. The Book of the Scottish National War
Memorial*, Bodley Head, London, 1931

Hendy, I., *Retrieving Wenty's Sturty Bird*, Black Dwarf Lightmoor, Witney, 2001

Hofschroer, P., *Wellington's Smallest Victory*, Faber, London, 2005

Holmes, R., *Tommy: The British Soldier on the Western Front 1914–1918*,
Harper Perennial, London, 2004

Keegan, J., *The Opening Moves*, Penguin, London, 1971

——, *The Face of Battle*, Penguin, London, 1978

——, *A History of Warfare*, Penguin, London, 1994

King, A., *Memorials of the Great War in Britain: The symbolism and
politics of remembrance*, Berg, Oxford, 1998

Lawrence, Dorothy, *Sapper Dorothy Lawrence: The Only English Woman
Soldier*, John Lane, Bodley Head, London, 1919

Leitch, M., *What Happened to Joe?*, Immingham Branch of the Workers
Educational Association, Immingham, 1995

Lloyd, D. W., *Battlefield Tourism. Pilgrimage and the Commemoration of
the Great War in Britain, Australia and Canada 1919–1939*, Berg,
Oxford, 1998

Macdonald, L., *Somme*, Michael Joseph, London, 1983

McCrorie, I., *Royal Road to the Isles. 150 Years of MacBrayne Shipping*,
Caledonian MacBrayne Limited, Gourock, n.d.

Marwick, A., *The Deluge: British Society and the First World War*, Bodley
Head, London, 1965

Middlebrook, M., *The First Day of the Somme*, Allen Lane, London, 1971

Milner, Laurie, *Leeds Pals: A History of the 15th (service) Battalion (1st*

Leeds) *The Prince of Wales' Own (West Yorkshire Regiment) 1914–1918*, Pen and Sword Books, South Yorkshire, 1998

Morton-Hardie, Mary, *A Cinder Glows: the story of a remarkable life*, Eric Dobby Publishing, Kent, 1993

Pollard, A. J., and N. Oliver, *Two Men in a Trench. Battlefield Archaeology – the Key to Unlocking the Past*, Michael Joseph, London, 2002

——, *Two Men in a Trench II. Uncovering the Secrets of British Battlefields*, Michael Joseph, London, 2003

Roberts, J. M., *The New Penguin History of the World*, Penguin, London, 2002

Schwarz, C. (ed.), *The Chambers Dictionary*, Chambers Harrap, Edinburgh, 1993

Seeling, C., *Fashion. The Century of the Designer 1900–1999*, Konemann Verlagsgesellschaft, Cologne, 2000

The Baroness de T. Serclaes, *Flanders and Other Fields*, George G. Harrap and Co. Ltd., London, 1964

Smithies, Carole, *The Barnbow Lassies: The Unsung Heroes of the Two World Wars*, MBE paper, Park Lane College, Leeds, 2000

Stornoway Gazette, *Sea Sorrow. The Story of the Iolaire Disaster*, Stornoway Gazette Commercial Print Division, Stornoway, 1972

Taylor, A. J. P., *The First World War*, Penguin, London, 1966

Terraine, J., *Mons*, Pan, London, 1960

——, *Impacts of War 1914 & 1918*, Hutchinson, London, 1970

——, *The First World War 1914–18*, Macmillan, Basingstoke, 1984

Wall, R., and J. Winter (eds), *The Upheaval of War. Family, Work and Welfare in Europe, 1914–1918*, Cambridge University Press, Cambridge, 1988

Winter, J., *Sites of Memory, Sites of Mourning. The Great War in European cultural history*, Cambridge University Press, Cambridge, 1995

Wynn, G. C., *If Germany Attacks: The Battle in Depth in the West*, London, 1940, quoted in R. Holmes, *Tommy: The British Soldier on the Western Front*, op. cit.

Young, J. E., *The Texture of Memory: Holocaust Memorials and Meaning*, Yale University Press, New Haven, CT, 1993

Websites

culturehebrides.com
cwgc.org
silentcities.co.uk
guardian.co.uk
The *Scotsman* digital archive at scotsman.co.uk
fylde.demon.co.uk.thankful.htm
hellfire-corner.demon.co.uk

Index

Index